CURMUDGUCATION

WHAT FRESH HELL

PETER GREENE

AUGUST 2015
Venangoland Press
Franklin, PA

Introduction

Curmudgucation started because I was in a mood.

In the summer of 2013, like many teachers in the field, I was trying to figure out what the heck was going on with this Common Core stuff. I had heard the rumblings for a while, but if you have been teaching for more than a week, you've always heard rumblings. Bureaucrats and other suits in faraway offices have always had bright shiny new ideas about how to tell teachers to do their jobs and Revolutionize Education. They spark, the flare, they fade away.

Initially, Common Core sounded like more of that. In fact, because it was supposedly created with the help of teachers, it seemed as if it might even be relatively benign. But I was curious, so I started reading.

And the more I read, the more I was stunned and amazed and horrified and, increasingly, cranky. And it wasn't just the Core—the more I read, the more I began to discover a giant web of interconnected reform ideas, and not only did they not seem like good ideas, but they seemed like actual bad ideas, not just unsupportive of education, but actively destructive.

Weirdly, so many people were not paying attention, or worse, paying attention and not getting it. Public education was being mugged, and not in a dark alley, but in broad daylight on a busy street, and while some people were trying to step in, the muggers just kept announcing, "We're just helping this nice old lady with her groceries," and people were nodding and saying, "Well, all right then. That's very nice of you."

It was (and is) crazy-making—bad ideas being pushed into education by amateurs with nothing to back them up but connections and money. Each new chapter would bring me back to the words of Dorothy Parker: "What fresh hell is this?"

There are not many facts in this book; for factual deconstruction of the reformsters, there are many great books out there, from *Reign of Error* by Diane Ravitch to *50 Myths and Lies* by David Berliner and Gene Glass to the works of Mercedes Schneider, Yong Zhao, and Jose Vilson. In this book I've collected pieces focused on the twisted reasoning and bent language used by reformsters. It's a complicated debate because inaccurate details are used in the construction of arguments that would give M C Escher a headache.

On top of that, sorting out all the sides and points of view was challenging. The right and left were suddenly allied, both in defending and assaulting public education (plus the usual assortment of crazypants loons on all sides).

Just sorting out positions became an exercise in extended research. I read so many blogs that I couldn't even remember what I read where—Diane Ravitch, Mercedes Schneider, Rick Hess, Anthony Cody, Valerie Strauss, anything that turned up in Google.

It was so much, and I needed to vent, and my colleagues and loved ones could only stand so much. So I turned to blogging. At first I wrote sporadically, but soon some sort of dam broke and the stuff just poured out daily. I was that proverbial guy who can't come to bed because he just found someone saying something wrong on the internet.

I had no idea what the blogging would lead to. If I had thought people were going to read what I wrote, I would have probably been a lot more thoughtful and perhaps a little less of an ass. But I wasn't looking for an audience; I was just looking to vent while collecting and working through my thoughts in one location.

That an audience found me is not any sort of testament to any writerly prowess on my part. There's an ever-growing crowd watching the reformster mess in amazed outrage. My most common audience reaction is some combination of "You said just what I was thinking" and "I thought I was the only one."

That an audience found me is also a testament to the people who helped me out and pushed me in front of a wider span of eyeballs. Anthony Cody gave me my first guest post in a real blog. Diane Ravitch, always extraordinarily generous with her massive audience, has made a regular out of me. The BATs on Facebook brought a ton of readers to my posts. Huffington Post invited me to re-post my stuff on their platform; it pays only in exposure, but I'm more interested in getting the word out than making big bucks. Anthony Rebora at Education Week invited me to get on board there after Anthony Cody moved on.

I owe thanks to many others as well. Since almost the beginning, Anne Patrick has been my free-lance proofreader, which is a huge task given my claws-in-mittens typing technique. Nancy Flanagan, Jennifer Berkshire, Paul Thomas, Valerie Strauss, Russ Walsh, Jason Linkins, Jose Vilson, Mercedes Schneider, Dan Katz, Jersey Jazzman, Rick Hess, Andy Smarick, Audrey Amrein-Beardsley, Sarah Blaine, Jonathan Pelto, and Stephen Singer have all lent aid, support, and/or inspiration at various times. And a huge hat tip to the Network for Public Education and the Education Bloggers Network. I even thank some of the folks on The Other Side like Charles Sahm, Andy Smarick, Rick Hess and Mike Petrilli, who help me to stay on my toes and remember that reformsters don't eat babies. I'm not trying to make myself look cool with a lot of name checking here—I want to be clear that my work on the blog benefits from and depends upon the work of hundreds of people in a widespread cause. I just really owe many other people.

My blogging in voice is personal because I think that's part of taking responsibility for what I say, but it's not about me. It's about public education.

In the spirit of transparency, I should note that there's nothing here that you can't read for free on the blog. Some pieces have been lightly edited, but this is old wine in a news skin, an attempt to get the word out to a different audience through a different medium (also, to let certain readers enjoy the convenience of paper).

As I type this, there are almost 1300 posts on the blog, plus the almosta-hundred over at View from the Cheap Seats, my blog for Education Week. This book is just a sliver of that. It leans mostly on pieces that are more personal. I shied away from the pieces that depend on links and quotes to make sense.

Most especially, I have to thank my wife and my mother, two of my most faithful readers, even when they don't entirely get what I'm rambling on about. I've tried to pick pieces that might appeal to them, for many reasons, not the least of which is that this book's primary purpose is a Christmas present for my mother.

If you are not a relative of mine or someone who already reads the blog (www.curmudgcation.blogspot.com), I encourage you to become informed and involved in whatever way you can. I bring nothing to the table beyond a lifetime of working in the classroom (where, I assure you, I am not God's gift to teaching) and prodigious amount of reading. But as a host of economists, thinky tank guys, assorted bureaucrats, and David Coleman have all repeatedly demonstrated, you do not need to have any special expertise to act like an expert. Public education is a marathon, not a sprint. Read up, speak out and step forward.

I Love My Job

Regular readers of the blogs (I believe there are at least three, now) probably expected that the headline was setting up some sort of sarcastic satirical rant. But no-- that's not where I'm going today. Because I do, in fact, actually love my job.

Sometimes it's the obvious stuff. A few weeks back I was hustling in overdrive overtime to pull together a hundred-plus students into a production of the annual variety show, standing in that big pre-show circle at all those faces excited and committed and simultaneously part of something brand new and also an eighty-four year tradition at our school. They had worked so hard and they were so excited and they created such a special night for hundreds of audience members and it was not possible for me to be any prouder of how each put his or her personal stamp of sweat and inspiration and talent and spark to those performances. How could anybody not love that?

Sometimes it's not so obvious. Today I was up in class and we were seguing straight from the difference between jazz hands and spirit fingers into what turned out to be an infomercial for the three uses of semi-colons (three! count 'em, three!) and we are all just enjoying ourselves while we nail this stupid punctuation nuance and I am thinking, damn, I have the best job in the world (although I'll admit I can see how not everybody would necessarily love that part).

Sometimes it pays off for decades. I teach in a small town, and while many of our grads leave the area, many don't, and many stay in touch. To see these people strive and grow and sometimes fall but then find a way-- it's an awesome thing. To see the many amazing ways in which a person's life can unfold, unexpected and not according to plan, and yet eventually finding its own way-- I tell you, it's watching my students grow and go into the world that has reassured me more than anything else in life that ultimately, for most people, things turn out okay.

And the generations. I see families unfold through generations and through years, see parents pass their own struggles and strength onto their children. I see parents and children trying so hard to figure out how to love and support each other, and I get to know both sides of their story. I mean, the line about touching the future because I teach is great, and I don't disagree, but I am also up to my elbows in the present and it's awesome. I get to work with real live living growing changing rising and advancing human beings. Not like doctors and nurses who see them when they're sick, or lawyers or social workers who see them when they're in trouble-- I get to see them when they are becoming themselves. I get to see them learn what it means to be fully human, to be who they are, to be in the world.

I am driven to understand just like I am driven to write and make music and ride a bike, and I am driven to connect other people to what I understand and to see what I can see through them. Like the guy shoveling coal into the furnace that drives the engine in the belly of a great ocean liner, I get to work next to the burning heart of humanity.

We talk about all the things that matter and all the things that don't, and we talk about how to talk about them, and we talk about how to bridge the gap between human beings, to share understanding, to pass on some of that heat from the burning heart. Every one of my students is a giant waiting to stand up tall, struggling to channel strength into those legs.

We read and write and do every piddly thing any English class ever did. We look into the literature and the paragraphs and the prepositional phrases and we try find some way to use it, some way to move forward, some way to grow and rise and embrace ourselves and the world.

It is not always pretty and it is not always neat and not always according to plan, and lord knows some days I am not very good at it for any number of reasons, up to and including that I'm an imperfect rough draft of a teacher. I may never retire because I don't think I can quit until I actually get really good at this.

The worst is to get distracted by the stupid stuff, and we are all awash in a sea of stupid distractions these days, and that's mostly what I write about. But I need to let myself know (and you, too, dear reader if you have hung on through all these paragraphs) that there is a reason I do this and it is bigger than all the stuff that I bitch and moan about. There's is more to this, to me, than the bitching and moaning. There is the energy in knowing and passing it on, there's the joy of grinding through the tight places to the places where the sky is fresh and clear, and there is absolute heart-shaking awesomeness of watching young humans grow and grasp and build and rise and become fully human and fully themselves.

Make no mistake. I love my job. I freakin' love my job.

Data Driven Drivel

The problem with the current data-collection fad is not that it collects too much data. It's that it doesn't collect enough.

Human beings are complicated and complex. All good teachers know that. It's why we collect data all the time. All. The. Time.

We go over a drill sheet on some simple skill. We call on students. We watch their responses. Did Johnny look puzzled or bored? Did Jane answer quickly, or do a lot of mulling? Did Ethel deliver and inspired insight or a lucky guess? Is Chris confused by the material or distracted by a fight with his best friend? Does Bob know how he got that answer, or did it come straight out his butt? We ask follow up questions, probe, watch carefully. We know there's a difference between a class that has a skill mastered and one that's just barely getting it, even if both classes get the same number of right answers.

We know all this because we collect literally thousands of data points, many of which boil down to verbal and non-verbal cues, and many of those we can interpret only because we've developed a relationship with the student. In the ten minutes it took to go over a simple worksheet, we have observed, gathered, sorted and collated thousands of data points.

These shiny new fancy data-collecting assessment whiz-bangs (available at a generous price from Pearson et al)-- how many data points do they collect?

One.

A score. A simple right or wrong number. They have to. It's all they can handle. If it's a complicated matter, they still reduce it to a fill-in-thebubble, right-or-wrong, one-data-point number.

This is why these things are de-humanizing. Because human beings are complex creatures who generate wild and vibrant webs of complicated information, a complex of behavior so varied and stunning that the very computers that are used to analyze it cannot even begin to imitate it.

The data-driven craze is like a doctor who wants to diagnose a patient. She has available every test, every diagnostic, every lab facility in the world. But instead, she just writes down the patient's height and weight and calls it a day. Or posts it on her data wall.

We need to stop saying that we are opposed to data-driven instruction, because we're not-- we've been doing it for as long as we've been in a classroom. What we need to start saying is that the so-called data-driving tools that we're being offered (or forced) to use are crap, producing a thin sliver of useless data, a mere drop compared to the vast waterfalls of data available from the beautiful, varied human beings who are our students.

To data-driving assessment providers, we have to say, "I'm sorry that you're only capable of measuring a minute fraction of what I need to do my job. But you have to stop saying that because X is the only thing you can measure, X is the only thing that matters."

Why American Public Education Is Worth the Fight

The US is a big gloriously polyglot mess of a country, stitched together out of pieces-parts from every other people on the planet. As such, we can only claim a handful of native art forms. Jazz, comics, maybe baseball. And true public education.

Only in America do we dump people from any and all backgrounds into the same building. Only in America do we let you pursue whatever dream of a future you can conjure up. Only in America have we put it down in law that one of your obligations as a citizen is to get an education.

We don't even make you vote, but we put the full force of law into making you learn to read and write.

We guarantee that every child, regardless of background and home life, will have at least one unrelated adult in his/her life who can provide good direction and model a healthy adult life. We guarantee that every child will have access to a place where every person is put in place to honor the needs of that child first and foremost-- not profits, productivity, or the good of the institution. As I tell my students every year, "You need to take advantage of this place. You will never again be surrounded by people whose only job is to look out for your best interests."

They say that home is the place where, when you go there, they have to take you in. But in America, there's one other place like that-- a public school.

American public schools collect everything there is to love and hate about our culture. American public schools display everything that is beautiful and everything that is broken about us as a people. American public schools are everything that we have to say about hopes and fears and aspirations for our future.

Given all that, of course American public schools capture all that is random and chaotic about life (as well as the very American fear and distrust of random chaos). As teachers, we know that we will leave a mark on the future, but we rarely know how. The moment that you built and planned and put all your effort behind vanishes into your students' pasts like a brief breath of wind, even as you discover that a few simple words you spoke decades ago have become a treasured guidepost in someone's journey.

American public schools are Democracy in action-- messy, tumultuous, contentious, inefficient, joyous, sprawling, striving, triumphant, rising, advancing, spirited, exhausting, reborn again and again and again. Do we contradict ourselves? Very well, we contradict ourselves. We are large. We contain multitudes.

I do not share warm-hearted stories. If you asked my students if I am warm and nurturing, they would laugh. But I believe in public education. I believe in it as an expression of our national character, and I believe there is nothing so awesome as varied young persons side by side finding their way to a greater understanding of themselves and each other, finding ways to be in the world, to be human, to be themselves.

Nothing else compares. Nothing. American public school will never be a neatly manicured hyper-orderly efficiently unified system because America will never be that kind of country. That's okay. It's not a bug; it's a feature. The fight will never be over, but American public education will always be worth fighting for.

Arne Duncan vs. White Moms

A classic Arne Duncan moment was his cogent analysis of why people are not putting on a smile, lying down, and letting the Common Core roll right over them. I want to just take a moment to unpack how many kinds of arrogant foolishness are rolled into that one little comment.

"It's fascinating to me that some of the pushback is coming from, sort of, white suburban moms who — all of a sudden — their child isn't as brilliant as they thought they were and their school isn't quite as good as they thought they were, and that's pretty scary,"

1) Why are we having this conversation?

Once again, Arne seems to have forgotten one of the central, important fictions of the Common Core-- that they are totally the result of a state initiative, and that they in no way represent a federal attempt to commandeer the state-based control of schools. If this isn't his program, why is he devoting so much time and fervor to defending it? Why aren't a bunch of governors running around defending the program that they developed all on their own that was in no way set up and nursed to life by the feds?

2) Moms? Really??

I thought these days it was supposed to be the GOP that dismissed contrary points of view simply by attaching them to women. "Ha ha. This is the crazy kind of objection you'd expect from one of those women. You know women, with their dumb vaginas and not-very-strong thinky parts. That's who comes up with this kind of stupid objection."

3) Plus "white" and "suburban"?? Did you skip politics 101?

Granted, this is a kind of genius play here. These are people who have it cushy, but they're not truly elite. We're trying to invoke the language of privilege, but not too much because that would land us in Arne's neighborhood. So "white suburban" translates roughly as "privileged but not as great as me." Arne is saying, "People who live on the mean streets-- they get it. People who have risen to the heights of power and wealth on their great merit (like, you know, me) get it. But these out-of-touch suburbanites (did I mention they were women) don't get it."
If you think I'm reading too much into points #2 and #3, imagine how this plays if Arne instead attributes these concerns to "blue collar fathers" or "working class black parents."

4) And then when you think for a second more...

Wait-- so only suburban Moms care about how well their kids are doing at school??

5) It's not me. It's you.

The administration has managed to cave and admit that maybe the ACA rollout didn't come off quite as planned and that maybe-- just maybe-- things weren't quite as originally advertised. (Predicted soon-to-bememe from the comment section of the WaPo article-- "Obamacore-- you can keep your school and teachers if you like them. Oops!")

But in the world of CCSS, there's still only one explanation for why people are upset about the results. Their perception of their school, the school's teachers, the education that they perceived in THEIR OWN CHILDREN-- all of those were at fault all this time, and now only the magic of the federal oops-- state standards can finally open their eyes.

Yup-- exposure to their offspring, with whom they presumably live, occasionally share a meal, even exchange the occasional grunts and greetings-- none of that could possibly give a parent an impression of how smart their child is. Only CCSS can reveal-- and surprise them with-- the truth. In Arne's world, there is no possible way that the bad results are even a teensy bit the result of an untested program poorly rolled out program. And that's why--

6) Randi Weingarten is actually right about something

The WaPo column contains a money quote from the AFT head, saying that the CCSS rollout is even worse than the ACA launch. And she's right. And she's right because the ACA rollout has allowed for course correction, changes based on conditions on the ground, and even an admission that some things need to be tweaked.

But in Arne-world, all problems, all objections, all difficulties with the CCSS have one explanation-- all you dumb civilians who don't know revolutionary genius when you see it. Especially those of you with vaginas.

The Wrongest Sentence Ever in the CCSS Debate

At Impatient Optimists, a Gates Foundation website, Allan Golston recently wrote a notable piece entitled "America's Businesses Need the Common Core." It's a notable column, not because it has anything new
to add to the discussion (it's a rehash of the usual pro-CCSS fluffernuttery), but because it contains this sentence:

Businesses are the primary consumers of the output of our schools, so it's a natural alliance.

As a semi-professional hack writer and fake journalist, I can tell you that it's a challenge to fit a lot of wrong in just one sentence, but Mr. Golston has created a masterpiece of wrong, a monument of wrong, a mighty two-clause clown car of wrong. Let's just look under the hood.

Output of our schools. Students are not output. They are not throughput. They are not toasters on an assembly line. They are not a manufactured product, and a school is not a factory. In fact, a school does not create "output" at all. Talking about the "output" of a school is like talking about the "output" of a hospital or a counseling center or a summer camp or a marriage. When talking about interactions between live carbon-based life forms (as in "That girl you've been dating is cute, but how's the output of the relationship?"), talking about output is generally not a good thing

Primary consumers. Here's another thing that students are not-- students are not consumer goods. Businesses do not purchase them and then use them until they are discarded or replaced. Students are not a good whose value is measured strictly in its utility to the business that purchased it.

Businesses are the primary consumers. Even if I correct "primary consumers" to mean something more human-friendly, this is STILL wrong. Businesses are NOT the primary recipients of the benefits of well-educated young humans, because the purpose of education is NOT simply to prepare young humans to be useful to their future employers. A good education prepares them to be good citizens, neighbors, voters, parents, and spouses. All of those people are stakeholders, too. And the number one stakeholder when it comes to the student's education-- that would be the student, whose education will prepare that student to get maximum use of his own personal constellation of skills to chart the life path that he chooses.

To shoulder yourself to the front of the great society-large crowd of stakeholders in education and declare boldly, "Yeah, we're more important than anyone else here" is a truly impressive display of ballsiness.

So it's a natural alliance. Let's pretend for a moment that this conclusion isn't predicated on the totally-wrong first clause. If business and education represent a natural alliance, then maybe business could start acting like allies instead of ham-handed paternalistic patronizing bosses. Pick the business of anybody on the Gates Foundation board of directors. Pick any one. Now imagine me, a teacher, showing up at the CEO's office and saying, "Hey, some of us at my high school formed a study group and we've come up with some recommendations about how your business should be run. And if you don't want to listen to us, we'll call up our friends in DC and make you listen to us."

I can imagine lots of responses. None of them would be, "Hey, you must be my ally!"

I thank Mr. Golston for managing to crystallize so much of what's wrong with the Gates-business crowd's view of the entire education and Common Core situation. I would like to also point out that there is some paternalistic elitist BS in this as well, because we're not talking about ALL education. This crowd will gain credibility with me the first time I pick up the paper and read about them marching into the main office of their child's exclusive private school and saying, "I pay good money to you guys in tuition and endowments, and I want YOU to become a pilot program for my school reforms. We're going to put all of these in place, here, where my child goes to school, so that I can show everybody else how great they will be."

No, if a sentence like Golston's turned up in the materials for an elite private school, the phone in that main office would be ringing, and it wouldn't be to deliver congratulations. Nobody would let a sentence this wrong come anywhere near their own child.

"Raise the Bar," or Not

While we're talking about watching our language--

Just in the afternoon, I've stumbled across the image of raising the bar on the education world about five different times. Here's what's wrong with "raising the bar."

Raising the bar is a perfect image for the idea of one-size-fits-all education. After all, it only makes sense if there's just one bar and it's set up in the only place where people jump. It's a metaphor that is repeatedly employed, and yet falls apart with very little examination.

Are we raising the bar for a high jumper, or a pole vaulter? Has to be one or the other, because here at the Common Core Track and Field Meet, there can only be one event.

What happens if we raise the bar for the 100 yard sprint? What if we raise the bar, but we set it up behind the jumping line? What if we raise the bar for the shot put? If we raise the bar for the limbo, isn't that rejecting excellence?

What if we raise the bar for swimmers? Should we raise the bar at basketball games, or should we raise the basket? Can we raise a bar at the band concert? Should we raise the bar for the dance group, or the drama club?

"Raise the bar" is the verbal equivalent of the oft-shared cartoon that shows all the different animals in school (the one where the fish fail because they can't fly). "Raise the bar" demands that we reduce the whole complicated business of education to one simple act that must be performed by every single student. "Raise the bar" insists that the whole wide range of human endeavor and achievement does not matter-- just the ability to get up over that bar. Use "raise the bar" with me, and I get the idea that your vision of what education is about is tiny and cramped and fails to reflect the full range of human awesomeness.

The Hard Part

They never tell you in teacher school, and it's rarely discussed elsewhere. It is never, ever portrayed in movies and tv shows about teaching. Teachers rarely bring it up around non-teachers for fear it will make us look weak or inadequate.

Valerie Strauss of the Washington Post put together a series of quotes to answer the question "How hard is teaching?" and asked for more in the comments section. My rant didn't entirely fit there, so I'm putting it here, because it is on the list of Top Ten Things They Never Tell You in Teacher School.

The hard part of teaching is coming to grips with this:

There is never enough.

There is never enough time. There are never enough resources. There is never enough you.

As a teacher, you can see what a perfect job in your classroom would look like. You know all the assignments you should be giving. You know all the feedback you should be providing your students. You know all the individual crafting that should provide for each individual's instruction. You know all the material you should be covering. You know all the ways in which, when the teachable moment emerges (unannounced as always), you can greet it with a smile and drop everything to make it grow and blossom.

You know all this, but you can also do the math. 110 papers about the view of death in American Romantic writing times 15 minutes to respond with thoughtful written comments equals-- wait! what?! That CAN'T be right! Plus quizzes to assess where we are in the grammar unit in order to design a new remedial unit before we craft the final test on that unit (five minutes each to grade). And that was before Ethel made that comment about Poe that offered us a perfect chance to talk about the gothic influences. And I know that if my students are really going to get good at writing, they should be composing something at least once a week. And if I am going to prepare my students for life in the real world, I need to have one of my own to be credible.

If you are going to take any control of your professional life, you have to make some hard, conscious decisions. What is it that I know I should be doing that I am not going to do?

Every year you get better. You get faster, you learn tricks, you learn which corners can more safely be cut, you get better at predicting where the student-based bumps in the road will appear. A good administrative team can provide a great deal of help.

But every day is still educational triage. You will pick and choose your battles, and you will always be at best bothers, at worst haunted, by the things you know you should have done but didn't. Show me a teacher who thinks she's got everything all under control and doesn't need to fix a thing for next year, and I will show you a lousy teacher. The best teachers I've ever known can give you a list of exactly what they don't do well enough yet.

Not everybody can deal with this. I had a colleague (high school English) years ago who was a great classroom teacher. But she gave every assignment that she knew she should, and so once a grading period, she took a personal day to sit at home and grade papers for 18 hours straight. She was awesome, but she left teaching, because doing triage broke her heart.

So if you show up at my door saying, "Here's a box from Pearson. Open it up, hand out the materials, read the script, and stick to the daily schedule. Do that, and your classroom will work perfectly," I will look you in your beady eyes and ask, "Are you high? Are you stupid?" Because you have to be one of those. Maybe both.

Here's your metaphor for the day.

Teaching is like painting a huge Victorian mansion. And you don't actually have enough paint. And when you get to some section of the house it turns out the wood is a little rotten or not ready for the paint. And about every hour some supervisor comes around and asks you get down off the ladder and explain why you aren't making faster progress. And some days the weather is terrible. So it takes all your art and skill and experience to do a job where the house still ends up looking good.

Where are school reformy folks in this metaphor? They're the ones who show up and tell you that having a ladder is making you lazy, and you should work without. They're the ones who take a cup of your paint every day to paint test strips on scrap wood, just to make sure the paint is okay (but now you have less of it). They're the ones who show up after the work is done and tell passerbys, "See that one good-looking part? That turned out good because the painters followed my instructions." And they're most especially the ones who turn up after the job is complete to say, "Hey, you missed a spot right there on that one board under the eaves."
There isn't much discussion of the not-enough problem. Movie and tv teachers never have it (high school teachers on television only ever teach one class a day!). And teachers hate to bring it up because we know it just sounds like whiny complaining.

But all the other hard part of teaching-- the technical issues of instruction and planning and individualization and being our own "administrative assistants" and acquiring materials and designing unit plans and assessment-- all of those issues rest solidly on the foundation of Not Enough.

Trust us. We will suck it up. We will make do. We will Find A Way. We will even do that when the people tasked with helping us do all that on the state and federal level instead try to make it harder. Even though we can't get to perfect, we can steer toward it. But if you ask me what the hard part of teaching is, hands down, this wins.

There's not enough.

from Why For-Profit Schools Must Stink

There are so many reasons to object to the privatization of public education, but it all comes down to the pie. It's the financial pie, a pie that can only be cut into so many pieces. There's a reason that we associate top-notch private schools with rich folks-- every time a Philips Academy needs a bigger pie, they just pick up the phone to their rich parents and their rich alumni and before you can say "Summer at the Hamptons," the school is awash in newer, bigger pies.

Not so in public ed. The size of the pie is set by a combination of legislators and taxpayers, and that's all the pie there is. And that means that private operators, whether they're operating a voucher school or a private charter or one of those public-private hybrid charters (public when they want money, private when anybody wants to see what they do with it), your business model has to acknowledge one fundamental fact. (This includes "noon-profits" that are really for the profit of well-paid executives.)

Every piece of pie served to the students is a piece of pie that the operators don't get to eat themselves. Every cent they spend on students is a cent they don't get to pocket. In privatized public schools, the interests of the operators are in direct conflict with the interests of the clients.

But when you only have so much money to split up, your motive is to find ways to spend less. And if you are a service business, spending less means providing less for your clients. Cheaper service providers. Cheaper services. Fewer services. You are never asking, "What's the best possible service we could provide our clients." Instead, you are asking, "What's the cheapest possible service we can get away with? Where is there a corner we can cut?"

The problem with the profit motive in fixed-payment service industries is not JUST that those in charge can only make money by finding ways to spend less on their clients. The more toxic systemic effect is that those in charge are pushed to inevitably see their clients as their biggest obstacle rather than their primary purpose. We know that attitude is lurking just over the horizon anyway-- how many of us deal with a business manager in our district whose attitude is that it would be easy to balance the budget if we didn't have to spend money on all those damn teachers and students.

For-profit schools are powerfully inclined to stink because they must foster an adversarial relationship between the owner-operators, the clients, and the employees. All of that takes place in an atmosphere of scarcity, of "having to do without." Add merit-based pay in which teachers must compete for their piece of the pie, and you get a school "community" that is anything but supportive and collegial.

Why Teacher Merit Pay Is Stupid

Sometimes we forget the obvious, so let me spell it out. Here's why teacher merit pay will never make sense.

In a business, here's how merit pay is supposed to work. Watch carefully:

1)   International Widgetmakers, Inc makes $1,000,000 more profit than originally projected.

2)   CEO Mr. McMoneygutz says, "Wow, that's great. Let us share this bounty with the hard workers who helped earn it in the first place."

3)   A large slice of the million bucks is divied up and handed over to grateful employees based on how much help they were in earning it.

In business, here's how merit pay sometimes actually works. Again, pay attention.

1)   International Widgetmakers, Inc makes $1,000,000 more profit than originally projected.

2)   CEO Mr. McJerkface says, "Hey, Board of Directors. You're so lucky to have me. You should give me a pile of that there extra moneys."

3)   A large slice of the million bucks is handed to the CEO and hardworking employees get screwed again.

Notice what each of these versions of merit pay have in common: An extra stack of money lying around. That's why companies having lean times don't give out merit bonuses-- because to give out bonuses, you have to have extra money.

So to discuss the wisdom of teacher merit pay, we don't have to talk about its motivational qualities, or its philosophical validity. All we have to ask this question:

When and where has it ever been possible to describe a public school system with the phrase "has an extra stack of money lying around."

When a company does well, that means, by definition, that it has made a ton of money. When a company does poorly, it has NOT made a ton of money. But the amount of money a school district takes in is exactly the same regardless of how good a job it does.

Reformy business guys know this. In fact, it is one of the things that drives them crazy, because it offends their very understanding of how the world is supposed to work, just as their notion that a school whose students get low test scores should get less money makes us see red. It is one of the bedrock fundamentals on which private sector and public ed people disagree. Much of what has happened in education reform can be understood as business guys doing their damnedest to force schools to conform to what they view as fundamental rules of the universe.

No school district has extra money. (In fact, no school district "has" any money-- it all belongs to the taxpayers.) The only way to have extra money would be for the district to say, "Taxpayers, our teachers did so well this year we'd like to collect an extra three mils worth of taxes so we can pay them appropriately." Call me crazy, but I don't see that happening.

Merit pay is extra money. There is no extra money. So what we're talking about in schools is not "merit pay," but "pay." Any school district proposing "merit pay" is really saying, "See this bucket of money? We are going to let you teachers compete to see who gets the biggest chunks of it."

This is certainly a creative way to rewrite salary scales. But it is not merit pay.

College Ready

One of the linchpins of proof among CCSS supporters is that Kids These Days are not ready for college. This is generally expressed in scholarly tones as "X% of college freshmen were in need of remediation" (and in more rhetorical tones as "OMGZZ!! The college freshmens are soooooo dumb that they need undumbification classes to be in the college!!") And this is proof that We Must Do Something, with "Something" defined as "slap CCSS into place."

Time for a lesson in metrics. This legendary unreadiness is usually expressed as "need remediation" which is turn is measured by "percentage of students taking remedial classes." Remember that.

This always sounds sciency because it comes out as number, but trying to pin down that number turns out to be a challenge. A wide variety of sources that I can't link to because this is a book throw out everything from 17% to 20% to a third of all entering freshies. Most of these sources do not compare the current figures to any from the alleged golden age of non-remediation. So can I at least suggest that the numbers are "controversial" or "contested" or maybe even "pulled out of a variety of different orifices"?

I'm not a scholar in the field. But as a high school teacher I have a buttload of anecdotal evidence that might explain this trend if it in fact exists (which I will concede it very well might).

Explanation #1. The college admissions process.

We used to tell our students, "You need to take college prep classes and do well in them if you want to get into college." We still tell them that, but they laugh at us as if we had just told them that sasquatch will eat them if they don't do their homework.

They laugh because every one of them knows somebody who barely passed non-college prep classes who was still cheerfully accepted into a college. Because at least in PA the college-age market is shrinking dramatically, and colleges are suffering dire financial straights because they can't find ~~enough parents to cut checks~~ enough searchers for higher knowledge and wisdom.

So when a local college prof starts in on "How can you send us these kids" my reply is always, "Look at his courseload and his grades. We told you exactly what you were getting. You accepted him anyway."

Explanation #2 College fund raising.

Funny thing about remedial courses at most colleges. They don't count as credit toward graduation. You do have to pay for them, though. So the more times a college can convince Joe Freshman that he "must" take Remedial Composition or Math or Hygiene, the more extra money they can bank.

For at least a decade I've been hearing stories about perfectly capable students who were told they must take a remedial course. Every once in a while they say, "No, I don't" and it never hurts them a bit. But imagine how many impressionable freshmen, alone in a college office without parental backup or sufficient knowledge of the system, are not able to stand up for themselves.

So have colleges start giving away remedial course for free, just to help their students succeed. Check what the enrollment numbers are like then. At that point, you can get back to me. In the meantime, remedial coursework is a great moneymaker for cash-strapped colleges.

Explanation #3 Marketing

We've been telling everybody that they just have to get a college education no matter what. It has been great marketing. It has brought lots of young folks into the market who are probably not well-served by the market. Meanwhile, America needs welders. Bottom line-- we should stop heavily recruiting people who are 250 pounds and 6'6" to become jockeys.

So I can believe that college readiness is, kind of, an issue. But you'll notice that none of my proposed causes can be addressed by a national one-size-fits-all top-down-imposed curriculum.

In fact, in many fairly significant ways, the reform movement has made things worse. For instance, standardized test writing is an abomination and teaching it undoubtedly makes students less ready for college. Definitely not a solution.

Memo to Three-Year-Old Slackers

To: American Three-Year-Olds
From: America's Education Reform Thought Leaders'
Re: Get to work, you lazy slackers

It has come to our attention that your older brothers and sisters have been showing up to Kindergarten completely unprepared for the requirements of a rigorous education. It is time to nip this indolent behavior in the bud. You probably don't even know what 'indolent" means, do you? Dammit-- this is exactly why Estonia and Singapore are challenging the US for world domination!

It's time for you to understand-- the party is over. We waited patiently for you to get potty trained and weaned off breast feeding on your own schedule, and that was probably a mistake because it led you to believe that you could just do things when you're good and ready. Well, no more. We're on to you. We saw you spend all that time crawling instead of walking because walking was just tooo haaard. Wah, wah, wah. We're done coddling you. The state has a schedule for you, and you are damn well going to get with it. You got to float around all free and easy in your Mommy's non-rigorous womb, and that's enough time off for anyone.

No, I don't want to see the pretty picture that you drew, unless you can explain what sources and data contributed to your compositional choices. You really need to be synthesizing two or more disparate sources for your pictures. And stick to the prompt-- I said draw a picture of an important Sumerian ceremony, not a bunny and a sun. And stop getting up every ten seconds to go look at something. You need to start learning how to focus properly. Sit in that chair and draw for the next ninety minutes without getting up.

Sitting will be good preparation for testing. Of course we're going to test you. How else will we know whether or not you are on track for college? Yes, I know your Mommy says she loves you and you can do anything, but what the hell does she know. Only a good solid expensive standardized test can tell us whether or not you are college material. Stop whining and get your pudgy little hand wrapped around that mouse. C'mon-- show some grit.

I know this is a lot to take in, and we really would have started last year when you were two, but frankly, all you would say was "no" over and over again. It's possible that the terrible twos are the educational barrier that we can't break past. But now you're three, and all we have to break you of is this tendency to be distracted by childlike wonder and joy, and this ridiculous desire to play all the time. We must get you ready for Kindergarten, or you will never get into a good college and then we won't have the workers we need to compete globally and our leaders will lose supreme command of the universe and our corporations will have access to fewer markets. You don't want that, do you? You don't know what "compete globally" means? See, this is what we're talking about. Go sit down and write a six-sentence paragraph utilizing multiple sources about economic developments in postagrarian societies, using non-fiction sources from government websites.

Look, kid. Everybody wants you to be Kindergarten-ready, so you've got to practice sitting inert, taking senseless tests, and being properly compliant. You need experience in going days at a time without playing, and I'm a little concerned that your napping is getting out of hand. And don't think your teacher is going to let you off the hook-- we know how soft and wimpy she is, and we've taken care of her.

Does everyone want this for all three year olds? Well, no, actually. Chad and Buffy, you can disregard this memo. Shaniqua and Bubba Jean-- you'd better listen up.

#AskArne & Spleen Theater

#AskArne is a video series on youtube that features Arne Duncan ~~spewing baloney~~ answering questions from theoretical teachers and other interested folks. It generally features the sort of straight shooting we've learned to expect from the USDOE, but the newly released "The Role of Private Funds and Interests in Education" could be used to fertilize all the fields in Kansas.

I am not going to be the first or last blogger to take a look at this, but the point of this blog is me to vent my spleen before I end up with little blown-up spleen parts all over my insides, so I am going to break this down anyway. I watch with the captions on and sound off because I think you get better face and body language reads. Also, I get hives listening to Arne's voice. I'll be using the closed captions as my transcript, so if somebody has bollixed that up, the bollixing will be reflected here.

This may be the toughest seven minutes I've ever watched my way through, but here we go...

Opening logo. I never really noticed before, but what the hell is that thing at the bottom of the tree? A flying snake wearing a beret?

Hey! It's Joiselle Cunningham and Lisa Clarke, teaching fellows from NYC and Washington state. "That means we are teachers on leave from our positions, bringing teacher perspectives to the Department." Oh, honey. I hope you do better work back in your classroom. They are standing at the National Library of Education, a thing I did not realize existed.

They're going to talk about private interests, and they cross fade into thanking Arne for taking the time to talk to them at this arranged interview that they were assigned by his office to conduct. This canned note of acting like he's a gracious guest instead of the ringmaster hits a nice, full false note right off the bat. Arne is sitting at a library table with the ladies in just-a-shirt, as if he's a Regular Guy and not a Very Rich Guy who likes to hang with Extremely Rich Guys.

So Lisa is going to ask the first question. And we leap right into it, asking if corporate-based philanthropists are playing too heavy a role in public education and if there's a corporate agenda at the Department of Education. This is a question she's "heard teachers asking" and the slight smirk that accompanies it suggests that the question reminds her of when her daughter asked if there was a monster in the closet. What I'm seeing is, "Please, Arne, calm the foolish fears of these silly people."

Arne is a good student who dutifully works important words from the prompt into the first sentence of his response. But as for that influence, "Nothing could be further from the truth." Not for the last time, I must applaud the special effects of the film. You cannot see his nose grow at all. "We listen to everybody," he says, and then proceeds to list a bunch of everybody's who are all the types of groups that cynics might call corporate-based philanthropy. "We try and spend a lot of time, "he continues incorrectly (it's "try TO spend"), "with teachers, listening to students, listening to community members." It's at this point that I start talking back to the screen. "Try harder, Arne." I say. My spleen is mollified. "A number of really important decisions we have made recently have been based on those conversations" he says, and then sticks the landing on the talking point about moving away from zero tolerance.

"Arne, let's stay on this for a second," says Joiselle, and I think it's cute the way she pretends to be controlling the flow of this conversation with her patron and boss. Then I hear "as we talk to teachers around the country" and I am momentarily wondering when the heck THAT happened. Was there a USDOE listening tour? Because I'm thinking that would be almost as much fun as a John King CCSS pep rally. Anyway, she's heard somewhere (everywhere?) that there's concern about private corporations and philanthropists that are involved in public education. What is the role of private dollars in public education? Which is a nice phrase, so kudos, uncredited writer.

"Sadly, education is underinvested in the vast majority of places this country." And then he's on to a list of things that schools need money for but I am busy brain-goggling. Wait! What? Because it appears that he is

A) admitting that schools are underfunded and therefor lacking in resources, which is funny, because in his ~~blaming~~ discussions of What's Wrong With Teachers and Schools and Teachers, this problem doesn't get much play ("We should be amazed and proud that our teachers achieve so much success with so little help from us," said no Arne
Duncan ever);

B) that when the government underfunds one of its agencies, the private sector should be picking up the slack. So, as roads and infrastructures crumble in PA, we should be getting corporations to pick up that tab. I myself am really looking forward to "The CIA, brought to you by Proctor and Gamble"

and C) that this private picking up of public slack is not a civic duty or a contribution, but an investment, aka thing you put money into with the expectation of getting more money out of it.

In short (okay, not really) I'm pretty sure Duncan just said, "Come buy up our public education functions. They're going cheap and offer great ROI."

AND (bonus round) he said it in the process of proving that private dollars do NOT have undue influence on public education. Which I suppose could be true, because "undue" just means inappropriate and (anti-surprise) Duncan thinks "due" influence = "pretty damn much."

So now my spleen is singing "Ride of the Valkyrie" but Arne says that you have to have good smart partnerships and you don't want schools to be isolated from the community, and that's not entirely stupid, so my spleen subsides once again. Schools as community centers. Yes, that's swell too. For example--

BAM. We will now list Swell Things That Corporate Sponsors Have Done. GE Foundation. Ford Foundation helped with labor relations? Joyce Foundation helped with teacher evaluation stuff (and that has been a rousing success, cries my spleen) which comes in the same sentence as reducing gun violence in Chicago which I don't think is meant to be related to teacher evaluations, although who the hell knows these days. Now we'll spend a relatively huge chunk of time on P-Tech (sponsored by IBM).

Then Arne unleashes "Again, all of this should be determined at the local level, not by us." And my spleen is amazed at the special effects, because you can not actually see the room disappear under a giant tidal wave of bovine fecal matter.

That somehow leads directly to a new idea-- that with all of this unmet need, for teachers and schools to bar the door and say that all these people are bad somehow or have an agenda of hurting kids or hurting teachers is just-- well, that has not been his experience. So there you have it. Arne's decision here is completely data-driven by one piece of data-- his experience. And schools need money, and these rich guys have money, so what else do we need to know anyway?

New question. We name check a couple of other Teaching Fellows who heard a question about private interests and the new testing stuff. And my spleen is sad, because it knows this is an important question and it expects to hate the answer a lot. Anyway, Lisa is saying that some people claim the new assessments are just about making money, and could you, Arne, tell us what you think about that, because we, as teaching fellows working here at the USDOE as well as being functioning literate beings on planet earth for the past several years, have no idea what Arne Duncan might say about the role of corporate interests when it comes to testing. And Lisa makes a pouty face, like she is sad to even have to bother this Great Guy with such a meanspirited inquiry. Seriously. My spleen thinks this is the worst infomercial ever.

Arne thinks that's an interesting question. He thinks the facts don't quite back up the worry and skepticism (so, only mostly back it up?) and here comes what I believe is an actual shiny new talking point. Here's the pitch-- schools have been giving oh-so-many tests anyway, and they were certainly made by companies, and golly, THAT was certainly expensive. But now we've got these consortia that can get those tests for you bulk, and THAT has to be cheaper (because the government always gets stuff for the best price) and economies of scale, dontchaknow. And you'll be glad to know that the test developers are working to some up with something that goes way beyond the bubble tests with critical thinking and writing, too. So yippee! More better tests! Saving money, so we can pump the leftovers back into the classroom. My spleen wants to run over to the pentagon to get a $10,000 hammer to smack Arne in the head.

New question-- Do states have a choice, Arne, with all this? And we are going to pretend that "this" means "tests." At this point my spleen begins to suspect that Pearson shot Arne's face up with a 50-gallon drum of Botox because how else could he get through all this without laughing, but it seems to be wearing off because he finds parts of this answer hilarious, like explaining that states can be part of one or both of the consortia or make their own tests out of everyday objects found around the house. But--again-- don't 50 states have more purchasing power together and also don't we want to be able to compare things all across the country and my spleen and I are vocal again, hollering, "Yes, Arne, I hardly know how to plan my lessons without knowing what the kids in fifth period English out in Medicine Hat, Wyoming, are doing!" Arne thinks states are free to do different things if they want to act like damn fools.

New question-- When guys like Bill Gates or Eli Broad start throwing money around, does that buy them a seat at the table? Joiselle asks this like she's in a hurry to get to the end of the question because it's a dumb question and he needs to kill it with fire. I unkindly suggest that the question is backward and would rather ask what Arne could do to get the USDOE a seat at Gates and Broad's table, but I can see I am living in disappointment here.

Arne says he has great respect for them and appreciates all their money. He smiles like he remembers the time they took him out for smoothies and let him lick their spoons. But no, they don't have a seat at the table. "You guys are the table," says Arne, and I think that's supposed to mean "You guys who are teachers" and not "You guys who are my departmental prop/lackeys" but it doesn't matter because my spleen just exploded in one bright flash of raging incredulity.

Teacher Lisa shares that she knows Gates did some work with teacher leadership stuff and so it's complicated, and I spleenlessly yell that, no, it's not complicated at all, but she goes on to say she'd really like us to engage each other and I'm thinking, yes, because after the many many many many many many many invitations teachers have received to be part of the CCSSreformy movement, we all just keep turning them down and refusing to offer any insights at all, and she is smiling a little bit like she can't believe she's saying this rotting raccoon carcass of a talking point either, but she'd like this conversation to continue, perhaps on twitter because she heard that worked really well for Michelle Rhee the other day, so let's use #AskArne to do that. And then she thanks Arne for showing up to this PR moment that he ordered, and we're on to credits and I am picking up pieces of my spleen from around the room.

You should not watch this. Nobody should. It is one of the most cynical reality-impaired dog-and-pony-with-a-paper-cone-pretending-to-be-aunicorn shows ever concocted, and now I have to go lie down.

A Peek at CCSS 2.0

Press release from 2017

The United States Department of Education (a wholly-owned subsidiary of Pearson International) is pleased to announce the new, improved version of the Common Core State Standards. Some of the highlights of this new set of standards include:

*We're pretty sure that Kindergarten simply isn't early enough to start the reading process, so we are proud to announce a program that starts this important educational experience as soon after conception as possible. Our problem with backwards scaffolding has been that we stopped too soon. How can we hope to compete internationally when our newborns have not yet been exposed to a dynamic and robust reading curriculum. **Phonics for Fetuses** closes that gap.

*DIBELS broke new ground with its program of having small children read gibberish. But why stop there. The new **SHMIBELS** program will require students to write gibberish. Students must produce ten pages of lettering without creating a single recognizable word (yet all completely pronounceable). The writing will be timed and matched against the Pearson master SHMIBELS list to see if students have produced the correct gibberish and not just any random gibberish. (Note: this program is expected to help target many future USDOE employees).

*Now that we have first graders writing multi-sentence essays, it's time to step up our game. **Novels for Nine-year-olds** brings the writing process to your fourth grade classroom. Students will follow a simple 450-page step by step guide that will help them create a novel that is page-for-page pretty much exactly like every other novel being written for the program. Rigor without creativity-- just the way we like it. (Note: Pearson will retain the publishing rights to all works created in this program)

*In response to continued complaints that focus on testing has squeezed out many valuable phys ed and arts programs, we are proud to introduce the **Physical Arts** program. For this program, offered during one day of the 9th grade year, students will draw a picture of a pony on a tuba and then throw the tuba as far as possible.

*By pushing subject matter further down the sequence, we expect to free up the entire 10th grade year for testing. Nothing but testing, every single day, all day. With that much testing, our students are certain to become the kinds of geniuses who can trounce our historic enemies, the South Koreans and the Estonians. We anticipate this becoming a rite of passage and popular cultural milestone as families look forward with joy and anticipation to the **Year of the Tests**. To those critics who claim that we have not offered support in the literature for this testing, we want to note that we have closely followed the writings of Suzanne Collins and Franz Kafka.

*CCSS 2.0 will feature even more improved data management. Infants will be fitted with a Gates Foundation data chip, while their social security number will allow us to link the vital health data with all online and economic activity. At the end of **Year of the Tests**, we expect to present each student with a document explaining what jobs he will hold, where he will live, who he is likely to marry, if he will be allowed to reproduce, and when he should expect to die (and of which causes).

Schools that manage to become fully certified in CCSS 2.0 will be designated a **Primary Testing School District.** We intend to make sure these are so widespread that every student will be able to have a **PTSD** experience. When every student in America has experienced some **PTSD**, then our nation will be truly great.

Please note that these standards are a totally legal state initiative, and our involvement is just as a supportive federal agency that thinks what you states are doing is swell. However, state participation in CCSS 2.0 is voluntary. States need not join up.

In related news, the administration would like to announce **Race to the Trough**. State will have the chance to compete for the right to receive their usual funding for schools, roads, airport staff, as well as any consideration for relief in the event of any future emergency. States may compete by being one of the first fifty to announce that all state department of ed functions are being handed over to the USDOE. Thank you for your support.

Should I Quit?

I've been there. A little over a decade ago, I was a local union president through contentious contract negotiations that started with contract stripping** and ended with a strike. I learned just how little some community members valued what we do. I learned it because some of them stopped me on the street or called me at home to tell me. And not just the foaming-at-the-mouth angry ones-- those were actually easier to take because I knew they were angry and upset by the situation and, hell, so was I. No, the tough ones were the people who wanted to explain to me in cool, calm, rational terms why teachers just didn't deserve the kind of money, autonomy or support that we were asking for.

So I stared into the abyss for about three years, and when it was settled, I started looking-- seriously looking-- at other career options.

I have asked that question-- should I quit?

I can't tell you how to answer that question for yourself, but I can tell you how I did, and didn't, do.

I didn't stay because I didn't want to be a quitter. Quitting doesn't make you a quitter, and staying in a situation that is toxic does not make you noble.

I didn't stay because I had to do it for the kids. I am not indispensable. I'm a pretty good teacher, and I can be replaced with another pretty good teacher. Some day I will have to be.

I would not quit because teaching made me unhappy. My job is not responsible for making me happy. My students are not responsible for making me happy or feeding me emotionally. The person responsible for my emotional health and happiness-- well, that's my job.

Quitting or not quitting, for me, came down to just one question-- can I do the work that I set out to do? I got into this profession to help students get better at reading, writing, speaking and listening. I got into this profession to help students become a better version of themselves, to help them find a way to be fully human in this world. So my question was, could I still do that work?

There are many things that can get in the way. A district that starves the classroom of useful resources. A set of rules that makes employment contingent on working against those goals. A building environment so toxic that the atmosphere prevents any growth. An environment so riddled with obstacles that simply getting past them leaves no energy left for actually doing the work.

In the end, being unvalued and disrespected didn't factor in my decision. Dealing with people who didn't get it didn't factor in. I could still do the work I had set out to do, and so I stayed.

My relationship with my job changed. I became more protective and feisty about my personal teaching mission. I became more willing to challenge authority or (because I have passive-aggressive behavior down to an art form) more willing to defy the system quietly to do what I believe is right. I got out of union leadership, which had brought me all too often in contact with the most difficult people both outside and inside the profession. And I became more deliberate in cultivating support systems and rewarding activities in my life outside the building.

It took a good three years for me to come back from the edge, to stop scanning employment ads and thinking, "Hmmm, maybe..."

As I said, I can't tell anyone else how to make this decision. I know lots of folks face it. I know big urban districts bring a level of bureaucratic cray-cray that my small district can only dream of. And I know most of all that the people who used to stop me on the street or call me at home now sit in state and federal capitals and even in the superintendent's office of some districts. The people who can make teaching miserable have unprecedented power. I don't begrudge anybody the decision to quit, and I try not to judge. It is an ugly new world. But no matter how ugly the world gets, it still needs teachers, and I still want to be one.

**Contract stripping is a negotiation technique where management proposes to cut off your arms and legs and then pretends that only cutting off your arms constitutes a "concession." It's a great way to negotiate without giving up a thing. In our case, the opening salvo of negotiations was to strip dozens of language items from the contract.

Should I Be a Teacher?

Every teacher faces that moment when a student announces, sometimes with fear, sometimes with excitement-- "I want to be a teacher!" This has become a touchy topic. All across the country, teachers are abandoning the profession. Our retention rate for new teachers is terrible, and every day seems to yield one more article entitled "Why I Had To Give Up" or "How I Was Driven from My Job" or "Holy Schniekies on a Schingle, I'm About To Rip All My Hair Out If I Don't Get Out Now." At times, it feels like we are at some creepy cabin in the wood where some monster keeps dragging teachers off into the dark, one by one.

So when some new blood announces his intent to join us in the isolated cabin, even the most dedicated teacher feels at least a small urge to say, "Run away! Save yourself!!"

I get it. I do. Even an only-partly-conscious teacher is aware of how much fire we are under in so many ways. And you don't have to be some kind of grizzled veteran (you know-- the kind we need to fire right away so that we can replace them with enthusiastic young temps) to know that in some ways, this is the worst it's ever been.

But I still feel sad every time I hear about one of my colleagues telling a student, "No, no. Whatever you do, don't become a teacher."

I still believe in teaching. I still believe in public education in this country. But at the same time, I don't think it's for everybody. Here are some warning signs that the profession might not be for you.

I don't like to rock the boat. If the people in charge tell me to jump, I won't even be lippy enough to say "how high?"

There was a time when teaching was a good profession for mildmannered go-along folks. That time has passed.

It's not just that you are going to have to stand up for yourself when you are directed to do things that are unethical, illegal, or just educational malpractice. At some point in your career, you are going to have to be an advocate-- perhaps the only advocate-- for a child. Filing the right paperwork and trusting the Powers That Be to do the right things will not be enough. That child will need a champion. Most of your students will need a champion.

I'm not advocating that you see yourself as some sort of knight in armor battling monsters under every rock. I'm not suggesting that you view all your interactions with administration as Us vs. Them antagonism-- that's just terrible for everybody. But you are going to be surrounded by allies and obstacles, and you must be ready to push through those obstacles, whatever form they may take.

I always liked [insert subject here] and now I guess what I can do with it is be a teacher.

No no no. Teaching is not a default profession. Not any more. If you think it's something you can just wander in and do because, well, it's a job, then teaching will eat you up and spit you out faster than a vegetarian with a mouthful of cow tongue.

It isn't just that you'll lack the toughness. It's that a teacher has to know what he's doing. By which I mean, you must know why you're teaching what you're teaching. You must know what the point is, what the purpose is. You cannot cover Chapter 2 from the Widget textbook because, well, that's what widget teachers do, you think. You will never be able to teach Chapter 2 effectively until you know why you're teaching it.

It is a long, long road from "I think I'll teach about widgets" to "I am going to teach this concept on page 13 in order to achieve this exact goal for my students.". If you don't know why you're standing in that classroom, there are many many highly authoritative sources just waiting to tell you the wrong answer.

We get summers off, right?

Oh, just go away.

I'll just try it for a while.

The Humane Society won't even let you just try out a puppy for a few weeks. And children are not puppies. The profession does not need drive-by do-gooders or edu-tourists ready to go slumming among the little people for a short time. A school building is just a building. A school is a community of teachers and students, and even the students are just passing through. Schools need teachers who are in it for the long haul, who will provide stability.

So don't date a single parent and tell the kids that you'll just play at being their step-parent for a little while. Don't propose to your girlfriend by saying, "Let's try out this engagement thing for a little while." And don't try being a teacher for a while. Do it, or go away.

So should I be a teacher? Seriously? Can I get an answer?

Teaching is hard work. It is no longer stable and dependable work, and the jobs are drying up. People will call you names and blame you for things you could never do anything about. The pay is not great, and there will not be some great outpouring of love and support to make up the psychic difference. On top of that, you will work in isolated circumstances and sometimes find yourself working for idiots who will evaluate you based on terrible, stupid systems.

Teaching is not the only job in the world that sets less-than-ideal conditions. There are lots of reasons that teaching sucks. But in this respect, it has merely become like many other professions, where the work is hard to get and hard to do. And the answer to "Should I do this" is the same for teaching as it is for jet piloting or deep sea diving or playing in a heavy metal polka band--

Do it if it's what you want to do.

If it's what you want to do-- HAVE to do-- then go for it. There will always be time to give up later if you must, but in the meantime, is this what you want to do? If so, do it! If it's what you must do, if it's what you're driven to do, if it's what you're passionate about doing-- then do it.

I became a teacher because I had to. I had to in the same way that I have to write and I have to make music and have to exercise. Because if I don't, I don't feel myself. Teaching, as crazy-making and challenging and frustrating and miserable as it can be, makes me feel fully me. It hooks me up to my students and my community and the world around me in a way that nothing else can.

It is work that must be done. I think of it a little like jury duty-- do you want this essential job done by somebody who treats it with serious dedication? Are you that person?

If it makes you feel something like that, damn the torpedoes and slap that pedal to the floor. Should you be a teacher? I don't know. If you WANT to be a teacher, then you should not let anything stop you, including grumpy old educators who are worried about the future. Would I do it all over again, if I knew what I know now? I sure as hell would. I am a teacher, dammit. Maybe someday I'll be ready to hang it up, but even if that day comes, I won't regret any of the days that came before. If you can imagine feeling like that, come join us.

Close Reading 2.0

Close reading is an example of how misshapen and distorted a teaching technique can become when it enters the gravitational pull of CCSS. The specific ways in which it has become misshapen tells us a lot about the shape of CCSS.

Where did close reading come from, anyway?

A search on good old google ngram tells us that the phrase "close reading" has been around since 1800 in some trace amounts, starting to climb post-WWII and steadily growing to a peak around 2000. This is not surprising. Calling a reading technique "close reading" is kind of like announcing your new athletic program, "fast walking."

But close reading as a technique for literary analysis began, according to some sources, in the 1920's under the tutelage of I. A. Richards, a forefather of the New School of criticism. You can google all this and pursue it at greater length. Take away that close reading is old.

It is also...well...vague. Or rather, broadly interpreted by many proponents over the decades. Some critics assert that Richards was taking a Skinnerian view of language, treating it as a behavior. And the path gets tricky because although Richards is sometimes considered important to the New Critics, the New Critics said they rejected much of his work, and then proceeded to pretty much follow it. Add to that the fact that so much of the groundwork was laid in the fertile but often hard-to-translate-into-plain-English soil of academia and hightoned scholarliness, and-- well, for our purposes, let's just note that close reading has been around as a technique for almost 100 years.

How does close reading work?

So what is it? There, too, we find a number of interpretations, and for every one of us who went to college to study Englishy Stuff, it all seems so vaguely familiar. My professors never said, "Okay, we're going to do a close reading of this text. Here's the official list of close reading steps. Follow them." I suspect my experience is not unique.

But on the occasions when I have heard about close reading, I recognized it pretty readily. Look carefully at the writer's language choices-- diction, tone, that good stuff. Know the context of his/her writing. Follow the syntax. In longer works, note the sequencing of words and ideas. Is it narrative or dramatic-- watch for specific choices accordingly.

In short, "close reading" is what many of us think of as "reading."

In thirty-five years, I've never told my students, "Okay, we're going to do a close reading now." But I direct their attention to how it makes a difference whether Frost writes "to stop without A farmhouse near" or "to stop without THE farmhouse near." We examine what Longfellow might intend in "Psalm of Life" and how the recent deaths of loved ones might inform that intention. We watch Twain eviscerate Cooper's inexact word choices. We search for allusions in the word choices of William Bradford. We try to pick apart that confounding twentieth chapter of *Light in August*.

So why is putting close reading with CCSS a big deal?

So when I first heard that close reading was coming to town, a-riding on the CCSS train, I thought, "No big deal. We've been doing that for years." Well, yes and no.

Close Reading 2.0 is a new animal. The new, improved, CCSS-ready version has some significant differences from the old-school version we thought we knew.

It's for hard things. In one of many training videos available on youtube, the teacher starts right in by noting that close reading is for hard things. It's kind of an odd assertion. As a teacher of pop culture, my bread and butter has long been giving close readings of ordinary pieces of writing. Twilight may be a work of light fluff, but a close reading of it unpacks how many truly indefensible and odious subtexts are lurking in its gooey pages. But no-- we are hearing repeatedly that we are supposed to use close reading for hard things.

It's for short stuff only. Short poems. Short excerpts. Little things. It's an aspect that I hardly know how to argue with, like a nutritionist who insists that we should only eat red food. I'm pretty sure there is some valuable literature out there that is more than one page long.

It must be read in a vacuum. Of all the cockamamie bits of malpractice that have been attached to reading under CCSS, this is the most cockamamied of all. The examples are legion. Read the Gettysburg Address without knowing anything about the Civil War. Read "A Modest Proposal" without being told anything about Swift or the poor of the time. Read *The Sun Also Rises* without knowing anything about The Great War (only, of course, don't, because it's a big long novel).

It's an easy game. Any English teacher can rattle off a dozen works that only fully give up their depth and riches if students understand a bit of context.

There isn't a real teacher of literature on the planet who thinks this is a good idea. These three restrictions tie the students' hands and force them to do readings that are, contrary to the buzzwords, an inch deep at best. With just a few quick additions, CCSS whizzes have turned Close Reading into Close Reading 2.0, whch is kind of like turning wine into vinegar.

So then why is Close Reading 2.0 here?

Why Close Reading 2.0? Simple. Reading instruction is hereby turned into test prep.

Standardized test excerpts are always short, usually inpenetrably hard (or the kind of dull that passes for difficulty), and always delivered without any context at all, not even the context of the rest of the work from which they've been untimely ripped.

Close Reading 2.0 is proof (piece of evidence #2,098,387) that CCSS was built to feed the testing beast. Close Reading 2.0 is authentic assessment turned on its head. You remember authentic assessment. It was just starting to flourish when NCLB plowed it under over a decade ago. The idea was that if you were trying to teach a particular skill, your assessment should come as close as possible to actually demonstrating that skill.

What we knew back then was that if you wanted to teach reading and interpreting a full, complex work of literature, you couldn't assess that skill with a bubble test. Now, instead, our Educational Overlords say that since the assessment is going to be a machine-scorable standardized test, then that's the skill we must teach. And so instead of actual reading, we are now pushed to teach standardized test reading, and to make it look like legitimate, we'll give it the name of an old and honorable practice.

Close reading? You reformers keep using that word. I do not think it means what you think it means.

Close Reading 2.0 is crap. Specifically, it is the kind of crap that only people who know nothing about reading or teaching could come up with. It is one more application of the idea that if we are only able to count X, then X must be all that counts. It is teaching redesigned to fit the test. It is educational malpractice. For English teachers, it is one line that we refuse to cross.

Choice & Cable

School choice is the ultimate education zombie, the argument that absolutely will not die. It has been shown time and again that there are so many things wrong with school choice-- soooooooo many things-- and yet from charter school profiteers to governors of New York, people just keep opening up the tomb and letting the corpse ramble around some more.

There are a host of arguments to be made, a raft of reasons to be debated, but today I'm going to focus on just one idea. We can hack on the limbs of this shambling horror some other day. But the whole idea of school choice is, at least publicly, based on a belief in market forces and how they will bring quality. Here's the thing:

Market forces do not foster superior quality. Market forces foster superior marketability.

We are awash in examples. Does anybody think the beer or soda markets are dominated by the companies who have created the best product? Or would you like to talk about VHS vs. Betamax one more time? But let's focus on a more immediate and instructive example. Let's talk about television.

When cable television arrived, it brought with it an explosion of channels. It was exciting-- 500 channels, and something completely different on each one of them. We had choice like never before. Even tv snobs could find quality channels that served their interest. Slowly but surely, all that changed.

The drive for market share created a slow-motion race to mediocrity. So today, A&E (that used to stand for Art and Entertainment) has dumped broadcasts of Broadway classics in favor of millionaire hicks. The History Channel produces less history, more Pawn Stars. Bravo, also started as a haven for the Arts, now is the home of endless trashy drama. Most famously, nobody wants their MTV for musical reasons any more. Channels increasingly tried to create a marketable brand, aimed at a broader sector.

The marketplace did not produce greater quality. It didn't even produce much more variety, but stamped variety out as channels chased the same market shares. And there's more.

That market can't even sustain itself. It turns out that when you offer too much tv choice, the individual choices aren't self-sustaining. That's why your cable company makes you buy bundles-- because if these channels had to sustain themselves with their share of the market, they couldn't. Cut the market up into enough slices, and it won't sustain any of them.

The other long-term effect of the marketplace is to create Big Winners. Because, of course, your 500 channels are all owned by about five corporations. So as in other marketplaces (like, say, the supermarket), you don't have real choices at all. As much as fans of choice love the marketplace, the marketplace hates choice and over time, in every industry, eventually erases it. No corporation sitting on top of the heap has ever said, "We should be sure not to gain too much control of the marketplace, because then we would create less quality." (That includes, especially, Microsoft).

There's an older lesson from TV as well. Remember the Beverly Hillbillies? They were a huge hit in the late sixties, and when they were canceled they were still ranked 33rd in the ratings. But they were canceled because they appealed to the wrong audience. Advertisers wanted to market to a hipper crow. Popular was not good enough. Popular with the right people was required. Not all customers are valued equally in the marketplace (and the value of hick-mocking TV can change in forty years).

There is no example, anywhere, ever, of the marketplace creating a drive for higher quality and better products. There is a sea of examples of the marketplace pushing for products that are cheaper, have lowest common denominator cookie cutter appeal, and aim at only some of the customers. None of these are characteristics that would enhance US public schools.

VAM for Dummies

If you don't spend every day with your head stuck in the reform toilet, receiving the never-ending education swirly that is school reformy stuff, there are terms that may not be entirely clear to you. One is VAM-- Value-Added Measure.

VAM is a concept borrowed from manufacturing. If I take one dollar's worth of sheet metal and turn it into a lovely planter that I can sell for ten dollars, I've added nine dollars of value to the metal.

It's a useful concept in manufacturing management. For instance, if my accounting tells me that it costs me ten dollars in labor to add five dollars of value to an object, I should plan my going-out-of-business sale today.

And a few years back, when we were all staring down the NCLB maw requiring that 100% of our students be above average by this year, it struck many people as a good idea-- let's check instead to see if teachers are making students better. Let's measure if teachers have added value to the individual student.

There are so many things wrong with this conceptually, starting with the idea that a student is like a piece of manufacturing material and continuing on through the reaffirmation of the school-is-a-factory model of education. But there are other problems as well.

1)   Back in the manufacturing model, I knew how much value my piece of metal had before I started working my magic on it. We have no such information for students.

2)   The piece of sheet metal, if it just sits there, will still be a piece of sheet metal. If anything, it will get rusty and less valuable. But a child, left to its own devices, will still get older, bigger, and smarter. A child will add value on its own, out of thin air. Almost like it was some living, breathing sentient being and not a piece of raw manufacturing material.

3)   All pieces of sheet metals are created equal. Any that are too notequal get thrown in the hopper. On the assembly line, each piece of metal is as easy to add value to as the last. But here we have one more reformy idea predicated on the idea that children are pretty much identical.

How to solve these three big problems? Call the statisticians! This is the point at which that horrifying formula that pops up in these discussions appears. Or actually, a version of it, because each state has its own special sauce when it comes to VAM. In Pennsylvania, our special VAM sauce is called PVAAS. I went to a state training session about PVAAS in 2009 and wrote about it for my regular newspaper gig. Here's what I said about how the formula works at the time:

PVAAS uses a thousand points of data to project the test results for students. This is a highly complex model that three well-paid consultants could not clearly explain to seven college-educated adults, but there were lots of bars and graphs, so you know it's really good. I searched for a comparison and first tried "sophisticated guess;" the consultant quickly corrected me— "sophisticated prediction." I tried again—was it like a weather report, developed by comparing thousands of instances of similar conditions to predict the probability of what will happen next? Yes, I was told. That was exactly right. This makes me feel much better about PVAAS, because weather reports are the height of perfect prediction.

Here's how it's supposed to work. The magic formula will factor in everything from your socio-economics through the trends over the past X years in your classroom, throw in your pre-testy thing if you like, and will spit out a prediction of how Johnny would have done on the test in some neutral universe where nothing special happened to Johnny. Your job as a teacher is to get your real Johnny to do better on The Test than Alternate Universe Johnny would.

See? All that's required for VAM to work is believing that the state can accurately predict exactly how well your students would have done this year if you were an average teacher. How could anything possibly go wrong??

And it should be noted-- all of these issues occur in the process before we add refinements such as giving VAM scores based on students that the teacher doesn't even teach. There is no parallel for this in the original industrial VAM model, because nobody anywhere could imagine that it's not insanely ridiculous.

If you want to know more, the interwebs are full of material debunking this model, because nobody-- I mean nobody-- believes in it except politicians and corporate privateers. The awesome blog Vamboozled by Audrey Amrein-Beardsley is a fine place to start.

This is one more example of a feature of reformy stuff that is so topto-bottom stupid that it's hard to understand. But whether you skim the surface, look at the philosophical basis, or dive into the math, VAM does not hold up. You may be among the people who feel like you don't quite get it, but let me reassure you-- when I titled this "VAM for Dummies," I wasn't talking about you. VAM is always and only for dummies; it's just that right now, the dummies are in charge.

"Why I Heart Common Core"

Hey. Everybody else is writing one. Why not me? Here's my teachercheerleading CCSS letter.

As everybody knows, US education has been descending into failure of Biblical proportions, leading to an entire generation of students who don't know enough to come in out the rain. We were facing world domination by Estonia and South Korea. Thank goodness a bunch of teachers got together, possibly teaming up with parents, to produce the Common Core State Standards which were totally not created by a bunch of guys from the major testing corporations. These life-changing and nation-rescuing standards were voluntarily adopted by 45 states who were in no way influenced by their desire to get their federal ed money and avoid the impending NCLB crash. In fact, these 45 states were so excited about voluntarily adopting CCSS, some of them did it before the standards were actually published.

Some wacko ~~tea partiers~~ ~~Obama haters~~ crankypants teachers have been raising a fuss, but a complete legit assortment of polls show that 75% of teachers support the standards, because standards just like these have been around forever. So these are just like the standards we had when we were sucking hard enough to take the chrome off a fender, but they are so totally different that we will now turn education completely around.

In my own classroom, Common Core Standards have been pedagogically transformative in a dynamically epistomological kind of way. My students are involved in deep and thoughtful activities that involve interaction, reflection, and involvement. We do projects. We have discussions. We use critical thinking. We read books, and when we do, we read carefully and deeply and discuss ideas about the book while using details from the book to back these up. We even write stuff, and sometime use computers and techy things.

These may sound like activities that teachers have been doing in classrooms since the dawn of time, but before CCSS, I made my students learn everything by rote and repetition. We used pieces of slate that we drew on with charcoal. If we used novels at all, we simply let them sit on the desk and gained insights into the contents by consulting our spirit animals. I mean, I had no idea that critical thinking even was a thing! It used to take me three months just to introduce regular old thinking. Also, grit and rigor. We are awash in grit and rigor, and I can see with my own eyes that the grit and rigor is transforming my useless young hooligans into future investment bankers. It's awesome.

CCSS has liberated me. Once I open my Pearson test book and set up the lesson that is carefully aligned to the standards for that exact day of the school year, I am free to put my own personal spin on it. I could deliver the lesson with a red shirt on, or I could wear a blue shirt. I could recite the opener with a thoughtful face or a happy face. I can part my hair on whatever side I choose. Teachers who say that the Core is restrictive are just cray cray. Because freedom is slavery.

Of course, teachers need time to adjust to these new standards of awesomeness, time to plan lessons around our new materials, and time to adjust students to having just skipped an entire grade of instruction. And maybe we could hold off on the tests until, you know, some are actually written-- though the tests are a necessary part of the learning experience. Also, seeing results from last year's single test will totally tell me what I need to emphasize with next year's students.

But even though the standards have never been tested, we can all be assured that they will make all students gritty and rigorous and college ready. Whether students want to grow up to be artists, welders, scientists, writers, actors, engineers, or stay-at-home parents, don't they all deserve to have the exact same preparation for those futures? But by giving them rigorous tests now, we can unlock all their dreams for the future. Because dreams, rigor, common sense, and effectiveness.

I am a more effective teacher now that I have a set of government and corporate documents to tell me how to do my job. Also, ignorance is strength.

If Not for Those Darn Kids

I was in a CCSS training, and the trainer stopped to make an observation about how Kids These Days lack discipline and order. She even illustrated it with a story about her own child. And a light bulb went on for me.

I have long considered that the Masters of Reforming Our Nation's Schools view children as widgets, as little programmable devices, as interchangeable gears, as nothing more than Data Generation Units. I had considered that these MoRONS were indifferent to children. What I had not considered was that reformers are actively hostile to children.

I have certainly heard people in the ed world complain about Those Darn Kids, and I have taught in the building with more than one person who blames all their classroom woes on terrible awful no good pretty bad students. I try to be understanding. If I hear it once or twice, I assume somebody is having a bad day. If I hear it many times, I assume somebody is a bad teacher.

But a hostile teacher is one thing. A movement that institutionalizes that hostility is a whole other level of awful.

After I wrote about my experience, other teachers shared more of the same. Tales of trainers talking about how Kids These Days need to be rigorously rigored into a state of rigor. And as I reread old materials, I could see the hostility bubbling beneath the surface.

Sometimes it is misplaced and out of date. There are still education commentators railing against the self esteem movement, and while I don't disagree with some of the criticism, it's like complaining that too many Kids These Days are spending too much time on their new computers and listening to the rap music. That ship has sailed, Grampa.

Sometimes it is not even beneath the surface. What is a "no excuse" school, except a school founded on the premise that Kids These Days are all hooligans that will take a mile if you give them an inch. Or even one of those new-fangled millimeters. And when Arne Duncan suggests that those suburban white moms have over-inflated images of the abilities of their coddled children, isn't he already suggesting that those over-protective parents need to step aside so their kids can be whipped into shape.

Or Frank Bruni's op-ed that unambiguously declared Duncan correct and opponents of CCSS a raft of child-coddlers: school is supposed to be unpleasant.

The narrative here is not a new one. See if you can recognize some of the key points. We live in a meritocracy that rewards hard work and grit. Therefor, anyone who is poor and unsuccessful must have failed to show merit, hard work, and grit. If we have a lot of poor people, it's because they are all slackers-- and it starts when they're kids. If we could get to them when they were little and whip them into shape, then poverty would be gone. **Fixing education would cure poverty.**

So to fix poverty, we have to toughen these little slackers up. They need to be toughly uncoddled with rigorous excuse-free punches to their tiny brains. **These children are one of the big obstacles to fixing our society (along with the teachers who won't properly kick their little asses).** And just look at how dumb and lazy they are! Look at all the factoids about the things they don't know, and the low test scores they get! **Back in my day,** students got such much better scores and, buddy, we knew stuff. These kids have to be brought up to snuff.

Is your kid wasting time playing? Stop coddling. Did a lesson make him so frustrated he burst into tears? Good-- maybe he'll start taking school seriously now. Did he fail his big test? Let that be a wake-up call for you. Is his spirit being crushed? Then his spirit is too weak and whiny, and his spirit needs to get its act together.

That this sort of program should originate in the halls of power and privilege is unsurprising. These are men who must believe that their own vast success is the result of their own merit and awesomeness, not luck, timing, underhanded gamesmanship or simply the result of a privileged background. Nor is it surprising that they don't subject their own children to Reformed School, because they know that their own children already possess the qualities of virtue that they are so ardently trying to beat into Other People's Children.

Is this is some sort of bizarro generational theater in which Boomers are trying to fix the children they believe Millenials are unfit to raise? Are Americans having another Calvinist flashback?

I don't know. What I do believe is that the reformy movement carries a strong thread of anti-child fervor (or at least anti-Other People's Children), and that this belief that children should be beaten into shape rather than cherished and nurtured.

Look, if you ask my students if I coddle them, they will laugh at you and tell you that I am the least warm, most unfuzzy teacher they've ever dealt with. I believe in many of the virtues that these virtuous crusaders espouse. I even believe that sometimes love means facing hard, painful things.

But I had a superintendent once who used to tell a story about a horse trainer who was asked about the secret of his success. He asked his inquisitors what they thought the first step was, and they made many guesses, all dealing with technical horse trainy actions. Said the trainer, "First, you have to love the horse."

How we can possibly teach students we don't love or respect or value is beyond me. How we enter a classroom with a program that assumes they are unworthy, weak, and fundamentally deficient, and then teach effectively is a mystery. And how we start with the belief that our students are essentially worthless until a hero teacher fixes them-- well, that encompasses so much arrogant, wrong-headed, ineffective and just plain evil mess. If that's our attitude-- or the attitude that we are supposed to embrace-- I know one more reason that CCSS reformy stuff is destined to fail.

Poop Sandwich

If you wanted to trick someone into eating poop, you would not just hand them a bowl of poop unless you also had a gun to point at the person's head.

No, it would be easier to trick them by hiding the poop inside something yummy like soup or a casserole. Or you could make a poop sandwich. Just hide the poop between two perfectly good slices of tasty bread (white, rye, pumpernickel-- for purposes of this metaphor you can use whatever bread you like, as I have no idea which bread would go best with poop).

Recently I wrote about (and by "wrote about," I mean "made fun of") the burgeoning science of grittology, and its earnest belief that we just need students who can Suck It Up.

Because here's the thing-- grit is not entirely a bad concept. I think many of my students could use a little more toughness, a little more faith in their own strength, a little more willingness to bounce back from disappointments and failures.

But grit as it is being presented these days is a big poop sandwich. The perfectly good bread of personal toughness and resiliency is being used to hide a bunch of poop about how schools and employers and corporations and government don't have to show any sensitivity or support to human beings-- if people can't handle being abused and mistreated, then it's their fault for not being gritty enough. Grit as it is currently being presented in the world of Reformy Stuff is just a big poop sandwich.

Standards are not an innately bad thing. But the CCSS are using the value of standards to mask some terrible one-size-fits-all badly-framed poorly-written poop. Having high standards? Also a good thing, but that value is used to hide the crazypants untested wrongheaded standards of CCSS. Having smart young people spend some time helping strengthen schools is not a terrible thought and teaching really is a noble profession, but TFA is using those values to hide an agenda of destroying the profession and aiding profiteering. Assessment is a necessary part of teaching students, but the values of assessment are being used to justify the most wretchedly awful program of high-stakes testing ever seen in human history. Teachers should be accountable to the taxpayers who pay our salaries, but that value is being used to mask an abusive anti-teacher evaluation program that is about destroying teaching as a career.

Those of us who argue against Reformy Stuff often find ourselves in some variation of the same conversation; we are pointing out the evils of some aspect of the whole wretched mess to someone who keeps saying, "But this part of it right here is totally okay!" It's just a variation on this conversation:

Pro-public school advocate: Do not eat that poop sandwich! It's a poop sandwich!!"

Other guy: But the bread looks totally okay.

People are coming around, slowly. They are lifting up the bread and declaring, "Hey! This is poop in here!" And reformers, getting greedy and sloppy, keep putting less and less bread with more and more poop, making their poopiness more and more obvious.

Of course, the next hard part comes later, because when you make a poop sandwich, you end up ruining a lot of perfectly good bread.

Why CCSS Can't Be Decoupled

Don't think of them as standards. Think of them as tags.

Think of them as the pedagogical equivalent of people's names on facebook, the tags you attach to each and every photo that you upload.

We know from our friends at Knewton what the Grand Design is-- a system in which student progress is mapped down to the atomic level. Atomic level (a term that Knewton lervs deeply) means test by test, assignment by assignment, sentence by sentence, item by item. We want to enter every single thing a student does into the Big Data Bank.

But that will only work if we're all using the same set of tags.

We've been saying that CCSS are limited because the standards were written around what can be tested. That's not exactly correct. The standards have been written around what can be tracked.

The standards aren't just about defining what should be taught. They're about cataloging what students have done.

Remember when Facebook introduced emoticons. This was not a public service. Facebook wanted to up its data gathering capabilities by tracking the emotional states of users. But if users just defined their own emotions, the data would be too noisy, too hard to crunch. But if the user had to pick from the facebook standard set of user emotions-- then facebook would have manageable data.

Ditto for CCSS. If we all just taught to our own local standards, the data noise would be too great. The Data Overlords need us all to be standardized, to be using the same set of tags. That is also why no deviation can be allowed. Okay, we'll let you have 15% over and above the standards. The system can probably tolerate that much noise. But under no circumstances can you change the standards-- because that would be changing the national student data tagging system, and THAT we can't tolerate.

This is why the "aligning" process inevitably involves all that marking of standards onto everything we do. It's not instructional. It's not even about accountability.

It's about having us sit and tag every instructional thing we do so that student results can be entered and tracked in the Big Data Bank.

And that is why CCSS can never, ever be decoupled from anything. Why would facebook keep a face tagging system and then forbid users to upload photos?

The Test does not exist to prove that we're following the standards. The standards exist to let us tag the results from the Test. And ultimately, not just the Test, but everything that's done in a classroom. Standards-ready material is material that has already been bagged and tagged for Data Overlord use.

Oddly enough, this understanding of the CCSS system also reveals more reasons why the system sucks.

Facebook's photo tagging system is active and robust. Anybody can add tags, and so the system grows because it is useful. On the other hand, their emoticon system, which requires users to feel only the standardized facebook emotions, is rigid and dying on the vine because it's not useful and it can't adapt.

The CCSS are lousy standards precisely because they are too specific in some areas, too vague in others, and completely missing other aspects of teaching entirely. We all know how the aligning works-- you take what you already do and find a standard that it more or less fits with and tag it.

Because the pedagogical fantasy delineated by the CCSS does not match the teacher reality in a classroom, the tags are applied in inexact and not-really-true ways. In effect, we've been given color tags that only cover one side of the color wheel, but we've been told to tag everything, so we end up tagging purple green. When a tagging system doesn't represent the full range of reality, and it isn't flexible enough to adapt, you end up with crappy tagging. And that's the CCSS.

It's true that in a massive tagging system like this, a Big Test could be rendered unnecessary-- just use all the data that's pouring in from everywhere else. Two reasons that won't happen:

1) While our Data Overlord's eyes were on the data prize, their need for tagged and connected data opened the door for profiteering, and once that stream is flowing, no Pearsonesque group will stand for interfering with it.

2) High stakes tests are necessary to force cooperation. To get people to fork over this much data, they must be motivated. We've seen that evolution in PA, as the folks in charge have realized that nothing less than the highest stakes will get students to stop writing the pledge to the flag on their tests and teachers to stop laughing when they do.

Decoupling? Not going to happen. You can't have a data system without tagging, and you can't have a tagging system with nothing to tag. Education and teaching are just collateral damage in all this, and not really the main thing at all.

Standardized Tests Tell Nothing

Testy stuff experts could discuss all of the following in scholarly type terms, and God bless them for that. But let me try to explain in more ordinary English why standardized tests must fail, have failed, will always fail. There's one simple truth that the masters of test-driven accountability must wrestle with, and yet fail to even acknowledge:

It is not possible to know what is in another person's head.

We cannot know, with a perfect degree of certainty, what another person knows. Here's why.

Knowledge is not a block of amber.

First, what we call knowledge is plastic and elastic.

Last night I could not for the life of me come up with the name of a guy I went to school with. This morning I know it.

Forty years ago, I "knew" Spanish (although probably not well enough to converse with a native speaker). Today I can read a bunch, understand a little, speak barely any.

I know more when I am rested, excited and interested. I know less when I am tired, frustrated, angry or bored. This is also more true by a factor of several hundred if we are talking about any one of my various skill sets.

In short, my "knowledge" is not a block of immutable amber sitting in constant and unvarying form just waiting for someone to whip out their tape measure and measure it. Measuring knowledge is a little more like trying to measure a cloud with a t-square.

We aren't measuring what we're measuring.

We cannot literally measure what is going on in a student's head (at least, not yet). We can only measure how well the student completes certain tasks. The trick-- and it is a huge, huge, immensely difficult trick-- is to design tasks that could only be completed by somebody with the desired piece of knowledge.

A task is as simple as a multiple choice question or an in-depth paper. Same rules apply. I must design a task that could only be completed by somebody who knows the difference between red and blue. Or I must design a task that could only be completed by somebody who actually read and understood all of *The Sun Also Rises*.

We get this wrong all the time. All. The. Time. We ask a question to check for understanding in class, but we ask it in such a tone of voice that students with a good ear can tell what the answer is supposed to be. We think we have measured knowledge of the concept. We have actually measured the ability to come up with the correct answer for the question.

All we can ever measure, EVER, is how well the student completed the task.

Performance tasks are complicated as hell.

I have been a jazz trombonist my whole adult life. You could say that I "know"many songs-- let's pick "All of Me." Can we measure how well I know the song by listening to me perform it?

Let's see. I'm a trombone guy, so I rarely play the melody, though I probably could. But I'm a jazz guy, so I won't play it straight. And how I play it will depend on a variety of factors. How are the other guys in the band playing tonight? Do I have a good thing going with the drummer tonight, or are our heads in different places? Is the crowd attentive and responsive? Did I have a good day? Am I rested? Have I played this song a lot lately, or not so much? Have I ever played with this band before-- do I know their particular arrangement of the song? Is this a more modern group, because I'm a traditional (dixie) jazz player and if you start getting all Miles on me, I'll be lost. Is my horn in good shape, or is the slide sticking?

I could go on for another fifty questions, but you get the idea. My performance of a relatively simple task that you intended to use to measure my knowledge of "All of Me" is contingent on a zillion other things above and beyond my knowledge of "All of Me."

And you know what else? Because I'm a half-decent player, if all those other factors are going my way, I'll be able to make you think I know the song even if I've never heard it before in my life.

If you sit there with a note-by-note rubric of how you think I'm supposed to play the song, or a rubric given to you to use, because even though you're tone-deaf and rhythm-impaired, with rubric in hand you should be able to make an objective assessment-- it's hopeless. Your attempt to read the song library in my head is a miserable failure. You could have found out just as much by flipping a coin. You need to be knowledgeably yourself-- you need to know music, the song, the style, in order to make a judgment about whether I know what I'm doing or not.

You can't slice up a brain.

Recognizing that performance tasks are complicated and bubble tests aren't, standardized test seemed designed to rule out as many factors as possible.

In PA, we're big fans of questions that ask students to define a word based on context alone. For these questions, we provide a selection that uses an obscure meaning of an otherwise familiar word, so that we can test students' context clue skills by making all other sources of knowledge counter-productive.

Standardized tests are loaded with "trick" questions, which I of course am forbidden to reveal, because part of the artificial nature of these tasks is that they must be handled with no preparation and within a short timespan. But here's a hypothetical that I think comes close.

We'll show a small child three pictures (since they are taken from the National Bad Test Clip Art directory, there's yet another hurdle to get over). We show a picture of a house, a tent and a cave. We ask the child which is a picture of a dirt home. But only the picture of the house has a sign that says, "Home Sweet Home" over the door. Want to guess which picture a six-year-old will pick? We're going to say the child who picked the cave failed to show understanding of the word "dirt." I'd say the test writers failed to design an assessment that will tell them whether the child knows the meaning of the word "dirt" or not.

Likewise, reading selections for standardized tests are usually chosen from *The Grand Collection of Boring Material That No Live Human Being Would Ever Choose To Read*. I can only assume that the reasoning here is that we want to see how well students read when they are not engaged at all. If you're reading something profoundly boring, then only your reading skills are involved, and no factors related to actual human engagement.

These are performance task strategies that require the student to only use one slice of brain while ignoring all other slices, an approach to problem solving that is used nowhere, ever, by actual real human beings.

False Positives, Too

The smartest students learn to game the system, which invariably means figuring out how to complete the task without worrying about what the task pretends to measure. For instance, for many performance tasks for a reading unit, Sparknotes will provide just as much info as the students need. Do you pull worksheets and unit quizzes from the internet? Then your students know the real task at hand is "Find Mr. Bogswaller's internet source for answer keys."

Students learn how to read teachers, how to divine expectations, what tricks to expect and how to generally beat the system by providing the answers to the test without possessing the knowledge that the test is supposed to test for.

The Mother of all Measure

Tasks, whether bubble tests or complex papers, may assess for any number of things from students's cleverness to how well-rested they are. But they almost always test one thing above all others-

Is the student any good at thinking like the person who designed the task?

Our students do Study Island (an internet-based tutorial program) in math classes here. They may or may not learn much math on the island, but they definitely learn to think the same way the program writers think.

When we talk about factors like the colossal cultural bias of the SAT, we're talking about the fact that the well-off children of collegeeducated parents have an edge in thinking along the same lines as the well-off college-educated writers of the test.

You can be an idiot, but still be good at following the thoughty paths of People in Charge. You can be enormously knowledgeable and fail miserably at thinking like the person who's testing you.

And the Father of all Measure

Do I care to bother? When you try to measure me, do I feel even the slightest urge to co-operate?

Standardized tests are a joke

For all these reasons, standardized tests are a waste of everybody's time. They cannot measure the things they claim to measure any better than tea leaves or rice thrown on the floor.
People in the testing industry have spent so much time convincing themselves that aspects of human intelligence can be measured (and then using their

own measurements of measurement to create selfjustifying prophecies) that they've lost fact of that simple fact:

You cannot know what's in another person's head

What goes on in my head is the last boundary I have that you cannot cross. I can lie to you. I can fake it. I can use one skill to substitute for another (like that kid in class who can barely read but remembers every word you say). Or I may not be up to the task for any number of reasons.

Standardized test fans are like people who measure the circumference of a branch from the end of a tree limb and declare they now have an exact picture of the whole forest. There are many questions I want to ask (in a very loud voice that might somewhat resemble screaming) of testmakers, but the most fundamental one is, "How can you possibly imagine that we are learning anything at all useful from the results of this test?"

In Praise of Non-Standardization

It is hard for me to argue with fans of national standards, because we hold fundamentally different values.

I'm opposed to CCSS, but unlike many other CCSS opponents, I'm opposed to any national standards at all. But it's hard to have that conversation because it comes down to this not-very-helpful exchange:

Standards fan: But if we had national standards, everyone would be on the same page. The system would be standardized. That's a good thing.

Me: No, it's not.

I'm not advocating the destruction of all rules and order. I'm not calling for the Land of Do-As-You-Please. But let me speak in praise of nonstandardization.

Standardization is safe. It's predictable. We can walk into any McDonald's in the country and it will be just like any other and we will know exactly what we will get. I am not excited about that prospect. Let me plop you into the center of any mall in the country and defy you to guess where you are. That's not a good thing.

Complete organization and standardization is complete boredom. A canvas painted by Monet is interesting precisely because it is disorganized. There's more of some paint over here, less of the other paint over there. A wall painted by Bob's House Painting is perfectly orderly and organized. It's also flat and featureless and nobody particularly wants to look at it; in fact, once it has dried, the homeowners will break up its monotony by hanging photos or decorations or a print of a Monet painting.

Take a glass of water and drop one drop of food coloring into it. At first it will be a group of stark swirls against a clear background. It will be disorganized, disorderly. It will also be cool, interesting. After a while, it will be completely organized and orderly. And boring and uniform.

Chaos and information theories tell us that disorder and entropy are not necessarily best buds, that in fact achieving order and increasing entropy actually go hand in hand. Progress and creation arise out of chaos.

We don't have to be all philosophysicsy about this. Look at the arts. Watch the following process repeat over and over and over again:
1) The prevailing standard has become moribund and stultifying.

2) A large group of alternatives suddenly arise, almost simultaneously providing a whole host of exciting alternatives

3) Eventually one or two emerge as the "winners."

4) The winners cement their status as the new standard by becoming more orderly, more formalized, more organized (but less energetic)

5) See step 1. Rinse and repeat.

This covers everything from the French Impressionist movement to the rise of varied forms of Rock and Roll and Pop in response to the easy listening of the fifties. Or the arc of the computer software and app industry.

It is not just that the non-standard makes the world beautiful and interesting. It is the non-standard that is necessary for human beings to rise and advance. It is the non-standard that allows us to be our best selves, to express whatever unique blend of human qualities that birth and circumstances bring to us.

The goal of standardization is the exact opposite of what is, I would argue, the business of human life. We exist as human beings to make our mark, to make a difference, to be agents of change, to put our unique fingerprints on the things we touch. The goal of the standardized human is to not make a difference, to not leave a mark, to interact in the world in such a way that it would not have made the slightest difference if some other standardized human had been there in our place.

Some loose standardization greases the wheels of society, gives us a common foundation to develop our individual differences. But to imagine that standardization is in and of itself a high and desirable virtue is to imagine that a foundation is the only thing we need in a house. So no, I don't see some sort of national standard as a worthy goal.

How Did CCSS Happen?

My wife is a smart person, and great and committed teacher. She's a reminder to me that for every one of us who have been wading in this stuff for what feels like ages, there are many other concerned professionals who feel like they just walked in on the second season finale of Game of Thrones and aren't sure how to figure out what the hell is going on.

I'm going to imagine this entry as a conversation between me and my wife. To all readers who are actually married to me, let me just say that this will be done with nothing but love and respect.

So where did Common Core come from anyway?

Well, back in 1983 with *A Nation at Risk*--

You promised this would not be like six seasons of How I Met Your Mother

Right. No Child Left Behind put school districts under a lot of pressure. We had to get a certain percentage of students to get above average scores on a standardized test every year. The above-average percentage ramped a little every year until 2009, when it ramped up like a sumbitch.

Same year George Bush was out of office, right?

Exactly. We were supposed to hit 100% this year, which meant that everybody was either going to be failing or lying. Schools were feeling highly motivated to do something else. It turned out that something else was already waiting in the wings. In 2009, the National Governor's Association and the Council of Chief State School Operators formed a committee to write standards. This whole process was pretty murky because A) it was done in secret and B) it involved people and groups that had already been working on this stuff for years. Most of the shadowy previous work was connected to a group named Achieve.

There were two groups that did the writing. Those 25 people included folks from the College Board, the ACT, and Achieve. There was also a feedback group of 35 people; 34 college profs and 1 classroom teacher. Some of those people quit in protest during the process.

They say these are so all students will be college and career ready. How do they know that?

At this point, nobody has seen a shred of the research or data that supports that. The Gates Foundation has paid the bills for most of the support for CCSS that you see, and Bill called this a "best guess" and that we would have to wait ten years to find out if it was right.

So why do they keep saying teachers worked on the Common Core?

As near as anyone can tell, some teachers were allowed to see drafts and provide comments. There's no shred of evidence to suggest that anybody paid any attention to what the teachers said. By the time they saw it, the work was already done.

And the states?

Yeah, they didn't have a leadership role here, either. You'll noticed people don't make the state-led, teacher-involved claim quite so much any more. Everybody who follows this stuff knows that it was federally pushed without the benefit of research or teacher input.

So if the states didn't really develop the Core, why did they adopt it?

You remember they were in a tight place, NCLB-wise. The Obama administration offered them a way out. Two, actually.

First, they could compete for free federal money by joining the Race to the Top. We didn't hear much about that in PA because it required a whole lot of people to sign off on the application, and in PA, they wouldn't. They wouldn't because there was a whole lot of mystery language in it. But if you wanted to compete you had to agree to do a couple of things:

1) You had to agree to collect a boatload of data.

2) You had to agree to being measured by beaucoups testing.

3) You had to agree to evaluate teachers by using testing data at least a
little.
4) You had to adopt some college and career ready standards and pretend
that you were helping develop them. This also meant in some cases that
you were agreeing to them sight unseen.

Wasn't it only a few states that won Race to the Top? What about the rest?

It was only a few. But that No Child Left Behind kept squeezing, and it became obvious that nobody in Congress was going to rewrite the law. Even though everyone could see we were headed for a cliff, nobody wanted to touch the stupid thing. But the administration said states could get a waiver and be excused from NCLB 100% above average requirements.

I bet the list of requirements to get a waiver sounds familiar.

Good bet.

So can't states just rewrite it to suit themselves?

The Common Core State Standards are actually copyrighted. States aren't allowed to change a thing, and can only add 15%. Now, whether that would just void the warranty or invoke fines or lose federal money or put a sheriff on the statehouse steps I don't think anybody knows. But you can't mess with them.

Can anybody ask them to change the standards?

Nope. There's no toll-free service number, no appeal process, no feedback system, no nothing. I don't know about the math, but the guy who wrote the English standards has a completely different job at this point.

So if this really wasn't the states bringing a bunch of teachers together to develop standards that would make sense for everybody, then why did this happen? Why would anybody do this?

The short answer is money and power and who knows. The long answer is a piece of writing for another day.

Coleman Speaks Out (Sort of)

Oh, the interwebs were alive with the sound of David Coleman today. His fervent presentation about the new, CCSS-infused SAT roused journalists (Wall Street Journalist), sort of journalists (Huffington Post), and tweetists (now we're on my level) galore. I read splintered quotes of Colemania, which must have merely scratched the surface, because I also read that his SAT speech earned the Standing O from the crowd in Austin

But I couldn't be there (I was busy, you know, working for a living). So now, using such classic faux journalist techniques as "Splicing Together Secondary Sources" and "Reading Real Journalism" and even one I like to call "Making Shit Up," I am going to bring you, loyal reader, David Coleman's presentation of the the ideas behind the New SAT!

Let's face it. The SAT is a doddering dinosaur of a test. Research just proved for the umpteenth time that it doesn't predict college success as well as high school GPA, and proving that is laced with loads of cultural bias has become a training exercise for freshmen-level research assistants. The old girl needs a facelift, a tummy tuck, and a boob job. It's not that I particularly care about the validity or usefulness of the test, but we are losing market share to the ACT and some colleges are starting to ignore us altogether. We've got a product to move, and that means releasing this year's hot new model to stir up the customer base.

So what have we done?

Well, that essay portion that colleges just kept ignoring because it didn't effectively test anything except a student's ability to locate the piece of paper-- that's gone. Well, "optional." If you still want to take it, knock yourself out.

But that won't matter because we are expanding writing in the rest of the test. Students are going have to write stuff based on documents from other disciplines-- in other words, none of that literature crap. God-- where we ever got the idea that anybody should read, like, that Shakespeare guy is beyond me. No, it'll be historical documents and biology charts and stereo instructions and quarterly earnings reports-- things that really matter.

Their essays will be evidence based. So all they have to do is come up with the correct interpretation of the reading, support it with the correct evidence from the excerpt, and assemble the evidence in the correct manner. This makes the SAT invaluable, because the ability to regurgitate a pre-determined single reading of a text is central to college studies. The ability to repeat what they're told is important for all American citizens, but real excellence is in being able to figure out exactly what we want them to say, and how, without us having to spell it out for them.

We're also going to get rid of all that fancy-shmancy vocabulary. We're chucking out words like "sagacious" and "ignominious" and putting in vocabulary like "empirical" and "synthesis" and "actuarial tables" and "return on investment."

Now, I know that many students in this country get an unfair advantage on the SATs by hiring private tutors and prep programs, and I feel that it is completely unfair that this going on. Specifically, I feel that it is unfair that this is going on and we aren't benefiting from it. But we have been learning from facebook and your grocery store customer card and every on-line retailer in the world, and we will be happy to provide you with some free test prep products and even a handful of other free services for a select few-- all you need give us in return is all your personal information and the chance to market many of our other products directly to you. See? We are just a big bunch of humanitarians.

Look, these tests have become "disconnected from the work of our high schools," by which I mean that I used CCSS to redefine what the work of high school should be, and I promised that it would line up with college, and now in this new job I get a chance to make my own prophecy come true. I don't just get to move the goal posts-- I get to declare that now a football game will be won by the team that hits the most home runs. Is this a great country, or what?

And to all you sunsabitches who griped about my Common Core work-- how do you like me now? One way or another, I am going to force you to teach what I personally think ought to be taught the way I think it ought to be taught. Your students pee themselves over the SAT-- they will beg and bully you to teach math and English the way I want you to in mortal terror that they'll get a low score and end up working as a part-time cart-bearing greaser at some Wal-mart.

I am David Effing Coleman. I'm an education amateur, but I'm a wellconnected one and I have personally redefined what it means to be an educated person in America. No more of this namby-pamby reading and writing about thoughts and feelings and ideas and the rest of that shit. From cradle to grave, you'll focus on the only thing that matters-- practical, literal stuff that helps people make money. "Beauty is truth, truth beauty"-- what the hell was that Keats character smoking, anyway? The liberal arts?? Who in the bloody blue hell needs the liberal arts???!

Yes, the SAT was a biased test. It still is-- but now it's biased the right way. My way. We've got the CCSS and the SAT lined up. Next we'll get your three-year-olds properly rigorized, and once that's happening colleges won't be able to keep from becoming the proper vocational training centers they're supposed to be. Quality of life? Quality of life comes from money, baby. Education has something to do with a greater understanding of our world and our humanity and how we make sense of them, how we express our deepest connections to each other and the universe in a process of discovery, expression and wonder that continues our whole life? You're killing me.

Look, an educated person is one who can do well the tests assigned by his betters, can fulfill a useful job for the corporations that hire him, and will behave properly for the government that rules him. If you wanted something more out of life than that, you should have arranged to be rich. In the meantime, enjoy the new SAT.

At least, that's what I imagine him saying today. I might have paraphrased a little.

Why the Hell Are We Racing Anywhere?

Race to the Top had been rather quiet as a brand until President Obama revived it in his new budget proposal. Unfortunately, the new iteration underlines the metaphorical problems with the nom de regulation. For a guy who launched his career by being a moving speaker, Obama has hit on a real tone-deaf clunker here.

This time, we are racing for equity, which means, I guess, that we are going to Race To The Top To The Middle. Seriously, how does this metaphor even sort of work? How does a race for equality work, exactly?

My first thought is that we are about to see a real-life Diana Moon Glampers to preside over a race in which the swift are properly held back. But no-- we're clearly supposed to be competing for excellence. Excellence in...not being any more or less excellent than anybody else??

But the metaphorical muddle that is Race To The Top To The Middle only raises a more important question which is-- why were we ever racing anywhere?

Competition in pursuit of excellence is highly overrated.

First of all, we only compete with other teams. The five members of a basketball team do not compete with each other to score the most baskets; if they did, they would be a terrible team and they would lose very much, and nobody would say, "Wow, those guys are really excellent!" Not even if they competed with great rigor.

So who is supposed to be the other team in this race? Other schools? We are supposed to beat other schools and teachers and students and leaving them whipped and beaten and in this way we will achieve excellence?

Or is it just possible that, in the education game, every American public school that uses teachers to educate American children-- that every one of those schools is on the same team and not in competition at all?

Second of all, even in economics and business, competition is really great until it isn't. Rockefeller created Standard Oil by absorbing competition, by buying up every last one of his competitors. At no point did he say, "You know what? For me to be really excellent, I need to have some competition." No-- he said, "In order for me to be really excellent, I need to control and organize most of this big, messy industry. Competition must go away." You know who else thought ending competition would be a good business strategy? Bill Gates.

Granted, Gates and a few others toyed with making their workers compete with each other. They stopped doing it, because it was bad for the team.

So don't tell me the business world loves competition, because they don't. At best, the people who are losing pay it lip service which lasts right up until they aren't losing any more.

And they aren't wrong. Rockefeller and Gates both brought order to industries that were messy and wasteful, industries that were throwing away valuable resources and opportunities fighting against each other. Competition did not improve the industry; it made it sloppy and inefficient.

Obama et al seem to believe that races advance all racers, just like Reagan's rising tide raised all boats (or trickled down on submarines, or something). They remain convinced that the folks in the back of the pack are only there because they are slackers, lazy, unmotivated, and that somehow the shame of losing will spur them to finally get their acts together. We've heard about compassionate conservatives. Here we see loveless liberals, compassion-free with a Nietzschian disregard for the under-menschen.

"But," they are going to protest, "we can't keep giving medals to everybody no matter what." And you know what? I agree. The selfesteemy movement to reward students just for having a pulse was a mistake. But our mistake was not giving medals to everyone. Our mistake was giving unearned medals to everyone.

"But," they are going to mansplain, "in the race of life, there are winners and losers." And I am going to say, not in school there aren't.

This is the problem with people who play too many sports. I'm a musician. You know what happens when you go to a concert and everybody plays their very very best? We don't declare one a winner and one a loser no matter what. We applaud like crazy, because when everybody does a great job, it's freakin' awesome!

In my classroom, there is no useful purpose for having a race. There is no useful purpose in declaring winners and losers. If all my students learn today, today everybody wins. And we don't have to race for that to happen.

Racing is a terrible awful no good very bad metaphor for what should be happening in schools. It is a stupid way to frame the whole business and cheap besides. Competition will not improve education-- not on the macro-national scale, not on the district scale, not on the building scale, not on the classroom scale.

We are not racers. We are builders. And building takes time and care and attention. It takes an understanding of your materials and the place in which you are building. It requires time and care and harmony and craft and attention. And every beam, every bolt, every square inch of surface matters. Every aspect of the building rests on and supports other aspects. And if you build a great building next to mine, it does not diminish me, but adds to my work.

Mr. President, I reject the language of scarcity, the language that says we will only support those who finish the race first, the language says that we are not a team, but a country of competitors in a dog-eat-dog world where there is only enough to support a chosen few. I am not going to race to any damn where.

How To Do Real Teacher Evaluation

The fans of Reformy Stuff are not wrong about everything. For example, they are correct that the general state of teacher evaluation in this country was pretty useless. Their mistake was replacing Inertly Useless with Actively Destructive. The old system was a simple two step process (1- check for teacher pulse; 2- award perfect score [edit-or, in some Bad Places To Work, award lousy score just because you want to]) while the new step is a little more involved (1- apply random groundless unproven mathematical gobbledeegook to big bunch of bad data; 2- award randomly assigned bad score).

Years ago, frustrated with the old mostly-useless model and before the current looney tunes empire took hold, a friend and I had started to rough out an evaluation system. Let me sketch out the basics for you.

What Should a Good Teacher Eval System Do?

1)   Provide clear expectations to the teacher. One of the wacky things about teaching is that everybody is sure that everybody knows what a teacher's exact job description is, and yet it invariably turns out that nobody agrees. In many districts, teachers enter their classrooms with no job description and no really clear idea of what is expected of them.

2)   Provide useful feedback and remediation. That includes setting the stage for meaningful remediation if it's called for. Only a small percentage of new teachers will be awesome right out of the box or clearly hopeless. Most are waiting to be guided toward either excellence or despair, and most districts depend on a system that I like to call "Blind Luck." I swear there are teachers out there whose careers could have gone a completely different direction if they had just eaten lunch with a different set of veteran teachers in their first few years.

3)   Provide the district with clear information on whether they need to retain, retrain or refrain from hiring permanently.

Assumptions in Building the Eval System

1)   Precise, observable data is the enemy of real, useful information. In the hands of hard data overlords, traits like "maintains good communication with parents" ends up being some numerical observable, such as "calls at least two parents every five days." Hard data fans like really precise measures, and so their data may be precise, but their conclusion is always wrong. Mr. McSwellteach may personally visit 150 parents a month or sing in a church choir with half of his total parental units. He may rely more on e-

mail because that's what his students' parents prefer. He may have an absolutely uncanny sense of when to contact the parents and when to leave them alone. He may, in short, be a pretty awesome parent communicators, but since the metric focuses on one specific, concrete, observable, measurable piece of data out of a thousand possible factors, it completely misses the real information here.

2)   People may not be able to explain a good teacher, but they generally know one when they see her.

3)   The best way to correct for individual bias in a survey is to collect information from many, many individuals. And anyway...

4)   You're trying to evaluate subjective qualities. This is like trying to evaluate husbands. Your husband from hell may be her perfect dreamboat. There are certainly some rough patterns of qualities that will emerge, clustered around a statistical strange attractor of some sort, but you will not be able to draw a box around a configuration and say, "Everything inside the line is good, and everything outside is bad." If that violates your world view or makes you uncomfortable, just suck it up and put on your Big Person Pants.

The Short Method for Real Teacher Evaluation

Hire a really good principal and let him do his job.

The Method Proposed for the Other 98% of Schools

The first step actually occurs before your district even gets started. This is where our consulting firm start-up was going to have to do some real work. Basically, you need a giant list, a huge constellation of teacher qualities arranged around some master categories such as Knowledge, Community Interaction, Classroom Management-- mostly the basic main qualities that we're familiar with. For each of the master qualities, a truckload of specifics, from "dresses up for work" to "enthusiastic with kids." Not that mostly these will not be specific enough for some of you-- it will be more "communicate well with parents" and not at all "makes two parent phone calls every four days." This massive menu of teacher qualities is where we start and launch into the following steps.

1)   Pull together a large committee. It will include teachers, students, administrators, community members, parents, business folks-- as much of a broad representation of the stakeholders as you can gather up. And then

using one of any of the many fine models for this kind of group work out there, your group is going to take the master list of traits and customize it.

2)   Customizing will cover two factors-- what to include, and how to weight it. It's here where your folks will decide, for instance, that in your community dressing up to teach doesn't matter at all, and that being kind to students is twice as important as being funny. You'll work this out on two levels-- which micro-traits will contribute what percent of the score for the categories (eg "strict disciplinarian" will make up 4% of the "Classroom management" category). And you will work out the relative weight of the master categories. You'll do this on the school level-- Content Knowledge may be 50% of your expectation for secondary teachers but only 30% for elementary, whereas Parent Relationship might run the other way. And hey-- if you want "Prepares students thoroughly for standardized tests" to be a huge factor, you can go ahead and do that.

3)   Congratulations. The process was long and hard and involved lots and lots and LOTS of discussion, some of it probably heated, but once you're done you have created a fairly detailed job description, a picture of what your stakeholders expect from a teacher in the district. Imagine, teachers, if on your first day someone had handed you a multi-page detailed and weighted list of the qualities and behaviors they expected you to display instead of a room key and hearty "Good luck!"

4)   Hey look! That big involved job description is also the evaluation form. All we have to do is give you a score for each line item, and we have already figured out how much weight that carries in your final evaluation.

5)   Who fills out your eval form? Well, some of you won't like this, but our answer was "Everybody." Other teachers, current students, former students (we thought it important to keep alumni in the loop for decades after graduation), admins, parents, anybody we can think of.

The eval forms can be filled with simple number scores, but we allow for narrative to be added if they wish. Will there be outliers-- cranky parent, jerk student, someone who just has an axe to grind? Sure-- but if our sample is large, small outliers won't screw anybody up, and the same software that's going to crunch (and possibly collect) all this data can also be taught to toss out small left-field samples. We could probably even teach the program to block folks who are consistently mischief-makers.

We had never quite figured out weighting as it applied to this portion. I'm pretty sure the principal should carry more weight than Billy-Bob Schnoodleman in 5th grade art class, but we hadn't quite worked out that kink when we stopped working on this. Put it in the to-do pile.

6)   Hey look! The evaluation results tell you exactly where your strengths and weaknesses are! And part of this process will involve establishing a in-school remediation work group-- folks who can be mentor and help other teachers with particular weaknesses that match up with their particular strengths. There's a piece for deciding when someone is, well, hopeless, but our focus is on strengthening people. But we'll stop there before I start in on my plan for creating teaching schools that work like teaching hospitals for doctors.

Why This Is Better Than What State and Federal Authorities Want To Do

1)   The goal is to help people improve rather than firing our way to excellence. FOWTE creates an ugly atmosphere in a building, and it doesn't really help because the replacement hire is only going to require you to start from scratch again. I know some reformy types think we can churn and turn TFA-style forever, but those people are idiots. With emphasis on building strength, we not only get better teachers, but we automatically build the atmosphere of collegiality, support, and quality work that makes a school a better place.

2)   The data comes from many many observations over much time, and not one forty-five minute squat and squint by just one guy. No evaluation system in the world can protect a teacher from an incompetent vindictive principal if he's the only guy who has a say.

3)   The data does not come from a bad standardized test that measures little of value and is useless as a teacher measurement tool.

4)   The system is transparent. Unlike VAM, which cannot be successfully explained and is apparently created by magic gnomes in a castle under the South Pole, this system is created and weighted in plain sight. Everybody knows what's going on.

5)   The system reflects local values. What's the story we keep hearing with the current crop of test-based VAMified evals-- that Mrs. McWunderteach has gotten a terrible rating even though everybody knows that she's an awesome teacher. We should be tapping the source of that "everybody knows," not the Data Overlord system. Does this mean that Teacher Excellence will look different from district to district? Well, yes. Of course it will-- because IT DOES!!

National Standards

I am aware that this system does not really give us a model for teacher evaluation and excellence that scales to the national level. That's one of the reasons I like it. It's actually a bit of a compromise, because if every single district used it, they would still be able to talk to each other, but they would still be free to do what seemed best in their own district ("Oh, is that how you scaled and weighted Content Knowledge for elementary? Here's what our sheet ended up looking like").

Yes, an Excellent Teacher in Buford, Montana might be a different set of measures and paperwork than an Excellent Teacher in Nicetown, Tennessee-- but each of those districts would have what they believed to be examples of excellent teachers. What would be better than that?

At any rate, we had this system well past halfway done when the New Evaluations started to emerge. But it still represents my idea of how a useful, authentic teacher evaluation would work, and is definitely my answer to, "Well, if you don't want to use this awesome teacher evaluation system of VAM and test scores and Danielson rubrics, then what DO you want to do?" This. I want to do this.

Bubble Answers for an Essay World

I have had the same conversation multiple times in the last week. I have had it with elementary teachers, secondary teachers, someone who works with young teachers, someone who works with college students. The crux of the conversation is something like this:

I do not know what to do with these [persons]. They do not want to understand. They do not want to discuss or explore. They just want to know what they're supposed to say or do so they can give the right answer and be rewarded.

We talk a great deal, especially during Testing Season, about the shortterm damage done by the Cult of Standardized Testing. The tears, the fears, the frustration, the damaged psyches, the wasted time, the sheer stupid uselessness of the test results.

But we also need to pay attention to the more insidious long-term damage being done by the Cult of Testing. It is changing a generation's very concept of what education is, of what it means to be an intelligent person, of how a learned person engages the world.

Standardized testing creates its own model of the world. In Testing Land, all answers to all questions already exist, and a Learned Person is proficient at hunting them down and bringing them back. In Testing Land, everything is already known. In Testing Land, a good student is one who can say what the Testmakers want her to say.

In elementary school, students learn How To Take Tests, which includes learning How To Do What The Testmakers Want. Children have to be taught to stop exploring, stop following their curiosity, stop running off whatever direction their lively minds take them. Stop chasing butterflies; sit down at your desk and do this practice sheet. Stop telling stories in that rambling circuitous narrative manner of a child, and start making your paragraphs exactly-four-sentence-long paragraph.

By high school, students have learned the purpose of education-- to teach you how to pass The Test. And you do that by looking at the choices you're given and picking the Right One. You look at the constructed response question and you follow the Right Formula for turning it into the response that you are supposed to write. Cheating becomes more prevalent because it's not cheating-- the task is to Get The Right Answer and turn it in, not to understand or comprehend or grapple with your brain-muscles. Just turn in the right answers.

Do not think. Do not engage. Your own thoughts and opinions will only slow you down. Go find the right answer.

When these students arrive at college, they meet a new expectation. Do some research. Write a paper. And in the process, construct a new piece of information. Create and present some knowledge that has never been presented before. The college student gapes. The professor might as well say, "Glorp a fleegle in blurgdorple." The college student asks a thousand variations on the same basic question-- "What am I supposed to do? What am I supposed to say?"

Some college programs are happy to provide that kind of lockstep guidance, and education programs, because they are preparing teachers for this Brave New Bubble World, are among the worst.

Folks, there are teachers out there in classrooms who have never created a single original teaching unit in their careers. They have taught from the book. They have used the packet of materials. When they need a worksheet or study guide, they go get one from the internet (students appreciate this a great deal because it makes it so easy to Get The Right Answer).

We are producing a generation of Bubblers, people whose understanding of understanding is bizarrely stunted. Yes, I know these sorts of students have always been with us, and I know old farts like me have always complained [insert Socratic quote about Kid These Days here]. But this is different.

We deliver nods to synthesis, curiosity, inquiry, exploration, the full range of Bloom-- but not really. We talk about higher order critical thinking skills-- but as only as techniques for divining what One Answer must be Bubbled. By presenting higher order thinking as just a way to solve the bubbling problem, we are systematically shutting down curiosity, inquiry, exploration, synthesis, construction, intellectual independence-- and it is working! At every level, we are seeing more and more people who are falling into lockstep, and not because they have been beaten into it, but because they think that's how it's supposed to be.

Life is not a bubble test. It's rich and complex and only reveals its full intricacy when observed from a million different vantage points. We are losing that, and as a culture we are poorer for it. I know that the education debates are often given to hyperbole, but I truly believe that when we fight the Cult of Testing, we aren't just fighting for quality of education, but for the very spirit and soul of what it means to be human, to understand and be in the world.

Is This CCSS Criticism Fair?

The supporters of Common Core have eaten so much cheese with their whine that we may have to call a whaaaambulance.

Their complaints have been percolating for a while, but the heat of the Louis C.K. flame-up has brought their big bowl of treacly tears to a roiling boil. The criticisms are not fair. Those stupid examples of bad assignments have nothing to do with the Core, and the terrible tests are separate from the Core, and an idiot misprint could happen to anybody no matter what federally-coerced education program they were trying to implement.

Do the Core supporters have a point?

Yes. Yes, they do.

All along, people have been holding up bad assignments and worksheets and lessons as examples of Common Core that could have come from anywhere. When supporters say that CCSS do not mandate particular stupid instructional strategies, they are correct. Reformsters who decry the linkage of standards and The Test are not technically wrong. And pinning a bad print job on the Core, as if no printers error could have occurred in a land of local control, is kind of silly. In short, trying to act as if no teacher or school district ever did anything stupid in the days before Common Core is a ridiculous argument.

However.

However. The Core supporters asked for this.

First. First, the creators of the CCSS wrote the damn things and then just walked away. They promised publishers and ed corporations a massive payday for anyone who would slap "CCSS Ready" on teaching materials, and then they walked away. And when those corporations started cranking out all manner of sloppy crap and calling it CCSS material, there was nobody minding the store. Instead of standing over their creation and saying, "Woah woah WOAH! Let's just all take it slow. You fellas line up and let us make sure you're getting this right," Coleman and the rest had clocked out and headed off to their own big payday, pausing just long enough to toss a "Have fun, boys" back over their shoulders.

Second, because the CCSS Reformsters made sure they had control of the playing field since day one, they made the rules. These are the rules they made:

* Making up shit to sway the public is okay (e.g. "You can trust the Core

Standards because they were written by professional teachers")

* Using people who control large audiences but have no actual expertise in education is fine. If they have a large audience, that's all the right they need to speak on subjects in which they have no professional expertise. Bill Gates and US Chamber of Commerce, meet Louis C. K.

* Blur the line between standards, curriculum and lessons as it suits you. CCSS supporters have referred to the Common Core Curriculum, touted Common Core Lessons, and talked incessantly about how the Core will guarantee that students in Alaska, Tennessee and Maine will all learn the same thing (a promise that sounds like it's about lessons and curriculum to most anybody). How did the public get the idea that the Core and all these lessons are different parts of the same big elephant? The people busy trying to cash in on CCSS told them so.

* Link the CCSS to the Big Tests. The federal gummint made testing and CCSS part of the same get-out-of-NCLB-jail-free card. Advocates for the Core told states that they HAD to have high stakes testing in place for the Core to do any good.

* Link the standards to teaching. Keep claiming that the standards will fix all the crappy teachers, that teachers will be held accountable for their work by the use of the Common Core. Publish glowing articles about how the Core has made Mrs. McUberteacher do the best teaching of her life because the core has transformed her classroom.

* Inflate the importance of piddly shit when it suits you. Throw around obscure baloney like PISA scores and keep telling the public that it's hugely importance. Blow up the statistical importance of classroom teachers to students success. Basically, establish the rule that any small detail that helps prove your point can be magnified a thousandfold.

* Directly connecting what the Core says and what students do. We've been told repeatedly-- the Common Core Standards mean that students will do more rigorous work. It will be hard. they might cry. But this Common Core work will be good for them. This rhetoric, repeated repeatedly, has established a clear and direct link between the standards in the Core and the worksheets on Johnny's desk.

* Teachers must teach to the test. You didn't mean to make this a rule, but you couldn't help yourselves. But how else will any sentient being interpret, "Your students will do well on this test, or we will flunk them and fire your

ass." Nobody-- NOBODY-- thinks the next line in that poem is, "So don't teach to the test."

* Mock opponents rather than engage them. As in, characterizing all CCSS opponents as tin hat crazypants tea partiers or whiny moms or lying teachers.

For years, CCSS supporters established that these would be the rules by which we conducted all discourse about the standards and their attendant complex of core-created crap. And now, those same rules of discourse are being used against them. Aspects of education that they repeatedly linked to Common Core? They would like those unlinked now, please. Stop calling us names and just talk to us! And let's start sticking to facts. Sorry, but that's not following the rules that have been in place for the past several years.

Are these rules fair? No, of course not. We've been saying so for years now. But you supporters always replied, "Tough shit. We're winning, so tough shit." Only as the tide has turned against you have you started saying, "Hey, let's talk about the quality of discourse in this conversation."

Too late, boys. I actually agree with you-- we do need a better quality of conversation to rescue public education from the Reformy Status Quo you've saddled us with. There are so many reasons of substance, importance educational reasons that CCSS etc should be scrapped beyond the sometimes-trivial odds and ends currently being torn apart. But you never created any way for that discussion to be had, no method for revision or review ever, and anyway, there aren't that many reasonable folks like me around, and for the time being, we're not going to carry the day.

Karma's a bitch, isn't it.

An Educated Person

"Don't you think there are things that every educated person should know?"

I hear this fairly often, generally in response to my stated disinterest in having Common Core standards in particular and national education standards ever in general. It's an eye-opening question for me , because even just a few years ago, I'm pretty sure I would have answered yes. But the current toxic educational status quo and its foundation of Making People Prove They Know Things has forced me to really examine my thoughts in this area.

The issue breaks down into three parts for me.

I. The List

In the English teacher biz, we wrestle with The Canon all the time, and that master list is always a work in progress. If you're old enough, you can remember the struggle surrounding the recognition that we might want to expand beyond the traditional list of Dead White Guys, but there have been many mini-arguments over the years, none of which have been conclusively settled.

But that's content. What about skills? Well, we agree on readingwriting-speaking-listening in principle, but in English-land there's ongoing debate about the usefulness of knowing grammar, and the process of writing (which was only "discovered" in the last forty years or so) is still metamorphosing. And in most places, the speaking-listening piece is a haphazard Rube Goldberg stapled to the airborne seat of our pedagogical pants.

And that's just my field. Multiply that by every other discipline. Factor in all the parents and taxpayers who believe that What Kids Should Learn is roughly the same as What We Studied Back In My Day.

But I do believe there are things students should learn, don't I? I mean, how else do I make decisions about what I should teach (because in my district, I make many of those decisions myself)?

Turns out, when I think about it, what I really have is a list of Things I think It Would Benefit a Person To Know.

I think any person would be better off knowing some Shakespeare. I think every person would benefit from being able to express him/herself as clearly as possible in writing and speaking. I think there's a giant cargo-ship-load of literature that has important and useful things to say to various people at various points in their journey through life.

But this is a fuzzy, individual thing. Think of it as food, the intellectual equivalent of food. Are there foods that everybody would benefit from eating? Wellll.... I would really enjoy a steak, but my wife the vegan would not. And given my physical condition, it might not be the best choice for me. On the other hand, if I haven't had any protein in a while, it might be great. And a salad might be nice, unless I already had a salad today, because eating a lot of salad has some unpleasant consequences for me. Oh, and I do enjoy a lobster, which is fairly healthy, unless I'm have to eat while I'm traveling-- lobster makes very bad road food in the car. You see our problem. We can agree that everybody should eat. I'm not sure we can pick a menu and declare that every single human being would benefit from eating exactly that food at exactly the same time.

Ditto for The List. I mean, I think everybody should learn stuff. Personally, I'm a generalist, so I think everybody would benefit from learning everything from Hamlet to quantum physics. But then, I know some people who have made the world a better place by being hard core specialists who know nothing about anything outside their field.

So if you ask me, can I name a list of skills and knowledge areas that every single solitary American must learn, I start to have trouble. Every mechanic, welder, astronaut, teacher, concert flautist, librarian, physicist, neurosurgeon, truck driver, airplane pilot, grocery clerk, elephant trainer, beer brewer, housewife, househusband, politician, dog catcher, cobbler, retail manager, tailor, dentist-- what exactly does every single one of those people have to know?

II. And Why?

Let's pretend there is a list. What is it for?

Do we want people to be more productive workers? Do we want them to be more responsible parents? Do we want them to be kinder, more decent human beings? Do we want them to be better citizens?

Then why aren't we trying to teach them those things?

One of the most bizarre disconnects in the current toxic ed status quo is the imaginary connections between disconnected things. We have to get students to score better on standardized tests, because that's how we'll become the economically dominant Earth nation. Ignoring for a moment the value of either of those goals, what the heck do they have to do with each other?

Reformsters are constantly telling us that we must drive to Cleveland because that's the only way we'll make it to St. Louis. If you want to drive to St. Louis, first, let's discuss whether we really want to go to St. Louis or not and next, if we agree, let's map a path to St. Louis, not Cleveland.

III. Enforcement

So even if I have my tiny list of things I think absolutely every person must learn, the small irreduceable list of content and skills that every educate person should know, I have another hurdle to climb.

Do I think the full force of law and government should stand behind forcing people to learn those things?

Should the federal and state governments say, "We think you should learn these things, and we will put the full weight of law behind that requirement. You will not be allowed to proceed with your life unless you satisfy us that you have learned the stuff on this list."

What is X such that I would stand in front of a diploma line and say, "Since you have not proven to me that you know X, I will not let you have a diploma."

"Don't you think there are things that every educated person should know?" seems like such a fair and simple question, but by the time I've come up with a short list of skills and knowledge for every single solitary human being, and then filtered it through the question of what deserves to have the full force of federal law behind it, my list is very short and extremely general.

Maybe you think that makes me one of those loose teachers who lets his students slop by with whatever half-assed work they feel like doing. You will have to take my word for it-- my students would find that assessment of my teaching pretty hilarious.

But The List approach is, in fact, List-centered, and I'm well-anchored to an approach to teaching that is student-centered. It is, I have become convinced, the only way to teach. We cannot be rulescentered or standards-centered or test-centered or teacher-centered or list-centered, *even though we need to include and consider all of those elements*. How to weigh and balance and evaluate all these elements? The answer has been, and continues to be, right in front of us. We balance all the elements of education by centering on the student. As long as we keep our focus on the students' needs, strengths, weaknesses, stage of development, hopes, dreams, obstacles, aspirations-- as long as we stay focused on all that, we'll be good.

What does every educated person need? Every educated person needs-- and deserves-- an education that is built around the student. Everything else must be open to discussion.

Charter$ & Ca$hing In

In the past, many charters were launched that focused solidly on providing unique and exciting educational experiences for their communities. These schools were innovative. These schools were connected to their communities. These schools were icing on the public school system cake. And these schools were run by chumps. There's only one question you need to answer to gauge the success of your charter school-- am I making money.

Here's how to properly cash in on the charter school movement.

Diversify!

Not the school-- your portfolio. Set up multiple companies. Create a holding company that owns the building, and charge the school rent and facilities fees. Create a school management company, and hire yourself to run your school. Form your own custodial contracting company. Write your own textbooks, and then sell them to yourself. Buy a loaf of bread and a jar of peanut butter and set yourself up as a lunch concession with ten dollar sandwiches.

Don't Overlook the Obvious

"Non-profit" just means "not wasting money by throwing it away on stockholders." Taking money hand over fist that you can't call profit? Just put it all in a big wheelbarrow and pay it to yourself as a salary. There's no legal limit to what you can be paid as the charter school operator. The only limits to your salary are the limits set by your own sense of shame. If you have no shame, then ka-ching, my friend. Ka. Ching.

Ain't Too Proud To Beg

Have a fundraiser. When you wave schools and children at people, they fork over money like crazy, whether you actually need it or not. The only way it could work any better would be if you found a way to work in the American flag and puppies.

Students Are Marketing Tools

Students have a job at your charter, and that's to make your charter look good and marketable. If they won't do the job, fire them. If they aren't for sure going to graduate, fire them before senior year (100% graduation rate makes great ad copy). If they are going to create bad press for disciplinary reasons, fire them.

Students Are Also The Revenue Stream

The other function of students is to bring money in while not costing any more than is absolutely necessary. Never take students with special needs (unless you can use them to make the school look good without incurring extra costs). If a student will require extra disciplinary or academic intervention, fire him.

Always remember, however, that students need to be fired during Firing Season-- late enough to hold onto the money they bring, but early enough that they won't hurt your numbers.

Only Use McTeachers

Personnel costs will eat up your revenue. Make sure your teachers are young, cheap, and easily replaced. Remember-- with the proper programs in a box, teaching requires no more training and expertise than bagging up an order of fries. Why pay New Cadillac wages when all you need are Used Yugos. It should go without saying, but they should never, ever be allowed to organize. Keep them too demoralized to cause trouble, and if someone insists on causing trouble, fire her. Pro tip: TFA can be a great source of people who don't even want to be teachers and will gladly take themselves out of your way.

Remember-- You Are A Public School

You are entitled to public money, public resources, public buildings, public anything you can get them to give you. Never pay a cost out of your pocket when you can get the taxpayers to foot the bill. You also want to accent the "public" in your marketing, as it helps reduce parents' reluctance to screw over the actual public schools.

Remember-- You Are A Private School

Never let anybody see your financials, ever. This is your business, and nobody-- especially not the taxpayers who pay you-- is entitled to know anything about how you run it. "Transparency" is a dirty, dirty word.

In general, rules are for chumps. Make sure you are only playing by the ones that best serve your ROI.

Make the Right Friends

It's true that not everybody can afford to buy, say, an entire legislature or the governor of a state, but even outside of New York, it's possible to use the giant pile of money you've accumulated to help important people understand what a great public service you're performing.

We've come a long way from the days when charter school operators made the mistake of thinking that their schools should focus on educating young men and women. In Modern Times, we better understand that a well-run charter operation can contribute to an important job-- the business of taking money away from undeserving taxpayers and putting it in the hands of the deserving rich. By focusing on the One True Function of charter schools-- making money-- you can develop a robust business that will make it possible for you to send your own children to real private schools that provide the kind of education that, thank goodness, you will never try to incorporate into your own charter operation.

Test (In)Security

One of the features of High Stakes Testing is a level of security usually associated with large bales of money, important state secrets, and the recipe for Bush's Baked Beans. On facebook, in the category of "Ethical Dilemmas Nobody Ever Thought She'd Face," teachers are arguing about whether it's okay to photograph or copy any of the PARCC or SBA exams. I have a thought-- but first, let me tell you a story.

Forty years ago I took a biology course called BSCS. That stands for "Biological Sciences Curriculum Studies," though we generally interpreted it as "BS College Style." To this day, the tests from that course are the toughest tests I've ever taken. I still remember sections of those tests (a village where they make pottery compared to a singlecelled organism, an experiment on a kangaroo rat) because they were so challenging. And these very tough, very challenging tests came with zero security.

In fact, we took the tests as take-home tests. People called their college siblings, friends who were taking college biology. We had test parties, and everybody came and hammered out the answers. And then, on the due date, we handed the test in. And then we took the same test (with questions rearranged) in class.

The tests were so perfectly built around the ability to think and reason scientifically, to interpret data, to build useful analogies, that no security was needed (and no, everybody did not get an A every time-- not even close). So here's what I think about high stakes test security:

If your test needs super-secret high-and-tight lock down security, it is a crappy test.

This applies to classroom teachers as well. The better I get at assessment, the less I need test security. My students pass on year after year, like tales of the Loch Ness Bigfoot, tales of various assignments that may crop up in my class (though the assignment list does vary from year to year). It doesn't matter. If I've done my job well, there is no place on God's green earth to go look up The Answer.

The PARCC and SBA make a lot of noise about how tight security must be in order to protect the validity of the test. Baloney. Aren't these tests supposed to be impervious to test prep, completely inaccessible to the world of memorization and rote? What these folks want to protect is their delicate ears and eyes, protect them from the onslaught of outrage and ridicule that would follow if the general public and professional educators got a good look at the test.

If your model of a test is a surprise, a moment in your course when you jump out from behind a bush a try to play "gotcha" with your students, you are doing it wrong. Tests should be an opportunity to apply knowledge, to ramp the whole process up one final step that really seats the knowledge or skill in the students' brains.

But the underlying assumption in the high-stakes test-driven movement is that there are skadzillions of bad teachers and the students they have failed to teach out there, skadZILLIONS of them, and somehow they are sneaking by and we are going to have to outsmart them so that we can catch them in their consummate suckiness. The high-stakes test-driven movement is not about education-- it's about finding proof, somehow, that public schools are failing. It is nothing *but* a game of "gotcha."

The super-duper secret security that surrounds the assessments is further proof of their suckiness. And, for what it's worth, the ethical dilemma of copying one of the exams is about the same as the ethical dilemma of photographing a policeman who is beating a suspect.

Transparency for Reals

Reformsters loves them some transparency. However, by "transparency" what they means is "we want to show your school scores and teacher VAM scores and other fun data-ish stuff to the whole world." But if that's transparency, then Phyllis Schlafly is a stripper. "Transparency" means that the man behind the curtain will pass out some numbers and we will treat them as revelation.

Well, bullocks to that. Here's how we could have some real transparency.

Test Transparency

Along with the score, all parents will receive the completed version of their child's test. A complete copy of the test, with their child's answers marked, plus a brief explanation of why the correct answer is correct.

Parents will receive a complete guide to correlating questions to test areas. IOW, "Question 5 measures the student's ability to make inferences from text." Both these and the tests will be available to any member of the public.

Scoring Transparency

If there is any sort of conversion process to turn a raw score into a final score, that process will be made public. Also available in print and on the net will be an explanation of how the cut scores were set. It should be in the kind of English used by actual human beings.

For tests that involve human scorers, that facility will be open to tours by any interested members of the public. The training manual for those scorers will also be published on paper and net. Scorers names and qualifications will also be available upon request. None of those workers will be under any sort of gag order whatsoever-- they can talk to anybody about any aspect of their work at any time. They can write operas about it and perform them on street corners.

If the test is assessed by computer, that will, first of all, not be a secret. Second of all, any documentation necessary to establish that the program is more dependable than a hamster in a box will be readily available.

Validity Transparency

All data supporting the assertion that the test is valid and reliable will be published in their entirety. Honestly, I don't know why these people are scared of this-- there won't be three people in the country who can bear to read through it. Likewise all data about the field testing of tests will be available for anybody who can stand it.

Data Transparency

All federal, state and local school entities will publish clearly and publicly what other entities will be using test data. All of them.

I actually like the idea of a requirement that every time a piece of your child's data changes hands (so to speak) or is used, the parents are emailed a notification. I balk on this only because I suspect everybody's email would quickly become unusable.

Financial Transparency

Every test will come with a clear indication of who is making money for it. The price per unit of the test will be printed on the front cover, just like a magazine. ("Hey Mom! We took a fifty dollar test today!")

All not-for-profit schools will publish in big bold letters how much they pay their various officials. Maybe on numbers across the back of a jersey that said officials must wear to work every day.

VAM Transparency

All VAM systems must publish their computing formulas in full. With a complete explanation. If the explanation cannot be understood by an average college-educated 22-year-old, the system must be thrown out and started over. All VAM systems must also publish any and all studies done to create the impression that VAM works.

In short, stop throwing numbers around an insisting that if they're numbers they must be True. If you want to be transparent, then stop hiding the heart and spine of this bogus data system in a dark black box.

Welcome to Common Core Hospital

Nurse Duncan: Welcome to Common Core Hospital. How may I assist you?

Chris: My name's Chris Wobble. I was just in a car accident. My arm seems to be broken in about three places.

Nurse Duncan: All righty, then. We just need to do some assessments here to see what shape you're in. As a major health care provider, your health data determines our success rate. Now first we're going to take your blood pressure. Let me just put the blood pressure cuff on your arm here...

Chris: Ow! Owwww!! Hey!! Holly mother of God! I told that arm's broken!!

Nurse Duncan: Sir, our standard procedure is to take the blood pressure with the right arm. Stop whining. Show a little grit.

Chris: Aaaaaaiiieeeeeeee!

Nurse Duncan: Goodness. Your blood pressure numbers are quite bad. Quite bad. We are going to have to address that with an immediate treatment plan. Bad blood pressure numbers are a sign of poor health. Often they are related to excess weight. Are you fat?

Chris: Do I look fat? Look, do you want to just weigh me?

Nurse Duncan: Oh, we don't have any scales here. We find that the blood pressure measure is all we need to determine patient health quality. Let's just continue with my questions. Are you suffering from any stress or anxiety over the last few weeks that might have elevated your blood pressure?

Chris: Well, my frickin' arm is broken!! But that only happened today.

Nurse Duncan: I think we must conclude that your blood pressure problems are the result of a sedentary lifestyle. Please answer the following multiple choice question. Which strikes you as the most likely cause of your sedentary lifestyle. A) Your apartment does not have a gym, B) Your apartment is too small to offer room for exercise, C) You only socialize by drinking at bars, or D) Meal selections at your regular restaurant are high caloric content.

Chris: What? What??!! Those don't even make sense. And I live on a farm.

Nurse Duncan: We'll just write down A.

Chris: What hell is wrong with you?!!

Nurse Duncan: Let me consult my individualized treatment options chart. (Fiddles with iPad). According to our individualized treatment chart, your personalized treatment program is a regular series of pushups to be performed daily. Could you drop and give me ten right now, please?

Chris: Are you insane? Can you not see that my arm has extra bends in it?
Nurse Duncan: The use of my own senses for diagnosis is strictly against hospital policy. By the way, if you could give me your drivers license, credit cards, and on line passwords, we'd like to copy those for our records.

Chris: Why do you need that information for anything? What are you going to do with it, anyway?

Nurse Duncan: Well, that's not really any of your business now, is it? And I must say, Chris, that this is a charter hospital, and if you are going to be difficult to work with or require additional treatment options or indicate that you are likely to yield poor results that would hurt our ratings, I will be counseling you out.

Chris: You mean I won't get any treatment?

Nurse Duncan: Oh no. You will still be able to seek treatment at the public hospital. You passed it on your way in-- that gentleman in the back of the pick-up truck out in the parking lot.

Chris: Man. Will he take my insurance?

Nurse Duncan: Well, he can have what's left of your coverage payment. We'll still be keeping our full fee here. Now, about those pushups...

Chris: Oh look!! Isn't that Mark Zuckerberg in the hall? Is that a check he's holding?

Nurse Duncan: What? Where?? (Runs out of room. Returns shortly, confused and sad). I guess I must have missed him. Now then, about those push-ups...

Chris: Oh, I totally did them while you were in the hall. Can I have a pain pill at least?

Nurse Duncan: We're happy to hand out pills, particularly if it will make you more co-operative. As soon as we've finished our consultation here. I need to give you a final blood pressure check to measure your progress during our visit.

Chris: Here, give me the cuff. I'll put it on myself.

Nurse Duncan: But you've put it on your foot, outside your boot.

Chris: Just get your data.

Nurse Duncan: Very well..........Hmm

Chris: Yes?

Nurse Duncan: (Picks up phone). Maintenance? Yes, the patient I'm seeing is apparently dead. Get someone down here to process the patient out before it counts against us.

Chris: Oh for the love of God.

Directory of Anti-Teacher Trolls

It may or may not be a good idea to attempt reading all the pieces responding to the Vergara decision, but it's definitely a mistake to read the comments section for any of them.

If there is any group that has been emboldened by the California court's fact-free finding against teacher job protections, it has been the legion of anti-teacher trolls. From mainstreamish media like Slate to the usual bloggy outposts, teacher bashing trollery is in high gear.

So this seems like the perfect time to provide a directory of the basic varieties of internet teacher-haters you may encounter. (And remember-- don't feed them.)

Childless Troll

I don't have any kids, so why should I be paying any kinds of taxes to pay teachers salary? Cut their salary back to where I don't have to pay any taxes ever. Mind you, I still expect my doctor, neighbors, fellow voters, and every employed person I ever deal with to be an educated adult. I just don't want there to be any schools. I don't know how that's going to work. You're so smart, you figure it out.

Public Service Troll

People should work with children for free because it's such important work (also, musicians and artists should never want to be paid). When teachers complain about salary and benefits, it's unseemly. If they really cared about the children, teachers would happily live in a cardboard box just for the warm glow of satisfaction that comes from teaching. When teachers complain about no raise for eight years or trying to support their family, it just pisses me off-- don't they care about the children??

"Those Damn Unions" Troll

It's the damn teachers union. Teachers all want to go sleep at their desks because the union will protect them. The union does nothing but protect bad teachers. In fact, the union actually goes out, recruits bad teachers, and then cleverly forces administrations to give these crappy teachers tenure. The union also elected Obama President, and they have the power to bend all elected officials to their will (except for Rand Paul). Union leaders have a giant pile of money that they like to swim in a la Scrooge McDuck; they use it to buy all the elections and all the power.

Teacher Hater Troll

Teachers are the single biggest obstacle to education today. They are only in it for the power and the glory. Well, no-- they also became teachers because they knew that would put them in the best position to interfere with the education of American students, which is every teacher's goal. Teachers hate children, and they hate learning, so they become teachers so they can devote their entire lives to destroying those things. It's perfectly logical.

Race To The Bottom Troll

The guy who cooks the fries at McDonalds does not have tenure or make any more than minimum wage or get vacations, so neither should teachers. The guy who dropped out of school in tenth grade and now works part-time at Mega-Mart doesn't have job security, and he barely makes enough to pay his cellphone bill, so why should teachers not have to struggle, too? There are employers in this country who force their workers to toil in unconscionable conditions; why should we fight to improve those conditions when we can fight to drag teachers down to that crappy level instead.

Sad Bitter Memories Troll

I hated high school. My teachers were mean to me. I remember a couple who picked on me all the time just because I didn't do my work and slept in class a lot. And boy, they did a crappy job of teaching me anything. I sat in their classroom like a houseplant at least three days a week, and I didn't learn a thing. Boy, did they suck! Crappy teachers like that ought to be fired immediately! And that principal who yelled at me for setting fire to the library? That guy never liked me. Fire 'em all.

Unlikely Anecdote Troll

There was this one teacher in the town just over from where I went to school, and one day he brought in a nine millimeter machine gun and mowed down every kid in his first three classes. The principal was going to fire him, but the union said he couldn't because of tenure, so that guy just kept working there. They even put kids in his class who were related to the ones he shot. Tenure has to be made illegal right away.

Just Plain Wrong Troll

Tenure actually guarantees teachers a job for life, and then for thirty years after they retire and fifty years after they die. It's true. Once you get hired as a teacher you are guaranteed a paycheck with benefits for the next 150 years.

Confused Baloney Troll

If you really care about children and educational excellence, then you want to see teachers slapped down. The only way to foster excellence in education is by beating teachers down so they know their place. Only by beating everyone in the bucket can we get the cream to rise to the top.

Like A Business Troll

You know, in every other job, you get judged on your performance and then rewarded or fired accordingly. Personally, I would have been a useless lazy bastard at my job except that my boss was always looking over my shoulder. People suck unless you threaten them. Nobody threatens teachers enough; that's why they all suck. All the best businesses like, you know, big investment banks like Lehman Brothers or energy companies like Enron-- those totally function on accountability.

Fake Statistic Troll

It's a known fact that 63% of teachers failed high school shop class, and 43% are unable to even dress themselves. If you have a bad teacher in Kindergarten, it's a proven fact that you will make $1 trillion dollars less in life; also, you'll be plagued with adolescent acne until you're 34, and your children will be ugly. 92% of high school graduates last year were unable to read, and 46% of those were unable to even identify the English language. Also, 143% of urban teachers are "highly ineffective" and 52% of those are "grossly ineffective" and 24% of those actually give off waves that cause metal surfaces to rust. I ask you, how can we continue to support public education under these conditions.

Tin Hat Troll

Teachers are part of the Agenda 21 agenda, and will be used as tools to turn students into mindless puppets who will smother their parents in their beds at night. You can read all about it in the Codexes of the Postuleminatti.

Charter School Troll

All of these bad things only apply to public school. In charter schools, all students develop a cure for cancer and build pink unicorns from ordinary materials you can find around the house.

Accountability Troll

There are still poor children in this country who are doing poorly in school. That must be a teacher's fault. Hunt that teacher down and fire him, repeatedly.

Incoherent Rage Troll

Teachers just all suck with the suckiness think they're so smarty pants with their fancy college edumacations and don't even work a whole year or a whole day even they just work an hour and then twelve months off every summer resting up from just babysitting which any moron could do so fire them all because, suck gaaaaahhh.

If I missed any, you can just sign on as a **Hey You Made A Serious Omission** troll in the comments below.

Dancing into the Apocalypse Why the World of Public Education Has Never Been Worse, and Why I'm Excited To Be a Teacher Anyway

How Bad Is It?

It is almost breathtaking to step back and try to take in the wide array of forces lined up against the great traditions of American public education.

State legislatures and courts are re-writing the rules of employment to end the idea of lifetime teachers, and an entire organization has been set up to replace them with an endlessly cycle of barely-trained temps.

Data miners are rewriting the entire structure and purpose of schools to focus on gathering data from students rather than actually educating them, treating them as simply future marketing targets.

A far-reaching network of rich and powerful men is working to take the public education system as we know it and simply make it go away, to be replaced by a system that is focused on generating profit rather than educating children.

Teachers have been vilified and attacked. Our professional skills have been questioned, our dedication has been questioned, and we have been accused of dereliction and failure so often that now even our friends take it as a given that "American schools are failing."

One of the richest, most powerful men on the planet has focused his fortune and his clout on recreating the education system to suit his own personal ideas about how it should work and what it should do. He's been joined in this by other wealthy, powerful men who see the democratic process as an obstruction to be swept away.

We have been strong-armed into adopting new standards and the programs that come with them. These are one-size-fits-all standards that nobody really understands, that nobody can justify, and that are now the shoddy shaky foundation of the new status quo.

And in many regions, our "educational leaders" are also part of the reformster movement. The very people on the state and local level who are charged with preserving and supporting public education are, themselves, fighting against it.

All education is now slave to standardized testing. We live in a bizarro world where we pretend that test results tell us everything from whether a seven year old is college material to whether teachers (and the colleges at which they studied) are any good. The future of teachers, schools, and students themselves, ride on these tests that, when all is said and done, measure nothing except the students' ability to take these tests.

The President of the United States of America agrees with most of the forces lined up against public education. At his best, he has simply stood by while public education has come under attack; at his worst, he and his administration have actively implemented policies to break down our public education traditions.

It is true, as some folks like to say, that public education has been tossed about by the winds of one edu-fad or another. Anyone who has worked for more than ten years can rattle off a list of Next Big Things that have come and gone while teachers closed their doors and kept working.

But this is different. This is worse. This wind comes with more political power, more widespread support, and more power to do real damage than anything before. If these people achieve all their goals, what's left will be a system that looks nothing like the American public education system, and teaching as a career will be done.

So Why Am I Not Bailing Out?

First of all, none of what I'm saying here is meant as criticism of people who have left the profession. You can't do what you can't do, and when you reach your limit, you have to make the choice you have to make. Not all of us have the same kind of strength, and we do not all face the same level of challenge. I can't speak for anyone else, but I can say why I still think it's worth the fight.

There has never been a tougher time for public education, and that means there has never been a time when teachers have been needed more.

Education is can't run on autopilot any more. I don't mean it shouldn't (though that has always been true), but that anything resembling an autopilot or inertia or just a gravitation in the right direction has been busted, shattered. Public education will take its direction from the people who fight to get their hands on the steering wheel. Teachers need to be in that fight.

Someone has to look out for the students. Someone has to put the students' interests first, and despite the number of people who want to make that claim, only teachers are actually doing it. The number of ridiculous, time-wasting, pointless, damaging, destructive policies that are actually making it down to the students themselves is greater than ever before. Somebody has to be there to help them deal with it, help them stand up to it, and most of all, help them get actual educations in spite of it.

I don't want to over-dramatize our role as teachers, but this is what professionals do. Police, lawyers, doctors, fire fighters-- they all go toward people in trouble. They run toward people who need help. That's what teachers do-- and teachers go toward the people who are too young and powerless to stand up for themselves. And for professionals, the greater the trouble, the greater the need.

The fact that public education is under attack just means that our students, our communities, need us more than ever.

Is There Hope?

Yes. Yes, there is.

The new high stakes test-driven corporate status quo runs on money, and money is not infinite. Particularly when resistance picks up and the ROI isn't looking so great. The big bold reformster programs all have one thing in common-- they have not produced any sort of success. Well, two things-- they also all required a big boost of money and "advocacy groups" to even happen in the first place.

The reformsters are not going to win, but neither are we going to simply set the clock back to twenty years ago. Our education system, our schools are going to be different, changed. And we will deal with that, too.

The reformsters are tourists, folks just passing through for a trip that will last no longer than their interest. They'll cash in their chips and move on to the next game. But we'll still be here, still meeting the challenges that students bring us. They've committed to education for as long as it holds their attention and rewards them; we've committed for as long as we can still do the work. They think they can sprint ahead to easy victory; we understand that this is a marathon.

I don't care if this is a passing storm or the apocalypse. I choose not to meet it huddled and hoping that I'll somehow be spared. And while we keep defaulting to battle metaphors, I'd rather not get into the habit of viewing every other human as an enemy that I have to combat with force of arms. I learned years ago that you don't wait for everything to be okay to do your dance and sing your song; you keep dancing and singing, and that's how everything gets closer to okay.

We can do this. We will do this. And our students will be better for it.

Inauthentic Reading Assessment

Does it seem as if test writers come up with the most obscure, boring, reading-resistant passages possible for standardized test? It's not just you. It's a deliberate choice, and not necessarily an ill-intended one, but the result is a completely unreal inauthentic reading experience that real humans don't have anywhere except on standardized tests.

One goal in test design is to steer the ship of assessment past the shoals of "prior knowledge." After all, if I'm Pittsburgh and my test includes a reading passage about the Steelers with questions about Troy Polamalu's career stats, I won't know if the students answered correctly because they read the passage or because they already know the stats.

So I am looking for a passage that my test-takers are unlikely to have prior knowledge about. In fact, since I'm trying to create a standardized test on the national scale, my third grade testing goal is to find *selections for which no eight year old anywhere in America would have prior knowledge*.

That's how eight year olds end up taking tests on selections explaining the village politics of ancient Turkey.

But let's look at just how inauthentic that is.

In school, we always present new material by connecting it to old material. We do this because A) we are trained educators and B) we are not idiots. The most fundamental way of absorbing new material is to connect it to what we already know. As teachers, we use that to our advantage, and we model it for our students. They aren't just learning to read-- they're learning how to learn. Part of the whole business of becoming an educated person is acquiring enough background that no matter what New Stuff we encounter, we have the foundation of knowledge to connect the New Stuff to Stuff We Already Know.

We also model attack skills, the skills needed to make sense of things that do not, initially, make sense. Ask somebody. And in the 21st century-- get out your device and look it up.

In real life, we read things we are interested in, which means we already have some prior knowledge about the content before we even start. And our real-world presentation of reading materials always involves some reader prep, from the blurbs on the back cover of a book to the pull-quotes and sub-headlines in non-fiction articles.

I just looked at a wired article about photochrons with a blurb calling them the instagrams of the 1800s, which is not exactly accurate, but it immediately communicates where we're going for everyone who doesn't already know about photochrons (aka "pretty much everyone"). That connecting idea would be a complete no-no in standardized test land, yet in the real world, it's exactly what a good editor does.

Where in real life do we ever pick up something that has no connection to anything we already know, and then read it without the ability to do simple look-it-up research to make sense of the hard parts?

Nowhere. The type of reading we demand students do on reading tests is a type of reading that isn't done anywhere except on reading tests. Well, and of course now, also, in all the classrooms that are trying to get students ready for these inauthentic reading tests. The perversion of close reading that insists on teaching students short excerpts with no scaffolding or preparation has nothing to do with teaching readers and everything to do with test prep.

It has been said many many times, but it's important enough that somebody should be saying it, again, every week. Reading instruction is a casualty of testing, twisted into test prep that does not teach our students how real readers read in the real world. It is not aimed at preparing lifetime readers, but at preparing test takers.

Teacher Time

Every profession measures time differently. Doctors and lawyers measure time in hours or vague lumps. Teachers measure time in minutes, even seconds.

If a doctor (or his office) tell you that something is going to happen "at nine o'clock," that means sometime between 9:30 and Noon. Lawyers, at least in my neck of the woods, can rarely be nailed down to an actual time. Anything that's not a scheduled appointment is "sometime this afternoon." Even a summons to jury duty will list a particular time which just represents the approximate time at which things will start to prepare to begin happening. Further up the Relaxed Time Scale, we find the delivery and installation guys for whom "Between 8 AM and 3 PM Tuesday," means "Not at all on Tuesday."

Meanwhile, in teacher land, 9:00 means exactly 9:00. Other professionals may round off, saying 9:00 when they really mean 8:57 or 9:08, but we mean what we say. If a class starts at 9:00 and ends at 9:51, we are getting our fifty-one minutes of class.

This is one of those things that non-teachers don't entirely get. If you work in an office, time is pretty flexy. If a meeting can benefit by running an extra ten or fifteen minutes, you just do it. But in most schools, when the bell rings, you're done. There is no little extra bit of time you can just throw into the work.

Consequently we tend to measure out our time in coffee spoons. One minute and forty-three seconds left in class? Okay, I can totally get three more practice sentences about participial phrases in before I remind them of tomorrow's assignment. Which is better than realizing that you've got two minutes and twenty seconds left for a three-and-ahalf minute piece of business.

Nobody in the business world feels any real difference between a fortytwo minute meeting and a fifty-one minute meeting, but most teachers feel a whole world of difference in that nine-minute gap. That's why the phrase "It'll just a take a couple of minutes," doesn't mean a thing to civilians, but makes a teacher's heart sink. I think it's also part of why civilians don't really understand what they're asking when they request or require that teachers add "just one more little" thing to the teaching day.

Other than the fact that it gives some teachers the uncanny ability to act as human egg timers, I'm not sure we benefit much from this heightened time awareness. Yes, teachers learn to be punctual, which is a virtue, I hear. But doctors and lawyers and other folks are fast and loose (well, loose) with time because for them, a task takes as long as it takes, whereas in teaching, a task takes as long as we get to do it.

It's a fantasy of mine to imagine a classroom in which I say, "Okay, class. We're going to work with dependent clauses today, and we're going to keep at it till everyone gets it." I understand that problems that go with that (Mrs. Numberwhacker is up the hall wishing I would be done with clauses so she can get started with quadratic equations), but one of the screwy things about how we're set up in this country is that the most fundamental organizing principle is The Clock. Not the students, teachers, or lessons, but The Clock. I know it's hard to think of another way to manage several hundred humans working on a hundred tasks under one roof, but a guy can dream. And if your school figured out a way to be student or task centered, I'd be fascinated to hear about it.

Without Tenure...

It's true that in the absence of tenure, teachers can (and are) fired for all manner of ridiculous things. That's unjust and unfair. As some folks never tire of pointing out, that kind of injustice is endemic in many jobs (Why people would think that the response to injustice is to demand more injustice for more people is a whole conversation of its own). That doesn't change a thing. Firing a teacher for standing up for a student or attending the wrong church or being too far up the pay scale-- those would all be injustices. But as bad as that would be, it's not the feature of a tenureless world that would most damage education.

It's not the firing. It's the threat of firing.

Firing ends a teacher's career. The threat of firing allows other people to control every day of that teacher's career.

The threat of firing is the great "Do this or else..." It takes all the powerful people a teacher must deal with and arms each one with a nuclear device.

Give my child the lead in the school play, or else. Stop assigning homework to those kids, or else. Implement these bad practices, or else. Keep quiet about how we are going to spend the taxpayers' money, or else. Forget about the bullying you saw, or else. Don't speak up about administration conduct, or else. Teach these materials even though you know they're wrong, or else. Stop advocating for your students, or else.

Firing simply stops a teacher from doing her job.

The threat of firing coerces her into doing the job poorly.

The lack of tenure, of due process, of any requirement that a school district only fire teachers for some actual legitimate reason-- it interferes with teachers' ability to do the job they were hired to do. It forces teachers to work under a chilling cloud where their best professional judgment, their desire to advocate for and help students, their ability to speak out and stand up are all smothered by people with the power to say, "Do as I tell you, or else."

Civilians need to understand-- the biggest problem with the destruction of tenure is not that a handful of teachers will lose their jobs, but that entire buildings full of teachers will lose the freedom to do their jobs well.

We spent a lot of time in this country straightening out malpractice law issues, because we recognized that a doctor can't do his job well if his one concern is not getting sued into oblivion for a mistake. We created Good Samaritan laws because we don't want someone who could help in an emergency stand back and let The Worst happen because he doesn't want to get in trouble.

As a country, we understand that certain kinds of jobs can't be done well unless we give the people who do those jobs the protections they need in order to do their jobs without fear of being ruined for using their best professional judgment. Not all jobs have those protections, because not all workers face those issues.

Teachers, who answer to a hundred different bosses, need their own special set of protections. Not to help them keep the job, but to help them do it. The public needs the assurance that teachers will not be protected from the consequences of incompetence (and administrators really need to step up-- behind every teacher who shouldn't have a job are administrators who aren't doing theirs). But the public also needs the assurance that some administrator or school board member or powerful citizen will not interfere with the work the public hired the teacher to do.

Tenure is that assurance. Without tenure, every teacher is the pawn and puppet of whoever happens to be the most powerful person in the building today. Without tenure, anybody can shoulder his way into the classroom and declare, "You're going to do things my way, or else."

Tenure is not a crown and scepter for every teacher, to make them powerful and untouchable. Tenure is a bodyguard who stands at the classroom door and says, "You go ahead and teach, buddy. I'll make sure nobody interrupts just to mess with you." Taxpayers are paying us for our best professional judgment; the least they deserve is a system that allows us to give them what they're paying us for.

Teachers in Thunderdome

One of the dreams of reformsters is a school system in which teacher employment is shaped by neither tenure nor seniority. When the time comes for cutting staff, administrators will just grab their Big Spreadsheet of Teacher Effectiveness Data, look down at the bottom of list, point at the name next to the lowest rating number and declare, "Okay-- that's who's getting laid off."

We've talked about the huge problems with the data generation methods that would go into such a list. But let's talk about the effect that such a system would have on teaching staffs.

The system would turn shrinking school districts into education Thunderdomes (only "two teachers enter, one teacher leaves" will have a slightly different meaning).

Some of the best educational ideas out there are pushing teamwork and collaboration, built on the idea that all of our students belong to all of us teachers. Not my kids in my room, and your kids in your room. Unfortunately, most VAM-based systems don't see it that way. My kids determine my fate, and your kids determine yours.

So do I really want to help you with your kids when that means making my own job less secure?

Look, I think the overwhelming majority of teachers are good people who went into teaching for the right reason, and I think they would have a hard time saying, "No, I won't give you any help in figuring out how to teach that skill to your class." But how does anyone overlook the fact that she has a family to help support, kids to feed and put through college, a mortgage to pay off-- how does anyone look at that and say, "Yes, I am going to actively work to make my employment less secure."

Our current system depends on both official and unofficial mentoring of new teachers. How many pieces of advice, handy lesson tricks, moments of moral and educational support can you bring yourself to share when every bit of help you give to someone else is a bit of hurt for yourself?

Who really, truly imagines that a teacher beaten and carried out of Thunderdome will go home and cheerily announce, "Sorry, kids, but no new clothes and no new vacation for you. But i'm sure you'll be glad to know that I lost my job to someone with better numbers."

How will Thunderdome affect hiring? After all, some districts include classroom teachers in the interview process. Will teachers sit in interviews and think, "Yes, I want to find someone good enough to take my job!" Or will it become a tricky business of finding someone who's good enough not to be a big chunk of dead wood, but not so good that they're a threat? And will administrations figure this out and shut teachers out of the hiring process entirely?

In Thunderdome, teaching assignments will be critical. In a shrinking district, student and class distribution will become a matter of professional life and death. With so much riding on it, what do you suppose the odds are that the process will become twisted, driven by concerns other than what's best for the children? How hugely important will it be to smooch your principal's tuchus? How ugly will it be when certain students are turned into human hot potatoes?

How will Thunderdome affect the collegiality, the collaboration, the success of all students? Will it promote the learning of all students, or will it exacerbate the problem of teachers huddling in their own classrooms, keeping for just twenty-five students the educational assistance that could have helped 100?

Yes, teachers are professionals, and caring people, and usually naturally inclined to help and support each other. But Thunderdome raises the stakes. Helping a teacher become as good as, or better than, you would not just be a blow to your ego or trigger some sort of existential crisis-- it would mean your job. We already have evidence (as if we needed any), via multiple test cheating scandals, that when you pit people's devotion to philosophical purity against their desire to feed their children, purity often loses.

Teacher Thunderdome is a dumb idea that would do huge, irreparable harm to schools and create obstacles to student success. There's an old saying about how, when you're in a pack of people trying to escape a bear, you only have to be faster than the slowest person in the pack. That is not a scenario conducive to teamwork. There may be fields where the road to excellence is a one-lane footpath that must is best traveled alone, but in teaching, excellence always depends on the support and assistance of a larger team. To create a system that cuts that team apart, that makes teachers compete with the people they should be sharing with, is just dumb.

The Financial Fantasies of Choice

Proponents of choice systems, whether they're talking about charters or vouchers, depend on certain financial fictions to make their case. Like beach-bound vampires wearing SPF 110 sunscreen, these robust and rigorous fictions just won't die. Let's examine some of these dancing unicorns of the choice world.

System Savings

In the 1960s, Pennsylvania strongly encouraged its many small township-based school districts to consolidate. It did so because of an obvious piece of common sense-- it is cheaper and more efficient to educate 100 students in one school building to spread them out over four separate buildings.

Choice systems sometimes hide the additional costs by transfering them to parents or corporate sponsors or fund-raising projects. Charters can also bridge the financial gap by slashing teacher pay and maintaining high turnover so that there's little to no cost for benefits and pensions; that's just transfering the additional costs of a choice system to the teachers who work in it. But the bottom line is that opening a whole bunch of schools to serve a population that previously fit into one is cost-ineffective and usually more expensive. There may be clever methods used to hide the additional costs, but it is still there.

Cost Per Pupil

Let's say you read a statement that a car is stolen every forty-four seconds in this country. That's a lot of cars to steal, and a tough crime wave to put a dent in. But hey-- that means that about 163 cars are stolen between 2:00 and 4:00 AM every day. Streets are pretty quiet then-- it would be easy to spot nefarious doings. So let's create a federal grant to stem the tide of auto theft in those early morning hours. It will save almost 60,000 stolen cars a year!

Except, of course, that it really won't, because every statement about how [Bad Thing A] happens every [unit of time] is a fiction, a way to present data that is easily understood. But there is no ring of car thieves out there carefully and precisely stealing a car every forty-four seconds.

Likewise, Cost Per Pupil is a fiction. It makes a neat number for comparison of different districts, but a $10K per pupil expense does not mean that East Podwallow Schools are actually spending precisely $10K on each student.

Choice fans like to treat the per pupil cost as if it's a stipend, a chunk of money set aside for each specific student. The money, they insist, does not belong to the taxpayer or the school district, but should follow the student around like an imprinted gosling. But the per pupil cost is not an education allowance from the government that can be put into any educational vending machine.

Public schools are brutalized by this fiction time after time. If Chris leaves my school, taking "his" $10K with him, my school's expenses do not decrease. We do not hire fewer teachers, run fewer buses, heat the building to a lower temperature, or turn Chris's textbooks in for a refund from the publisher.

This remains true if ten of Chris's friends (and another $100K) leave the school. Or twenty- unless by some bizarre coincidence all twenty leave from the same classroom. And by the same token, when ten more students move into the district, the budget does not increase by $100K.

These statistical fictions have a place, particularly in comparison. If one city has a car stolen "every day" and another has them stolen "every twelve hours," it helps me decide when to park. And if Blorgville Schools spend $10K per pupil and East Woggle Schools spend $18K, that tells me something about how the districts are different. But it does not tell me that each student in East Woggle has a literal $18K paying for her education.

Disenfranchisement

That Cost Per Pupil amount is not an allowance paid to students by the state, and to treat it as such is to disenfranchise every taxpayer who contributed to it. Parents and students are not entitled to clutch that not-actually-a-stipend and claim, "This is mine. My school choice is only about me, and not about anybody else."

It is about other people. It's about the students left behind in the public school that is now some number of dollars poorer. And it is about the taxpayers who now have no say in how the money they invested in public schools will be spent. Every taxpayer is a stakeholder, because every citizen hopes to live in a country filled with educated people.

"Schools take money from taxpayers without giving them a say," protest the choice fans. That is simply untrue. School board members are elected, and taxpayers have a say (aka "vote"). That's true everywhere except in places like Newark and Philadelphia, where the public has been shut out of the democratic process, and you can see in those places just how bad this sort of disenfranchisement gets.

Apply the same argument to the army, and we would have soldiers trained and equipped by the taxpayers going back home and saying, "I am only going to protect my own house."

Zero Sum

A choice advocate once told me that I should stop talking about this issue as if it were a zero sum game. But it is a zero sum game. The tax dollars involved are finite. Money taken for one school must come from another school. And if we try to run two homes on a strict one-home budget, we are playing a zero-sum game that guarantees disappointment for some players.

There are many fine reasons to consider at least some aspects of a choice system. But we can't have those conversations until and unless we drop the financial fantasies and are honest about the true cost. Feel free to start in the comments section here.

Why Teachers Can't Have a Seat at the Table

This month has been declared New Conversation Month by reformsters. Teachers are being offered (in vaguely non-specific ways) some sort of seats at various tables. Unfortunately, this largesse underlines just how much teachers have not been included in conversations about public education. Every step of the way, every part of the discussion, teachers have not been included.

I got to wondering-- why not? I mean, there are only so many possible explanations. Knowing why teacher voices have not been pursued or included would tell us something about reformster attitudes about teachers and illuminate the relationships at the heart of how public education works in this country.

So let's consider the possible reasons that teachers are not, and have not been, at the infamous table. What are the reformsters thinking?

Teachers would sidetrack the process.

If we're going to get things done, we must begin with the end in mind. The conversation is not, for instance, whether charters would be a good solution or how to make charters a good solution. We're talking tactics and strategy, not inquiry and philosophy. So it's not "How could charters most effectively enhance education in a community" but "We know we want to get charters into this area. How do we make that happen?" Ditto for high stakes tests, Common Core, data mining, tenure stripping, teacher evaluations and evaluation-driven (aka less) pay.

Teachers might want to question those premises, try to open up for discussion things we just don't need to discuss.

Teachers lack our shared vision.

We need people who see the same things, who share the same vision for remaking Amerucan public education. Teachers by and large lack that vision and would detract from the focused unity we need to do What Must Be Done. We certainly don't need to waste time and energy arguing about what must be done or why it must be done. Teachers are way too attached to traditional models; it's almost as if they think traditional public education in this country actually works instead of recognizing that our premise of total educational failure is Totally Truthy. Proof shmoof. If they won't get on the bus with us, leave 'em behind.

In a proper society, one does not bargain with the help.

It was a sad day when the Captains of Industry and Commerce were forced to start dealing with unions. Yuck! The proper order of things is that the People in Charge determine the best action to take, and then the employees do as they're told. Bill Gates does not have to sit down and talk corporate policy with the Microsoft janitorial staff, General Patton did not consult with privates about military strategy, and the People In Charge of Education should not have to sit down and talk with teachers. It's true that teacher's unions sometimes become such a nuisance that they have to be listened to, but we're working on that.

Teachers are beneath us.

Arne Duncan plays basketball with the Reformster-in-Chief. The corporate titans of reformsterdom hobnob with the rich and famous. The hedge fund operators of reformsterdom deal with heads of state and juggle millions of dollars. We reformsters are big, important, rich, powerful people. Why the heck would we want to sit down with a bunch of women who make thirty-five grand a year and who manage milk money for a roomful of seven-year-olds?

Look, these policy decisions have to be made at very high levels. Teachers just don't belong there. After all, they're just... teachers.

We aren't friends with any teachers.

We like to work with people we know and like and trust. We don't know any teachers. It nothing personal. There isn't anybody at the table whom we don't already know and like and trust. Don't call them cronies. They're just people who Are On The Same Page.

Teachers suck.

Teachers have totally screwed up American education. Some huge percentage of them are grossly incompetent (and as soon as we tweak up the right evaluation process, we'll chase them out). They don't know a thing about how to educate children, and a huge percentage of them don't even want to. They just want to hand out worksheets and sit on their big fat tenure-enhanced butts. Everything that's wrong about public education is their fault. We're cleaning up their mess. Have them help us? No, thank you-- they've done enough already.

Okay, maybe they don't suck. But they lack expertise.

Teachers don't have expertise in dealing with educational theory and policy. They're just teachers. They sit around and run off worksheet copies and drill students in math facts and make sure that kids line up for recess. They help teenagers put up crepe paper for school dances. Teachers simply don't know enough about education to be involved in education policy discussions.

Okay, maybe they have some educational expertise, but this isn't about education.

This isn't about education. It's about how things really get done, and that comes down to politics, power, and money. Teachers don't know anything about how those work. Just sit out in the hall, honey, while the big boys take care of business.

Teachers will try to protect their at the cost of our goals.

Our goals include redefining teaching as a job that people only do for a couple of years, for middling pay with no retirement benefits. To make school finance more "nimble" and to provide better ROI, we need to transform teaching from a lifetime profession into a short time job. It would also be great if we could neuter their damn union. There's a ton of money tied up in education, and we want it, and some of that money is tied up in personnel costs. We need to get money away from the schools in general and the teachers in particular, and in our experience, nobody likes having money taken away (lord knows, we don't). We expect that a lot of teachers and a lot of union people will object to this, and we don't want to listen to their damn whining all the time.

Teachers will harsh our buzz.

It is just such a huge bummer when you think up a cool idea for how schools should work and teachers chime in with "That's a stupid idea that will never work blah blah facts blah blah blah research" or "Yes, that's a good idea which is why we've been doing it for the past twenty years." How can we enjoy feeling like great thought-leaders and education revolutionaries when people keep interrupting with that shit?

We totally included teachers.

We searched all over for teachers who agreed with everything we have to say and were totally willing to go along with us every step of the way. We have included those teachers. Well, at least, we've allowed those teachers to be spokespersons for us. They've been great and have given us no trouble at all. What else did you want?

You didn't get your invitation? Hmm. It must have gotten lost in the mail.

We totally meant to invite you guys. Did you check your spam filters? Our secretary must have messed up. Man, we wondered why you weren't here.

Are there any other possible explanations? In particular, are there any that don't smell of disrespect or disregard for public school teachers? I'm stumped. Maybe **We knew you were busy with Real Important Stuff and we didn't want to bother you** is a possibility, but I don't think I've ever read anything that would suggest it.

No, to really have a new conversation, there's a message that reformsters are somehow going to have to get out. It would go something like this:

You know what? We made a mistake. We now realize that teachers are deeply committed to educating our country's children, and as America's leading education professionals, they need to be not just part of this conversation, but leading it. After a few years of trying to reshape public education, we realize we need to change our stance. So we are here to listen to you, teachers. How can we help you achieve the best results for our public school students?

To their credit, some reformsters have picked up on pieces of that. But we're not there yet.

The Market Hates Losers

Fans of market forces for education simply don't understand how market forces actually work.

What they like to say is that free market competition breeds excellence. It does not, and it never has.

Free market competition breeds excellent marketing. McDonald's did not become successful by creating the most excellent food. Coke and Pepsi are not that outstandingly superior to RC or any store brand. Betamax was actually technically superior to VHS, but VHS had a better marketing plan.

The market loves winners. It loves winners even if they aren't winning-- Amazon has yet to turn an actual profit, ever, but investors think that Bezos is a winner, so they keep shoveling money on top of him. And when we enter the area of crony capitalism, which likes to pretend it's the free market, picking winners becomes even less related to success. Charter schools were once a great idea with some real promise, but the whole business has become so toxically polluted with crony capitalism that it has no hope of producing educational excellence in its present form.

But then, the market has only one measure for winning, and that is the production of money. The heart of a business plan is not "Can I build a really excellent mousetrap?" The heart of a business plan is "Can I sell this mousetrap and make money doing it?"

There is nothing about that question that is compatible with pursuing excellence in public education.

The most incompatible part of market-driven education is not its love of money-making winner, but its attitude about losers. Because the market hates losers. The market has no plan for dealing with losers. It simply wants all losers to go away.

Here's the problem. I teach plenty of students whom the market would consider losers. They take too long to learn. They have developmental obstacles to learning. They have disciplinary issues. They may be learning disabled. They have families of origin who create obstacles rather than providing support. What this means to a market-driven education system is that these loser students are too costly, offer too little profit margin, and, in their failures, hurt the numbers that are so critical to marketing the school.

In PA, we already know how the market-driven sector feels about these students. It loves to recruit them by promising a free computer and a happy land of success where nobody ever hounds you about attendance and all homework can be completed by whoever is sitting by the computer. But sooner or later, those students are sloughed off and sent back to public schools. And by "sooner or later," I mean some time after the cyber-charter has collected the money for that student.

The market sheds its losers, its failures (well, unless they can convince some patron or crony that they are just winners who are suffering a minor setback). Schools cannot.

For the free market, failure is not only an option, but a necessity. Losers must fail, be defeated, go away. For a public school system, that is not an option. Only with due process and extraordinary circumstances should a student be refused a public education. And certainly no traditional respectable public school system can simply declare that it has too many loser kids, so it's going to shut down.

The free market approach to schools must inevitably turn them upside down. In a free market system, the school does not exist to serve the student, but the student exists to serve the interests of the school by bringing in money and by generating the kinds of numbers that make good marketing (so that the school can bring in more money). And that means that students who do not serve the interests of the free-market school must be dumped, tossed out, discarded.

To label students losers, to abandon them, to toss them aside, and to do all that to the students who are in most need of an education-- that is the very antithesis of American public education. The free market approach to schools will no more unleash innovation and excellence than did 500 channels on cable TV. What it will do is chew up and spit out large numbers of students for being business liabilities.

Free market forces will not save US education; they will destroy it. To suggest that entrepreneurs should have the chance to profit at the cost of young lives is not simply bad policy-- it's immoral. It's wrong.

Living in a Non-Standardized World

My school was closed today. We're closed every year on this day because it is the weekend of our local small town festival. This is our local holiday.

Like many small town festivals, we have hung ours on a thinnish peg. John Chapman, aka Johnny Appleseed, lived here for a while in the distant past, and so our festival is Applefest.

We close down the main drag on Saturday and Sunday. There's a 5K race down the main street of the city and back. There's a car show on Sunday which fills that same street. There are roughly a gazzillion vendors in the park, selling everything from Ecuadorian sweaters to handcrafted clocks to Jesus painted on roof slate. There's a whole street of local service group vendors, right across from the farmers' market. The local theater group schedules a Big Show for this weekend (this year it's Chicago, which I'm directing but must modestly admit that, thanks to my cast and orchestra, it kicks ass). Last night my school sponsored our high school hall of fame induction dinner. Today my wife and I got up early to go to the apple pancake breakfast at the Catholic church.

Applefest was partly invented and has partly grown organically. When I was a tadpole, it was an afternoon of small crafty booths. Now it's a three day festival that shuts down the whole town and brings in tens of thousands of visitors. Maybe hundreds of thousands. There's not any good way to judge.

Why am I talking about this? Because it's an example of how life in a non-standardized world looks.

No amount of "town festival standards and practices" guidelines would have helped a bit, either in the creation of the festival nor in its growth and execution. Most especially, it would not have improved the experience of it.

There are thousands of small town festivals like ours (and a few hundred big city festivals trying to capture the same small town feel). They all have many similar features, and yet they are all different. If you teleport me into the middle of any of them, there isn't the slightest chance that I would mistake it for our festival here. They are all specific to place. You cannot just move seamlessly from one to another without it making a difference.

But they are most of all specific to people. Folks come back for Applefest to see people. In an hour of walking, I will touch on a hundred different relationships. This morning I saw dozens of current students. I saw some old friends and classmates of my own. I saw a student from a decade ago who wanted to tell me that she is now a middle-school English teacher and she sometimes channels me in class. I do remember her from back in the day, and her story becomes one more to add to the file of "People do grow up and turn out okay even if that future is not obvious when they're sixteen" stories.

So when people start talking about standardization in schools as if it is self-evident that standardization is a Good Thing, Applefest is the kind of human experience I think about. How can standardization possibly make human experience better? Why would it be any sort of improvement to be able to move from one place to another without it making a difference? Why is it a good idea to make human experiences more the same? And how, in a world where the foundation of all human activity is the relationship and interactions between various specific individual human beings-- how can standardization even happen without trying to render unimportant the very things that make us human?

If there's anything Applefest doesn't need, it certainly doesn't need a state or federal or "expert" authority to come in with some sort of standards for how to do this better. We don't need to standardize the events or the experience or the people. My experience this morning of walking around town with my wife was unique and singular and absolutely unstandardized.

Schools are a product of the place in which they exist and the people who walk their halls. Some may struggle, and some may face large challenges. Standardization is not the solution to any of those challenges. Standardization is not what makes the world go round. Standardization is not what makes life rich and full and worth living. And if standardization does not enhance the experience of being human in the world, how could it possibly enhance the experience of school.

College-ready Five Year Olds

We periodically hear of the notion of college-ready five year olds. Not that they are ready to go to college while still that young, but that we can clearly tell in kindergarten whether these children are on the collegiate trajectory or not.

Recently a pair of teachers attempted a response to Carol Burris's Real Clear Education interview. Since the two work for Student Achievement Partners, a group started by CCSS architect David Coleman and financed by Bill Gates, what the two SAPs is not exactly a surprise.

The kindergarten SAP argues that her students (at her select charter school in Oakland, California) are able to do super-hard things that let her know that they are ready for college. In particular she is arguing for having kindergartners count to 100. She does not clarify whether she uses the technique of Rote Repetition of the Numbers With No Idea What They Mean or the technique of Counseling Out Students Who Can't Count To 100.

I'm excited about being able to ID college-ready five year olds. This presents a host of opportunities including the chance to start applying to college at age six. I mean, my high school juniors and seniors get very stressed about the whole application process. Imagine how much more relaxed and focused they could be if they had locked up that collegiate spot by age seven. They are just childhood as an excuse to be lazy anyway.

Of course, deciding college that early would really mess with David Coleman"s College Board SAT revenue stream. There's a pretty hefty industry driven by the general college-seeking panic of teenagers and their parents, so even as Core boosters claim that we can determine the college prospects of small children, reformsters once again face two challenging choice:

1) Shift the industry around to monetize the new impact areas or

2) Pretend they don't understand the implications of what they're saying.

For cradle-to-career railroad, it's a big number two all the way.

Mind you, they've occasionally admitted that they really do want to be able to predict the adult life of a small child with a "seamless web that literally extends from cradle to grave." But nobody who A) knows who Big Brother is or B) wants a future in American politics is going to hold up that infamous Marc Tucker "Dear Hillary" letter and say, "Yes, this is what we should do." Not out loud.

Reformsters could argue that the very notion of being able to place a five year old in a college is silly because, of course, any number of things in his life outside of school could happen in the next thirteen years to interfere with his college readiness-- but they can't make that argument because then they would have to admit that life factors outside of school affect the child's education.

No, we have to pretend that the educational journey is a train-- one track, one beginning and ending, everyone traveling along the undeviating, uninterrupted trail.

So if that's true, why wouldn't we fill out those college applications at the end of kindergarten? If all students are going to meet the same standards at the same time, and we can tell whether kindergartners are on track, and there's only one track, why isn't that good enough?

I suspect that in a dark moment of honesty, some reformsters would say it was good enough, that they already knew that Chris was destined for a life of corporate servitude and all we're doing is waiting for the sapling to grow large enough to harvest.

But in the meantime, reformsters will at once pretend that it's not absurd to declare a five year old on track for college, even as they fail to acknowledge the implications of that college-ready declaration. If we know that a five year old is on track for college, why not sign her up now? The answer-- sort of-- is that reformsters can't explain why a five year old's college application is absurd without also explaining why reform itself is absurd.

How We Pay Public Servants-- and Why

We have always paid public servants a flat fee, untethered to any sort of "performance measures." That's because we want public service to be completely disconnected from any private interests.

Fighting Fire with Money

Imagine if, for instance, we paid fire fighters on sliding scale, based on how many of which type fires they put out at a certain speed. This would be disastrous for many reasons.

Fire fighters would refuse to work in cities where there were few fires to fight, because they couldn't make a living. In cities where there were commonly multiple fires, fire fighters would look at each fire call through a lens of "What's in it for me?"

For instance, in a system where fire fighters were paid based on the value of the flame-besieged property, fire fighters might view some small building fires as Not Worth the Trouble. Why bother traveling to the other side of the tracks? It's only a hundred-dollar blaze, anyway. Let's wait till something breaks out up in the million-dollar neighborhood.

In the worst-case scenario, one of our fire fighters depending on performance-based pay to feed his family may be tempted to grab some matches and go fire up some business.

Perverse Incentivization

Occasionally we've seen these kinds of perverse incentives in action, and we don't much like it. The areas of the country where you take extra speed limit care at the end of the month because the local police have a quota to meet. The neighborhood where cops have to roust a certain number of suspects a week to keep their job ratings. Nobody thinks these are examples of excellence in public service.

In fact, we have a history of playing with private police forces and private fire companies. We don't much care for how that works out, because it creates a system that provides excellent service-- but only for the customers who are paying for it.

The idea of public service is to create a class of people who are above self-interest and who do not respond to a single boss. We are outraged when abuse of police power happens precisely because we expect the police to act as if they work for everyone, and to put their dedication to that service above any single interests, including their own.

That's the definition of public service-- service roles that are stripped of any possibility of incentives other than the mandate to serve the public good. That's what we mean by "professional"-- a person who puts all personal self-interest aside and focuses on Getting the Job Done. Trying to motivate a public servant with self-interest inevitably tends to pollute the professional setting with the very self-interest that we're trying to get out of there.

Incentives and Suck-ups

Here's the thing about performance incentives. They always come from actual individual humans. In business that's okay, because the humans are already the bosses.

In public service, we often talk about performance incentives as if they fall from the sky, descending fully-formed from some on-high objective source. They are not. They, too, are developed by actual individual humans. And those humans will invariably encode their own values and priorities into the incentives.

"I like red houses. I think they are more valuable," say our fire company evaluators. "That's why I live in one. And that's why a good fire company always gives priority to saving red houses first."

Performance incentives for public service always-- always-- involve substituting the values of the few for the values of everybody. Fire fighters are supposed to save save everybody's homes. Police are supposed to protect every citizen. The US Postal Service is supposed to deliver to every home. They are there to serve the public, and that means everybody. Public servants are supposed to support the values of all citizens. Any performance based evaluation reward system will prioritize some citizens' values over those of other citizens.

A Public Service Performance Based Incentive System In Action

You know which public servants have a fully-realized performancebased pay system in place?

Congress.

The CEO of International Whoomdinglers says, "That Senator Bogswaller has done an excellent job of looking out for the things we believe are important. He ought to keep his job. Send him a big fat check."
The head of the Society for Preservation of Free-Range Spongemonkeys says, "We appreciate the hard work that Representative Whangdoodle has done looking out for spongemonkeys. He deserves a raise. Send him a big fat check."

You (and the members of the Supreme Court who are paying attention) might call this corruption, but it's just a Performance Based Incentive System, and the high regard with which Congress is held tells you how well a PBIS mixes with public service.

But But But

But a Performance Based Incentive System put in place by the government would not be run like the hodge-podge of private interests you describe incentivizing the US Congress, you say.

And I say, baloney. We already have a Performance Based Incentive System that says you're a better school district if you sell more of the College Board's AP product line. The PBIS testing system being used to incentivize students and teachers and schools-- that system is entirely a product of private corporate interests.

The only difference between an private incentive system, like the one that runs Congress, and a public one, like Race to the Top, is whether the people with money and power have to manipulate a government middle man or can go straight to the source.

Under the Umbrella

I teach mostly juniors, sometimes seniors. There are a few things I tell them every year.

One is to make the most out of senior year, because it is the last time they will be surrounded by people who are paid to put the students' interests first. It's the last time they'll be in an institution that is organized around their concerns, their interests, their needs. After that, they're in the open market. They will always be dealing with people who are trying to sell them something.

The PSAT will collect a ton of information about them so it can turn around and sell that data to colleges. Colleges will try to sell them, particularly if they are highly desirable ~~customers~~ students. Employers will try to get the use of their talents without having to pay much for it, and politicians will piss on them and tell them it's raining so that the pols can keep their jobs.

But here, under the umbrella of the public school, my students have nothing that I need to survive or make a living. I have no reason to do this job except for the reason I took this job in the first place-- to serve the best interests of my students.

It Doesn't Make Any Difference

It makes business-oriented reformy types crazy that the way I do my job doesn't make any difference to my pay. I understand the terror for them there, but that Not Making A Difference is actually the point of how we pay public servants.

It doesn't matter it's a big fire or a small fire, a rich person's house or a poor person's house-- the fire department still does their job. It doesn't matter whether I have a classroom full of bright students or slow students, rich students or poor students, ambitious students or lazy students-- I will still show up and do my job the best I know how. I should never, ever, ever have to look at a class roster or a set of test results or a practice quiz and think, "Dammit, these kids are going to keep me from making my house payment next month."

Why I Won't Suck

Reformsters are sure that human beings must be motivated by threats and rewards, and that the lack of threats and rewards means that I can too easily choose to do a crappy job, because it won't make any difference. They are wrong. Here's why.

1)   I knew the gig when I started. I knew I would not get rich, not be powerful, not have a chance to rise to some position of prominence. There was no reason to enter teaching in the first except a desire to do right by the students.

2)   Teaching is too hard to do half-assed. Do a consistently lousy job, and the students will eat you alive and dragging yourself out of bed every day will be too damn much. There isn't enough money to keep people flailing badly in a classroom for a lifetime. Just ask all the TFA dropouts who said, "Damn! This is hella hard!" and left the classroom.

And Most Importantly

Threats and rewards do not make people better public servants (nor have I ever seen a lick of research that suggests otherwise). Threats and rewards interfere with people's ability to get their job done.

Threats and rewards motivate people to game the system.

And any time you have a complex system being measured with simple instruments, you have a system that is ripe for gaming. In fact, if your measures are bad enough (looking at you, high stakes tests and VAM), your system can *only* be successfully operated by gaming it.

So, No Accountability At All?

Heck, no. You need to keep an eye out for the grossly incompetent, though they will often self-identify (I've made a huge mistake) and take the next stage out of Dodge. Beyond that, you just go watch and pay attention. If you're my administration, you're welcome in my classroom at any time for as long as you'd like to stay. No, don't bring that stupid checklist. Just watch and listen and use your professional judgment. If you think I need to fix something, let's you and I talk about it. How will bringing in extra layers of bureaucracy and government make that system work any more smoothly?

Man, This Is Running Long

Agreed. Sometimes these posts get away from me.

Bottom line-- the comparison to private enterprise performance based incentive systems is bogus. Those systems may be appropriate in corporate environments where we want to enforce a bias in favor of certain actors and outcomes-- where some people are in fact more important than others.

But in public service, performance based incentive systems are contraindicated. They by nature enforce a particular bias and cannot help but tilt the system in favor of some customers over others.

The system we have does, in fact, make sense. We stand our public servants beside a door and we say, "I'm going to pay you to stand here and wait as long as it takes and help whoever comes through that door. It doesn't matter who comes through that door-- nothing is going to affect your pay, so that's a settled and done deal-- just concentrate on watching that door and helping whoever walks through it."

Are You Still Here?

God bless you.

The Public Charter School Test

If you glance through the blog, you might conclude I hate charter schools. But like many critics of the current charter wave, I don't object to the idea of charters at all. Once upon a time, charters were actually a pretty good addition to the public education landscape.

The potential is still there. But to unlock it, charteristas will have to make true the mantra they keep repeating, that charter schools are public schools.

Charter schools, the modern version as represented by K12 and Success Academies, are not public schools at all. If they really want to earn the "public" label, they need to meet these four requirements.

Transparent Finances

As a taxpayer, I can walk into my local school district office and ask to see everything there is to see about the district finances. As a taxpayer, I'm entitled to a full accounting of how my money has been spent. To be a true public entity, you can't just take public funds-- you must give a public accounting of them as well.

That also means oversight. The modern charter is all too often tied up in all too shady financial dealings. Baker Mitchell of North Carolina is only the most recent example of a charter operator who uses a nonprofit charter to funnel money to his own private firms. It is Modern Charter 101 -- set up charter school, hire yourself, your family, your friends to do everything from managing the school to washing the floors. And rent the building and equipment from yourself. K12 routinely uses public tax dollars to mount advertising campaigns.

A true public school is always strapped for cash, and taxpayers are always keenly aware of where that money comes from. When negotiating contracts, spending money on big ticket items, even deciding to outsource janitorial services, our school board members are subject to plenty of input, feedback and general kibbitzing from the people who will pay for all those things.

Meanwhile, modern charters have famously gone to court to keep state auditors from getting a look at their books. That is not how a public institution behaves. If you're a public school, your finances must be completely transparent.

Accountability to the Voters

Boy, do I ever get charter operators frustration on this count. My ultimate bosses are a group of educational amateurs who have to win election to stay in charge of me. It's a screwy way to run a business-- what other enterprise requires professional experts to work at the beck and call of people whose only qualification is that they managed to garner a bunch of votes? Oh, wait. I remember an example-- the entire local, state and federal government of the entire country. Because we're a democracy.

Reed Hastings famously articulated the modern charter operator position-- elected school boards are a nuisance. They're unstable and change their composition and therefor their collective mind. What schools need is a single CEO, a kinderfuhrer who can swiftly and boldly make decisions without having to explain himself to people, particularly voting people who can remove him from power if they don't like his answers.

This is not how public institutions are supposed to work in a democratic society. Yes, as some folks periodically rediscover, democracy is terribly messy and inefficient. But the alternative is efficient long-term mediocrity or short term excellence (followed by crashing and burning). Neither is an appropriate goal for a stable society, and neither is appropriate for running a school system meant to serve all citizens, regardless of their income or social status.

If the voters of your school district do not have a say in how the school is run, you are not a public school. It does not count if your tsar or board of tsars is appointed by a state-level elected official. If there is no way for local voters to change the school's management through local means, it is not a public school.

And yes-- that means that there are places like Philadelphia and Newark where the schools are no longer public schools in anything but name. Leaving the name alone-- that's how you steal an entire public school system from the public it is supposed to serve.

Play by the Rules

The charter movement, even the traditional one, has been all about getting around bad rules. This has never made a lot of sense to me, this business of government saying, "We've tied up public schools in so many dumb rules that we need a different kind of school as an alternative." Why not say, "We've tied up public schools in so many dumb rules that we are now going to rescind some of those rules. Because, dumb."

The "we need charters to escape dumb rules" argument is like filling up your own car with Long John Silver's wrappers and empty coffee cups and one day saying, "Well, damn. This car's a mess. Guess I have to buy a new car." If you've made a mess of things, clean up the mess!

So I'll agree that there are some public school rules that charters shouldn't play by, because nobody should have to play by them. Important note: I can identify these rules because they interfere with a teacher's ability to provide quality service for students.

But there are other rules charters don't want to have to play by. For instance, "hire licensed personnel" seems to be a popular corner to cut (the Gulen folks seem to trip over this one a bunch). Likewise, modern charters like skirting that nasty union rubbish, which helps with holding onto the option to terminate any "teacher" at any time. This is not about providing superior schooling for students; this is about maintaining a more easily controlled workforce that will be cheap and kept in line.

It goes back to that whole damn democracy thing. Modern charter operators want to be able to rule their company like a Bill Gates or a Leona Helmsley. They do not want to have to govern a public service trust like a Congress or a President, held ultimately accountable to a separate court or electorate (though don't worry-- they're working on that system, too).

Public schools are a trust, a service to the communities that house them and the country that holds them. If you want to be a public school, you have to play by the public school rules. You can certainly set up a private school outside those rules, but that's what it is-- a private school, not a public one.

Serve the Full Population

The same modern charter trick has been documented over and over. Behind every charter school miracle is a charter school that gets rid of students who might hurt their numbers.

They say that home is the place where, when you go there, they have to take you in. But in America, there's another place like that-- the public school.

A public school accepts every student. A public school does not bar a student for being too expensive to educate. A public school does not push out a student who gets lousy test scores. A public school must accept every single student who shows up on their doorstep, barring only those who reach a criminal level of threat to others (and sometimes not even that).

No school that turns students away, pushes students away, counsels students out, or even has the option of considering these actions because there is some other school that *must* take the student-- no school that does these things can call itself a public school. No school that has a student population substantially different from the student population of the area it serves can rightly call itself a public school.

I was tweet-challenged on this point the other day with the issue of magnet schools. That's a valid point-- a school designed to focus on the performing arts cannot be expected to have the same percentage of tone-deaf, stage-inept non-performers as the rest of its neighborhood. But magnet schools have a very specific, very explicit mission that clearly defines how their population will differ from the larger group. A performing arts school mission does not say "To foster great student arts, plus keeping out any ELL students, too." The careful focus was in fact one of the things that could, and did, and does, make classic charters great.

But another characteristic of modern charters is that they rarely have such a clearly defined mission. And certainly none have a mission that makes explicit upfront, as magnet schools do, exactly which students they plan to include and exclude. As far as I know, no modern charter has a mission statement that reads, "We will give a mediocre education to all poor kids except the ones who are difficult or have developmental problems or who can't hit our numbers."

You can certainly be selective about which students make it into your school (and get to stay there), but if you do, you are a private school. A public school accepts all students.

Public School and Virtue

I am not saying that you must meet all four of these requirements to qualify as a ethically upright and educationally sound school. I can think of several private schools that flunk all four tests (though all have far more accountability measures in place than many modern charters), and they are perfectly good schools. But they are private schools, not public schools.

I can think of some charter schools that pass all four tests. They are classic versions of charter education, and they deserve to be called public schools.

But to call the Success and Imagine and K12 and Hope-on-a-Shingle and all the rest of the hedge-fund backed, politically connected, ROI ROI ROIing their big financial boat modern charters may be many things.

But they are not public schools. Not. Public. Schools.

Education Is Not Medicine

One of the popular new reformster talking points is to compare standardized testing to diagnostic testing at the doctor's office. This comparison is total baloney, and reformsters need to retire it immediately. They are just making themselves look silly. Let's break it down.

Students are not patients.

Students are not patients who need to be "cured" of the "disease" of not knowing stuff. There is nothing about that comparison that holds up. Disease attacks a healthy body and breaks down tissues and functions that were previously fine. Which part of that sounds like a student not understanding how to multiply doubly digit numbers or misunderstanding how to find verbs?

Doctors choose the tests.

The doctor uses her professional judgment to determine which tests will be administered. The doctor uses her professional judgment looking at the symptoms, the nature of the patient, and the possible issues that might be involved. And then the doctor decides which test to order because

There are many tests.

Doctors do not have a single one size fits all diagnostic test that is given to all patients, regardless of whether they are complaining about a sore chest, a broken leg, or a high fever. The test is chosen to fit the situation (again, using the doctor's professional judgment). For that matter, for every test the doctor chooses to give a patient, the doctor also choose NOT to give a large number of tests to that patient. There is no medical analog for a high stakes one size fits all test to be given to all students.

Doctors can still see.

When I went to the doctor with the flesh of my knee split open, my doctor did not say, "Well, it looks like the flesh of your knee is split open, and I might be looking at the patella right there, but let me run some tests, first." He definitely didn't say, "First, I have to give you this exact same test that we give every single patient who enters the hospital no matter what the issue seems to be." Because, as it turns out, my doctor has A) eyes and B) sense. So he sewed up my knee. Some times the correct diagnostic test is no test at all, because A) eyes and B) sense.

Results are timely.

Depending on the urgency of the situation (as determined by the professional judgment of the doctor), the results will come back in a timely manner. If you get your broken leg x-rayed in May, your doctor expects to see the images before September.

Judgment beats test

When the test results return, the doctor makes a diagnosis and prescription based on his professional judgment. The test provides data; it does not make a prescription. "The test says I have to prescribe paxil for you," said no doctor ever. The doctor's judgment is not subordinate to the test results.

Doctors know when to quit

My doctor does not shorten my treatment so that he has time to give me more tests. If he has to make a choice between more treatment for my problem and more testing, more testing does not automatically win.

No stakes tests.

The diagnostic tests that a doctor orders do not become part of the job evaluation of the doctor. The hospital board does not call a doctor in and say, "100% of the limbs you ordered x-rays for this year were broken. Therefor we find you ineffective and you're fired." Nor do we use the test results to judge the hospital. And we especially don't use the test results to judge people in some other department who never even saw the patient.

So stop comparing high stakes standardized tests to diagnostic medical tests. They are not comparable and the analogy is extraordinarily weak. Find something else better to compare high stakes standardized tests to, like cumquats or people who insist on talking loudly on their cell phones in public places.

Journeys and Destinations

Yesterday was, of course, Halloween Party day in my wife's classroom. My wife teaches first grade, which is one more reason that I suspect she is some sort of earthbound goddess, except that there couldn't possible be enough earthbound gods and goddesses to account for all the elementary teachers out there.

As with most days, her job yesterday seemed to involve lots of Reassurance. Her students made a ghost out of paper plates and crepe paper strips, and where six year olds with scissors go, disappointment follows. And so, reassurance. Your ghost's mouth didn't turn out the way it was supposed to? It'll be okay. The strips somehow ended up different lengths? It'll be okay. You glued your ghost's arms where his hair is supposed to be? It'll be okay. And that's before she even gets to the Big Stuff-- a little guy was dropped at school without his costume for the big Costume Parade. His mom promised she'd drop it off at the school later. And he waited. And she didn't.

We're extra careful with newborns because their skulls aren't fully formed. Eventually those plates will become hardened and tough and fully protective, but for a while their little brains are just hanging out there, unprotected, vulnerable, and easily hurt.

Well, the same things is metaphorically true of young hearts, but the time frame is much longer. Eventually their protective covering will get hard and tough, but for the time being, their hearts are just hanging out there, unprotected, vulnerable, and easily hurt.

Some of her students arrive already equipped with a powerful fear of Being Wrong, and so she has to reassure them (because when six year olds have soooo much to learn, they do make mistakes). Because when you're afraid to make mistakes, you're afraid to try. It's a long journey, and if you have to stop and fret over every single step, the journey is awfully difficult.

So, reassurance. It's okay to make a mistake. It's okay to be wrong. We just keep trying. We haven't figured it out yet. We don't have it yet. We'll get it. It'll be okay. We're still growing.

It seems natural to explain that a wrong answer or a mistake or a scissor cut that doesn't go according to plan-- none of these things are the end of the world or an unbearable disaster. We'll pull ourselves together. We'll try again. We'll learn from this setback. Doesn't that sound like the message we'd want any six year old child to absorb?

It'll be okay. Let's pick ourselves up, dry our tears, try this again until we figure it out and make it work.

But it is, of course, the exact opposite of what is hard-wired into the test-and-punish regimen that reformsters are installing in schools. The gods and goddesses like my wife are picking kids up, setting them on their feet, drying their tears, telling them that they are alright and they can keep moving forward on their journey, but the reformsters are in these children's faces snarling, "Here's a test. You get one try. Get it right or you're a big fat failure." By the time they're eight, some states want to punish those kids with (proven ineffective) consequences for one set of wrong answers on a single standardized reading test.

It's not just educationally unsound. It's mean, hard-hearted unkindness meant to break children down instead of building them up.

It's not that I want to value the journey to the exclusion of the destination. Those of us who teach writing wrestle with this balance-- it's good to work on your process, your technique, your journey; but ultimately you have to produce a piece of writing and be judged on that result. I don't post rough drafts on this blog.

But when we're talking about fostering the growth of little humans, I believe we must value the journey over the destination, because that's life. Life is mostly journey, and what we think of as destinations are little rest stops along the way. Those stops, those achievement, those checkpoints are great and important and lord knows we don't want to drive around aimlessly and never arrive anywhere, but life is mostly the journey. Where we get is important; I'm not so sure that it's more important than how we get there.

So we have a duty to teach young humans about how to journey through life with strength and confidence and skill. We need to teach them how to grapple their way to solutions, how to attack and attack and attack again whatever problem faces them. And you know-- I don't even think that many reformsters disagree with what I'm saying. But you do not measure any of this with a single one-and-done one-rightanswer-for-everyone standardized test. A snapshot test is all destination and no journey.

Despite test boosters claim to the contrary, there is nothing in life-- nothing-- that resembles the standardized test model. Your boss does not walk into your office and say, "Okay-- here's a problem I want you to solve. You have ten minutes. Your solution will determine whether I promote you or fire you." Someone does not walk up to you and say, "Hi, stranger. You have ten minutes to decide whether we should remain strangers or get married." All right-- I take it back-- there are some things like a standardized test. We call them disasters, or tragedies. A dam breaks .A car crashes. A gunman walks into your school. Is that what standardized tests are supposed to prepare students for?

This is just one more way in which standardized tests utterly fail to measure any of the things we say we care about. Attaching high stakes to them only make them worse. When everything is riding on one set of answers to questions that you only get to wrestle with once, there is no absorbing data from the results and attacking again. There is no learning to grow from that moment. There's nothing but a declaration of winners and losers, and nothing that even the most powerful goddess can tell the losers that blunts the standardized stab at their open hearts.

The standardized test and punish system is not just anti-education. It's anti-human. Our children deserve better.

Every Teacher Should Be Bad at Something

Like most teachers, I've worked at a variety of side jobs, from radio dj to musician to newspaper columnist. But I may have learned the most from my time at a catalog order call center.

This was not one of those cold call phone banks, but a call center where customers called us to place their orders. Our job was to get the ordered placed as quickly and pleasantly as possible, then provide them with a few opportunities for further purchases at the end of the call. Our job was to try to get them to pick up another item or two, and then "while their order was processing" (it was all on computer-- we were already looking right at it) try to sell them either a shop-withus club membership kind of thing, or a kind of medical supplemental insurance. I worked at the job a full summer and through many months part-time thereafter.

I was not good at this job. I was bad at this job. I was punctual and never missed a shift, which they liked, but I was a terrible salesman.

Now, I'm not a master of any of the trades I've messed with. I'm an okay musician, a passable writer, a fair-to-middlin' radio guy-- the list of things that I can do well enough goes on and on (nor am I by any stretch of the imagination the best teacher in my building). But I had never done a job before at which I was just plain not good.

It wasn't long before I noticed how Being Bad was affecting me.

I came to dread being there, walking through the door, driving the car to work. While there, I wanted to be somewhere else. There can be big down time between calls; rather than just sit and soak in the place, I would throw myself into reading. Any distraction-- a chatty caller, an entertaining co-worker-- was consuming. I would negotiate deals between myself, my bladder and the clock (forty-five more minutes and I will go pee).

Part of my brain just wanted to somehow discount the whole experience, to come up with ways to dismiss what I was doing so that my failure was somehow proof that I was smarter or better or cooler or just generally above this. If I could treat it as a ridiculous joke of a job, the fact that I wasn't any good at it wouldn't matter. If I could find flaws in the people who were long-time successful employees, then I wouldn't have to feel bad about myself. A part of my brain dropped whatever it usually did and devoted itself full time to creating excuses, both macro and micro, and another portion started working full time on odd routines just to give me back some sense of control over y situation. A part of my brain was doing anything it could to avoid reaching an unwelcome conclusion about myself based on my apparent inability to succeed at a seemingly simple task. A part of my brain worked on telling me reasons it just didn't matter that I wasn't good at this-- after all, the real part of my real life was outside the company's four walls. I knew I was a perfectly capable, intelligent human being with a useful array of talents-- but none of them were doing me any good and it was hard to not frame my mismatch for the job as a deficit on my part.

After a while, I became used to failing. When the screen popped up that held my script for selling the club membership, I would flinch and just try to get through to the moment when the customer would reject my offer and we could move on. The more I failed, the more it was impossible to imagine anything but failure, and the more I envisioned failure, the more I wanted to avoid entering that wrestling match with the job that I just knew I would lose.

My employers were great. I was gently coached, pleasantly directed, and given encouragement. It did not help.

There is just a spiritually corrosive quality to having to go back, day after day after day, and throw yourself into something that you aren't very good at. Yes, I'm sure I could have grabbed my bootstraps or sucked up my testicular fortitude or put my head down and driven through--and I knew that, and the fact that I couldn't do any of that just became one more badge of failure in the job.

However, the whole experience did have one useful aspect, because I realized right off the bat who also dealt regularly with feelings like mine.

My students.

This is why I now say that all teachers should not only get a job outside of school, but also have the experience of being bad at something.

My lower functioning students have to get up every day and go to a place where all day long, they are required to do things that they are bad at. They have to carry the feelings that go with that, the steady toxic buildup that goes with constantly wrestling with what they can't do, the endless drip-drip-drip of that inadequacy-based acid on the soul.

It's up to us to remind them that they are good at things. It's up to us to make a commitment to get them to a place of success. It's up to us
NOT to hammer home what they already know-- that there are tasks they aren't very good at completing.

I don't know how much longer the company would have tolerated my low bonus sale numbers, but my lack of scheduling availability was enough to end my phone career. That's okay. The extra money was nice, and I have no doubt that being a bad telemarketer made me a better teacher. And I have some great stories (you have not lived until you have helped a little old lady order a personal intimate massage device by phone), but I will save those for another day.

Questions for Professional Development

Once upon a time, when teachers and outside presenters gathered together for PD, there was a sense that we were All In This Together. We were there, as teachers, to provide a public service through educating students, and the presenters at PD were there to give us some tools to help do that job.

Those days are gone.

Now we are surrounded by people who view public education not so much as a public service but rather as a giant money tree waiting to be pruned, and here they come to professional development sessions, shears in hand. We've always had our share of PD run by people who served up heaping plates of condescension with a side of contempt sauce, but PD increasingly resembles a sort of unarmed assault on teaching staffs.

This creates a new professional dilemma for teachers. Instead of asking "How can I apply this in my classroom," teachers are asking themselves, "How much longer can I keep from saying something unprofessional and rude?" Unfortunately, some teachers don't want to be impolite, and so PD behavior often runs to vacant smiling and nodding, with honest reactions to be reserved till afterwards.

Some presenters are just trying to do a job, but others really are the barbarians at the gate who deserve to be met with resistance. Here are some questions to ask in PD to separate the wolves from the sheep.

Which company is producing this product, and how do they expect to make money from it?

It's not that the desire to make money is automatically evil. This is not a gotcha question. But the question goes to motivation and long term costs. We used to assume that programs and materials came from kindly gnomes that created it all in workshop somewhere and gave it away because it made them happy to do so. Nowadays virtually every program or tool that comes into a district is somebody's proprietary product, and we need to remember that their primary purpose is not to make our lives swell, but to make enough money to make the business worthwhile.

If you are making money from the sale of widgets, I have to cast a dubious eye on your claim that it's really the widgets that will revolutionize learning. If you're giving me free software that will require us to renew licensing every two years at full cost, you're not really giving me free anything.

If you're here to help, that's great. If you're pretending to help when you're just here to sell us something (or to sell us *on* something the district already bought), I reserve the right to treat you like the huckster you apparently are.

What is your teaching background? Do you have any other special expertise in the material you're presenting?

There is apparently some sort of law requiring all PD presenters to work the phrase "when I was in the classroom" into their presentation, as well as some claim to having been a teacher at some point. Unfortunately, those phrases can be thrown around by both of the following presenters:

Presenter A: Taught a couple of years, possibly as TFA temp. Couldn't hack it. Couldn't wait to get out and start real job.
Presenter B: Taught for a couple of decades. Enjoyed the work but eventually decided to move on to a new career.

The distinction is important, because Presenter A doesn't know what the hell she's talking about. Furthermore, Presenter A has tried to claim a kinship with the audience of teachers that she hasn't earned. Put these together and you get Presenter Whose Word Cannot Be Trusted.

What proof can you offer that these techniques/programs/materials are actually effective?

If you can't get a straight answer to this, that's because the straight answer is most likely, "None." If you get an answer such as "research says," it's fair to ask exactly which research and exactly how did the researchers arrive at this conclusion.

The other teachers in the room may hate you for prolonging the session. Tough. Too many teachers still think that if something's being pitched in PD, it must be legit good practice. Hell, there are too many teachers who still think that the Common Core was written by teachers and based on solid educational research. One of the side effects of reform has been the removal of any sort of quality-based filter between profiteering companies and the rest of us.

If we are going to be champions for our students and their educations, we have to stop accepting the judgment of people with barely an iota of our professional expertise. We have to start casting a critical eye on every program that tries to slink through the door.

Why don't you answer that question now?

This must be part of PD 101. When somebody asks a difficult question or raises an issue that the presenter was hoping wouldn't be brought up, just say, "That's a really good question, and I'd like to talk to you more about that at the break." The goal is to avoid dealing with any contentious issues in front of the whole group. They might get the wrong idea, you know.

A person who can't give you a clear answer either doesn't have one or doesn't want to. Neither is acceptable. If you want to implement your stuff in my classroom, you need to give me an answer.

In many schools, PD has become an assault on teachers' standards and practices, and we should no more sit politely through the worst of it than we would politely sit through an explanation of why our minority students are inferior. Simply ignoring the people who come to coach teachers in educational malpractice isn't working. Standing up and telling them to go to hell is probably a poor employment choice.

But we can always ask questions, and we should, pointedly and repeatedly. If that makes PD sessions a little uncomfortable, so be it. We have a responsibility to our profession and our students to call out powerful baloney when it presents itself.

It may not stop the baloney advance. Pennsylvania years ago shifted state level PD from an attitude of "We want to win hearts and minds" to one of "Sit down, shut up, and do as you're told." It's hard to slow down a steamroller, but we don't have to lie down and make it easy on the destruction crew.

Ask the questions.

The Big Picture

Why do we have these policies that don't make sense? Why does it seem like this system is set up to make schools fail? Why do states pass these laws that discourage people from becoming teachers?

My friends, colleagues and family ask these kinds of questions all the time. So my goal today is to step back and try to fit the pieces into the larger picture. If you have been paying attention, you already know this stuff, but perhaps this post will help someone you know who's trying to make sense of reformsterdom. Here, then, is my attempt to show the big picture.

The Perfect Storm

The Current Education Reform Wave is driven by a joining of two major impulses in the US. Neither of them are new, but over the past decade they have come together in ways that are proving powerful.

Growing steadily (at least since *A Nation at Risk*) has been a desire for **Centralized Efficiency** in education. Their basic narrative has always been that American schools are failing, and what is needed is strong, clear-headed, direction from People Who Know Better. The rise of massive computer based data capabilities and the internet's ability to lock together widespread organizations first led the CE folks to believe they could actually do it.

And then, they realized that they could do even more. The infamous Marc Tucker letter lays it out as clearly as anything-- we could create a cradle-to-career pipeline, a massive planned track fed by mountains of data. Through computer-based testing and data gathering, we could track each individual starting shortly after birth, so that we could design an educational program that would perfectly prepare each person for a productive place in society.

To do that, we'd need to get every possible data source plugged in, and for the data to mean anything, we'd have to have all schools doing basically the exact same thing. Standards could be used to tag and organize every piece of data collected about every student. This suited people who see US education as a slapdash, sloppy, disorganized mess of many different schools doing many different things (this bothered them as much as your pictures hanging cockeyed in the den drive your OCD aunt crazy). But all of that would require massive planning and infrastructure far beyond what government could politically or financially manage.

This dovetailed perfectly with the other powerful impulse-- the desire of **Educational Privatization**. Public education represents a huge, huge mountain of money that has historically been unavailable to corporate interests. Companies have been forced to jockey for the crumbs of book contracts here and there, or occasional consultant work. Now, making the Centralized Efficiency dreams come true would also provide corporations with unprecedented access to that mountain of money. This was also appealing because many business-folks find their sensibilities offended by the unbusiness-like running of US education.

Combining these two impulses finally opened up the possibility of remaking the entire US education system in a new image. Just as Rockefeller had brought vertical integration to the oil industry by owning everything step of the process from oil wells to consumer marketing, reformers envisioned a fully integrated system that generated financial returns at every step of the educational process while simultaneously organizing education around a centrally planned and controlled system. It is an unholy marriage between the worst aspects of socialism and capitalism, but to make it happen, certain steps must be taken.

Opening the Supplier Markets: The Mystification of Education

Producers of educational materials have long had to live on the fringes of education, subject to the individual preferences of thousand upon thousands of individual school districts. Texas was a hint of how sweet life could be-- a place where you just had to make a textbook sale to one central authority. Could the whole country become Texas?

Well, yes, kind of, and Common Core was key. Get everybody on the same page, and everybody needs to buy the same books. Common Core was envisioned as a way to get everyone teaching the same stuff at the same time, and therefor content providers need only align themselves to one set of expectations. Instead of trying to sell to thousands of different markets, they could now sell to a thousand versions of the same basic standardized school district.

The less obvious effect of the Core was to change the locus of educational expertise. Previously teachers were the educational experts, the people who were consulted and often made the final call on what materials to buy. But one message of the Core was that teachers were not the experts, both because they had failed so much before and because Common Core was such a piece of "high standards" jargon-encrusted mumbo jumbo that you needed an expert to explain it.
Educational experts were no longer found in the classroom. Now they are in corporate offices. They are in government offices. Textbook creators now include "training" because your teachers won't be able to figure out how to use teaching materials on their own. More importantly, teachers can no

longer be trusted to create their own teaching materials (at least not unless their district has hired consultants to put them through extensive training).

Meanwhile, testing programs, which would also double as curriculum outlines, were also corporate products (which require such expertise that teachers are not allowed to see or discuss their contents), and every school must test as part of an accountability system that will both force schools to follow the centralized efficiency program and label them as failures when their test scores are too low, as well as feeding data into the cradle-to-career pipeline.

The entire supplier market for education had become the sole property of the book publishers, who could market more efficiently while reinforcing the Centralized Efficiency picture of exactly what should happen in schools. And teachers were shut out of the process because they would only gum up the works.

Opening the Provider Markets: Breaking the Government Monopoly

But owning the entire supply chain was not enough. There was a ton of money to be made by running the schools themselves. Attempts to bleed money from the system by the use of vouchers had been repeatedly slapped down by the courts and simply not borne fruit

But another mechanism was already in place-- charter schools. Charter schools have been a way of using public tax dollars to finance an independent school for ages. Now the privatization crowd could harness this business model. It was ripe and ready; Clinton-era tax laws made the ROI from investing in charters wondrous. Charters were a ready-made tax shelter, a way to get solid investment results while looking like a do-gooder to boot.

But the market for schools was covered and controlled by the public school system (except for Pre-K, which was ripe for the plucking). So that nut had to be cracked. The government "monopoly" on schools had to be broken.

First, it had to be shown that public schools were failing. That job was half done, because Schools Are Failing had been the mantra since Nation at Risk. But people still tended to believe that their own local school was pretty good. We needed more proof. Common Core has been used as its own proof-- we need these "higher standards" because schools suck, and teachers never teach reading or critical thinking and look how bad our test scores are. Standardized testing, particularly testing that was poorly done, instigated before the actual standards that it was supposed to measure, and using cut scores set politically rather than educationally, could help "prove" that schools were failing. There was also a focus on how college unready students are.

The beauty of testing is that since test results generally line up with economic class, the schools that would fail would be the schools of the poor-- the people also least able to muster resistance to school takeovers. The discovery of failing schools for the poor also allowed reformers to adopt the language of the civil rights movement (and in a bold move by the Obama administration, to use civil rights law to enforce school reform). Real school failure could also be hastened by simply cutting money and resources for poor schools.

There have been attempts to create other means of failing schools. (The parent trigger law was one that never quite worked out.) But the result is always the same-- the discovery that a school is failing does not lead to meetings with the parents, teachers and administrators, but instead leads to hiring turnaround experts or charter operators or consultants. When a school "fails," somebody is going to make money from it. The more schools we can prove are failing, the more money somebody can make. And of course the rising tide of school failure has been the excuse for the Obama administration to make "open more charters" a requirement of waivers. And when more charters open, more resources are taken from public schools, adding to the ways in which they can fail.

Opening the supplier market also means breaking the geographical limits. The rhetoric of making sure that students are victims of their zip code is about opening up markets, about making it possible for charters to recruit from outside a defined geographical area.

Opening the Teaching Market: The De-professionalizing of Teaching

It drives corporate privatizers crazy that A) the biggest operating expense in schools is staff and B) that they can't simply hire and fire as they wish. It drives central planning fans crazy that teachers insist on doing whatever they feel like doing instead of all teaching the same things the same way at the same time. How could both groups effect change?

One step we've already discussed. By creating a system in which teachers are no longer the experts on what they teach or how to teach it, reformsters turn teachers from educated professionals into content delivery workers. You don't need a building full of education experts-- just one or two to direct the rest of a staff of drones. Use a boxed program like engageNY-- anybody who can read the script and the instructions can teach students.

Teachers frequently scratch their head and ask, "Are they TRYING to drive people out of the profession? " Well, probably, yes. Teach for America "teachers" are not a stop-gap measure-- they're the ideal. They don't stay long enough to get raises, and they don't saddle the district with any expensive pension costs. And they're young and healthy, so even insurance costs are low. Teachers who spend a lifetime in the profession are an expensive nuisance; what we need are a regular supply of compliant short-timers.

We can facilitate that by, of course, doing away with tenure and any other job protections. And systems like merit-based pay allow us to manage costs effectively and limiting the amount of pay that will be handed out. A low-paid, easily-replaced staff that serves at the pleasure of management provides optimum control of expenses and "human capital." These reforms can be applied to public schools as well, forced by budget cuts.

We can accelerate the process by taking the failure we are imposing on schools and blaming it all on teachers. The low scores that poor students always get-- teachers' fault. We can keep framing it as praise (teachers are the most important part of schools), but what's really being said is that everything that goes wrong is a teacher's fault. If there's a lot of failure, it must be caused by bad teachers-- and that's why school leaders must have the tools for hiring and firing at will.

And we can turn schools of education training into parking lots or basic training for delivering teacher-proof programs.

Is this some sort of conspiracy?

Am I suggesting that there is some sort of vast conspiracy? No. I'm not a believer in vast conspiracies. Hard to organize. Cumbersome. But all it takes for all of this to happen is people in power who believe that applying free market business principles are innately good, teamed up with people who believe that centralized standardization.and efficiency are innately good. There's a network of such people in power, and while some of them undoubtedly are motivated by greed and ambition, I believe that some of them simply believe they are giving schools a good hard dose of reality, of How The World Really Works.

The end effect is the same. Ignore the rhetoric. Watch what they do and what the effects are. Everything happening in education reform is about 1) reducing the autonomy and local control of schools and 2) mining the school system for every cent of economic advantage. Education reform has literally nothing to do with providing quality education for America's children.

Meaning and Standardized Writing

One of the most unsuccessful initiatives of the Great Education Makeover is the attempt to reduce writing to a skill set that can be assessed by a standardized test.

Making language is like making music-- there is definitely a technical component, but technical mastery is not enough. I can play all the notes on the page and still be boring, lifeless, and unengaging for any audience. I can write something that fits the technical definition of an essay, and it can still be a terrible piece of writing.

All writing is problem solving, and like any problem solving activity, the most important step is defining the problem that you intend to solve.

The vast majority of student writing failures are not actually composition failures, but thinking failures. I often tell my students that they are having trouble with an assignment because they are starting with the wrong question. They are asking "what can I write to satisfy this assignment" or "how can I fill up this piece of paper" or "what can I use to fill in five paragraph-sized blanks," and these are all the wrong question to start with.

The correct problem that writing should solve is "How can I communicate what I want to communicate in a meaningful way?"

I choose "meaningful" because it's a fuzzy word. We may find meaning in being moved emotionally or challenged intellectually. Whatever meaning may be, our goal is to create an experience for another human (and because writing is also time travel, that other human might even be our future self).

There are certainly technical aspects to this operation. In fact, much of the history of literature is the history of writers inventing new techniques and forms to better communicate meaningfully. But technical skills by themselves are not only meaningless, but have no purpose if not used for some meaningful pursuit. That's why you don't pay money to sit in a concert hall and watch great musicians run scales and warm-up exercises.

The standardized testing approach to writing, both in "writing" assessments and in the open-ended response format now creeping into other tests, gets virtually nothing right at all. Nothing. The goal is itself a meager one-- let's just measure student technical skill-- and even that is not measured particularly well. Test writing is the opposite of good writing. The problem the student is trying to solve is not "How do

I create a meaningful expression" but "How do I provide what the test scorer wants to see" or "What words can I use to fill up this space."

Students are supposed to react to the prompt or stimulus (yes, I've seen that word used, as if students are lab rats) with the appropriate response, and their response should not be side tracked by any attempt on their part to make the response meaningful. It is literally meant to be meaningless, as if stripping meaning from writing somehow leaves us with pure, measurable technique. This is like somehow sucking the bones from a human being on the theory that without the skeleton in place, we can get a better pure measurement of muscle tone.

Every teacher of writing has been saying the same thing for years-- standardized writing tests encourage and reward bad writing. "So what?" comes my least favorite response. "If they're really good writers, they ought to be able to fake the testing stuff, right?" Wrong on two counts.

First, while great writers may be able to "fake it," less great writers may not, and all writers run the risk of becoming hornswoggled into believing that Bad Writing is really the ideal. "Faking it" assumes some understanding that we're imitating something bogus. I'm concerned about students who don't recognized the bogus nature of test writing.

Second-- even if they can fake it, that's not a good thing. This is like saying that people who are really good at kissing their spouses would probably be equally good at kissing any random stranger. And, well-- do we really want anybody to be good at that? If the best kiss is one filled with meaning and significance, then why would we want to send the message that good kissing is just a matter of the right pucker and moisture and what it actually means is not even on the table. Who cares whose lips you're smooshing up against as long as your technique is good? Who cares about context or purpose or intent or any of the rest of it? Just pucker up and smoosh facial areas.

Sure, there are technical minimums that have to be reached. "Don't smoosh your lips against your partner's eyeball" is probably good technical kissing advice. "Don't write sentences composed entirely of prepositions" is also good advice. But as the ever-awesome Les Perelman has repeatedly demonstrated, standardized tests have a huge tolerance for meaningless gibberish that is technically proficient.

I remained convinced that it is absolutely impossible to create a useful cheap standardized test for writing. The repeated attempts to do so are a destructive expression of a nearly nihilistic impulse, the thinking of people who believe a picture of a bear rug is as good as a bear.

Common Core Testing Ignores Common Core

Some commentators applauded me for giving it to Common Core writing the other day. But in all fairness to the Core, the standardized testing that is being used to beat students, teachers and schools into submission, often completely fails to test the Common Core at all. One of the gigantic Jabba the Hutt sized fantasies pushed by reformsters is the one where they say, "See these standards over here? This Standardized Test will totally whether we're meeting those standards or not."

There are two failure points between the anchor standards and the tests themselves.

Anchor standards? Those are the broader, more global final destination of the standards, the Stuff of which College and Career Ready Dreams are made. They lead us to the grade-specific standards within the Core, and let's just say that often something is terribly, terribly lost in the translation. But that's a whole other post for a whole other day.

The second failure point is the one at which the grade-specific standard is somehow "measured" by a bubble test-- excuse me! we're totally past bubble testing-- a point and click question. Reformsters blithely assume/insist/pretend that nothing is lost, and that the standardized tests accurately measure if students are in line with the anchor standards or not.

But let's perform a little thought experiment. Let's look at the twelve anchor standards for writing, and let's imagine how we would assess those standards, and see if we imagine anything that looks at all like the mass-produced standardized tests currently serving as the pointy stick in the eye of education.

Write arguments to support claims in an analysis of substantive topics or texts using valid reasoning and relevant and sufficient evidence.

First we'll need a substantive topic or text, so, a text of some length and complexity. Any analysis and claim-making will require either some prior knowledge about the topic, or the opportunity to acquire that knowledge. So from beginning of the topic/text intro to the end of handing in the essay, I'd expect to spend at least a week. "Valid," "relevant" and "sufficient" are all subjective judgments and therefor would have to be made by somebody very familiar with the topic/text.
After all-- how do you know an observation about existential angst in
Moby Dick is valid or not unless you're familir with both existential
angst and Moby Dick?

Write informative/explanatory texts to examine and convey complex ideas and information clearly and accurately through the effective selection, organization, and analysis of content.

Again, how can you evaluate this skill without having the student do this very thing. The "accurately" as well as the "effective" again require expertise on the reader's part in order to assess.

Write narratives to develop real or imagined experiences or events using effective technique, well-chosen details and well-structured event sequences.

Big wig lingo for "tell a good story." "Effective," "well-chosen," and "well-structured" are all subjective calls. Would you rather read Hemmingway, Dickens, Studs Terkel, or Carl Sagan?

Produce clear and coherent writing in which the development, organization, and style are appropriate to task, purpose, and audience.

A difficult artificial task, as we are either writing for an imaginary audience, in which case we'd better hope we imagine it the same way the test-makers do, or we are writing for our real audience, either a minimum-wage test-scorer in a assessment sweat shop, or, God help us, a computer. What if the development or organization that's most appropriate is many, many pages?

Develop and strengthen writing as needed by planning, revising, editing, rewriting, or trying a new approach.

A great nod to the process writing approach, which I actually believe in. To properly assess this will again take a least a week. Editing and revising thirty seconds after writing is really just a more involved first draft technique.

Use technology, including the Internet, to produce and publish writing and to interact and collaborate with others.

I'm stumped. I don't even know how I would imaginarily assess this. You could, I suppose, use the popular on-line course technique of requiring the student to start X discussion threads and respond in Y others, because that always leads to scintillating authentic conversation. Again, there's a time frame here that I find daunting for standardized assessment.

Conduct short as well as more sustained research projects based on focused questions, demonstrating understanding of the subject under investigation.

Once again, how could you possibly reduce this to a mass-produced, mass-taken, mass-scored assessment? I suppose you could tell every single student to get out her netbook and research ferrets right now, but I'm afraid the infrastructure demands alone would make this a nowin.

Gather relevant information from multiple print and digital sources, assess the credibility and accuracy of each source, and integrate the information while avoiding plagiarism.

Also, lead a large angel square dance on the head of a pin. This will be an assessment that takes several days and is held in a library? It surely won't be assessed by listing several resource excerpts and requiring students to select the "correct" information from each of the minisources. It's an admirable standard, but it is completely unassessable in a standardized test.

Draw evidence from literary or informational texts to support analysis, reflection, and research.

At this point, I believe the full assessment will take roughly three months.

Write routinely over extended time frames (time for research, reflection, and revision) and shorter time frames (a single sitting or a day or two) for a range of tasks, purposes, and audiences.

No, never mind. It will take all year.

It's the same problem, over and over and over again-- the standards have to be assessed by someone whose professional judgment is equal to the task of dealing with highly subjective measures, while the activities involved are time-consuming and very open-ended. If I look at the writing strand of the CCSS, and I look at any of the High Stakes Standardized Tests out there, I can confidently state that those tests measure exactly NONE of these standards. Those tests have nothing at all to do with these standards. These standards might as well say "Student will spin straw into gold and use the gold to knit flipper mittens for the Loch Ness Monster," because the high stakes standardized tests are testing other things entirely.

Yes, I could lead a spirited argument about the standards themselves, but that's another post. Today, I want to underline one simple idea-- when reformsters say that test results tell us how students are doing on these standards, they are big lying liars who lie large lies.

Duncan in Denial

There are many portions of Arne Duncan's educational policies that are... what's the word? Counter-intuitive? Not aligned with reality as experienced by most sentient beings? Baloney? There are days when I imagine that the energy Duncan expends just holding cognitive dissonance at bay must be enough to power a small country (like, say, Estonia).

But nowhere are Duncan's powers of denial more obvious than in his deep and abiding love for Value Added Measures. Arne loves him some VAM sauce, and it is a love that simply refuses to die. "You just don't know her the way I do," he cries, as the rest of us just shake our heads.

At this point, VAM is no spring chicken, and perhaps when it was fresh and young some affection for it could be justified. After all, lots of folks, including non-reformy folks, like the idea of recognizing and rewarding teachers for being excellent. But how would we identify these pillars of excellence? That was the puzzler for ages until VAM jumped up to say, "We can do it! With Science!!" We'll give some tests and then use super-sciency math to filter out every influence that's Not a Teacher and we'll know exactly how much learnin' that teacher poured into that kid.

The plan is simple and elegant. All it requires is two simple tools:

1)   A standardized test that reliably and validly measures how much students know
2)   A super-sciency math algorithm that will reliably and validly strip out all influences except that of the teacher.

Unfortunately, we don't have either.

We know we don't have either. We are particularly clear on the degree to which we do not have the second. Scan the list of reformster programs, and while you can find plenty of principled disagreement on most points, there is no part of the reformster education platform that has been so thoroughly, widely debunked as VAM-for-teacherevaluation. The National Association of Secondary School Principals has taken a stand, and if you read their resolution, you'll find not just a philosophical argument, but a list of striking debunkers. The American Statistical Association has made its own statement in opposition. A peer-reviewed study paid for by the Gates Foundation itself, the granddaddy of all reformster backers, declared in no uncertain terms that VAM tells us nothing about teacher quality. The blog Vamboozled (by Audrey Amrein-Beardsley) provides unplumbable depths of VAM-busting research and essays.

At this point, even the Flat Earth Society would be reluctant to endorse VAM as a measure of teacher effectiveness.

NO portion of his policy has been so thoroughly disproven, and yet no portion of his policy has earned more of Duncan's loyalty. He stopped saying "Common Core" out loud. He at least pretends to be cooling off on testing. Even he has to admit that some charters have issues. And data collection has become the love that dare not speak its name. But VAM still owns a place close to Arne's heart.

Witness the most recent doubling down on VAM, in which Duncan not only pledges his allegiance to the flagging monster, but announces his intention to extend its reach, taking the already invalid VAM ratings of individual teachers and taking a giant leap backwards to use them to evaluate the college that trained that teacher. Is there anybody else who can present this idea with a straight face?

Why would someone who professes such love for data and critical thinking stay so attached to a policy that is supported by neither? Why does Duncan insist on such a mountain of denial?

Well, I can't pretend to see into his brain. But I can see that if Duncan were to admit that his beloved VAM is a useless tool, a snub-nosed screwdriver with a briar-encrusted handle, then all his other favorite programs would collapse as well.

Everywhere we turn in reformsterland, we keep coming back to teacher effectiveness. Every one of the policies and programs either begins or ends with measuring teacher effectiveness. Why do we give the Big Test? To measure teacher effectiveness. How do we rank and evaluate our schools? By looking at teacher effectiveness. How do we find the teachers that we are going to move around so that every classroom has a great teacher? With teacher effectiveness ratings. How do we institute merit pay and a career ladder? By looking at teacher effectiveness. How do we evaluate every single program instituted in any school? By checking to see how it affects teacher effectivesness. How do we prove that centralized planning (such as Common Core) is working? By looking at teacher effectiveness. How do we prove that corporate involvement at every stage is a Good Thing? By looking at teacher effectiveness. And by "teacher effectiveness," we always mean VAM (because we don't know any other way, at all).

If our measure of teacher effectiveness, our magic VAM sauce, is a sham and a delusion and a big bowl of nothing, then a critical piece of the entire reformy puzzle is missing. We have no proof that we need reform, and we have no method of proving that reform is working (we already have means of measuring reform's effects, but we don't like those because the answers are not the ones we want).

Duncan has to hold onto his belief in VAM because without it, the whole ugly sweater of reform starts to unravel even faster than it already is.

VAM is the compass by which reform steers. To admit that it is random and useless would be to admit that our political leaders have been piloting the ship of education blindly, cluelessly, haplessly, that they are steering us onto the rocks and that they have no idea how to get us anywhere else. Either that, or they would have to admit that they've known all along exactly where they were taking us, and the VAM compass has just been a big fat lie to keep the passengers quiet and calm. Either way, admitting VAM is a fraud would be inviting (further) mutiny, and Duncan can't do that any time soon.

Who Measures the Rulers?

Nobody squawked much when it was announced that Pearson had won the bid to develop the framework for the 2018 PISA test. The PISA, you will recall, is administered by the Organization for Economic Cooperative and Development every three years, leading directly to a festival of handwringing and pearl-clutching as various politicians and bureaucrats scramble to squeeze statistical blood from the big fat turnip of test results.

And yes, Pearson just won the right to design the 2018 edition. Given that back in 2011 Pearson won the contract to develop the 2015 PISA, the new contract is not a shocker. Given that Pearson is marching toward becoming the Corporation In Control Of Universal Testing, this barely qualifies as a blip. They have the GED. They have the PARCC. They have dreams of managing via computer every test, testlet, and testicle that exists.

There are many problems with that, but one of the fundamental issues is the one raised by this post's title. When one person with one ruler does all the measuring, how are we to know if he's correct?

If we want to confirm the accuracy of our Pearson measuring tool so we check it against our Pearson standards device and make sure those results line up with the Pearson Master Assessment-- well, at the end of all that, what do we really know?

If Pearson tells us that our six-inch long baby pig weighs 500 pounds, how are we to discover that it's a lie? If Pearson weighs our bag of gold and tells us it's worth $1.98, and they own all the scales, how do we know if we're being cheated?

It doesn't matter whether the people who make the rulers are devious or incompetent-- if there is no one left to check their work, how do we know the true dimensions of anything? If Pearson makes all the tests and keeps assuring us, "Yessiree, this test lines up with our other test and fits in with the main test, so we can assure you that this absolutely measures true learning or complete education or intelligence or character or what matters in a human brain or the strength of a nation's education program," how do we check to prove whether that is true or not?

Who watches the watchmen? Who measures the rulers? To whom does Pearson answer, other than stockholders? I'm hoping we don't wake up some morning to discover the answer is "nobody."

Womb to Workplace Pipeline Under Construction

In the education field, we've been talking about the government's interest in a Cradle-to-Career, Womb-to-Workplace, Conception-toCadaver pipeline for some time. But if you keep your focus on what the Department of Education is up to, you may have missed the news that the Department of Labor is already well into the construction of the Not Yet Teething to Not Still Breathing database.

It's called the Workforce Data Quality Initiative. This was a series of grants given to various folks as part of a "collaborative partnership" between the Departments of Labor and Education. Here are the main objectives of the WDQI:

1) Use every piece of workforce data imaginable, from Unemployment Insurance wage records to training programs for veterans and those with disabilities to adult literacy programs.

2) Fix it so workforce data can be matched up with education data "to ultimately create longitudinal data systems with individual-level information **beginning with pre-kindergarten** through post-secondary schooling all the way through entry and sustained participation in the workforce and employment services system."

3) Get more data. More!

4) Analyze the performance education and training programs.

5) Provide easy to understand "information" so that consumers can choose training and education programs.

Oh, and there's one other "output" expected from the Diapers-to-Dust database.

Additionally, WQDI grantees are expected to use this data analysis to create materials on state workforce performance to share with workforce system stakeholders and the public.

So when a corporation needs some drones to enhance their labor pool, they will be able to just check the Fetus-to-Fertilizer data pool and order up whatever it is they want.

So if you are dealing with people who think all this talk of a Big Brothery Huggies-to-Depends pipeline is crazy talk, just get on line and look at the department's website. But don't look for anything happening in the news about it. The fourth round of grants was announced last June; this is already well under way. Your seat on the Onesies-to-Donesies railroad is probably already labeled, tagged, and reserved for you.

My Public School Sales Pitch

In an America stuffed with charter schools, how would I make a pitch for a public school?

I don't mean how would I argue the ins and outs and dollars and cents of policy decisions. I don't mean how would I, for instance, try to talk the GOP out of turning ESEA into the Charter and Privatization Act of 2015. I'm not talking the big idea macro-scale argument about the place of modern charters in education.

How would I look a parent in the eye and make my pitch for them to choose public school over a charter? Well, I haven't polished this up into a slick video or fileted it down to billboard-ready copy yet, but here's the basic outline of what I would say.

Here's why you should send your child to your public school.

Stability.

I will promise you that at the end of this year, at the end of next year, at the end of your child's educational career, even if that's thirteen years from now, this school system will still be here. You will never arrive at our doors and find them suddenly locked. You will never spend a single part of your year scrambling to find a new school to take your child in. As long as your child is school age, we will be here for her. You will never have to discover that we have decided to stop teaching your child because we can't make enough money doing it.

Shared expertise.

Our teaching staff has over a thousand years of collective teaching experience. You may think that those thousand years don't matter if your child is in a classroom with a second-year teacher, but they do, because that second-year teacher will be able to share in the other 998 years' worth of experience any time she needs to.

Our staff will also share the experience of teaching your child. Your child's classroom teacher will be able to consult with every other teacher who works with, or has ever worked with, your child. We do not routinely turn over large portions of our staff, nor do we depend on a stable of green young teachers.

Commitment.

We are committed to educating your child. Only in the most extraordinary circumstances will we expel him, and we will never "counsel him out." We will never require a minimum performance from him just to stay in our school.

Ownership.

Our public school is owned and operated by the voters and taxpayers of this community, your friends, neighbors, and co-workers. The charter school is not. This public school is overseen by an elected board of individuals who live here and who must answer to voters. The charter school is not. When you have a complaint, a concern, an issue that you want to direct attention to, the people who run this school must have regular public meetings at which you must be able to air your concerns. The charter is a business, run by people who don't ever have to let you into their board room.

How we spend your money.

We have no expenses that are not related to educating your child. We will never spend less on your child so that we can pay our CEO more. We will never cut programs for your child so that we can buy a nicer summer home or a bigger boat. And we buy in bulk, so we can buy more resources, more programs, more variety, more choices under one roof. Nobody here is trying to make money from your child's education; we are simply trying to provide the best education we can, as directed by the elected representatives of the voters and taxpayers of this district.

And if you don't believe us, you are free to examine our financial records any time you wish. We will never hide them from you.

The public school difference.

I know that you must consider the best interests of your child. I also know that not every public school system does a perfect job of delivering on each of these promises. But as you are considering that charter school alternative, ask the charter school folks these questions:

Will you promise me that this school will still be here the day my child graduates?
Will you promise me that my child will be taught by the same group of highly experienced teachers throughout my child's school career? Will you allow me to see your financial statements any time I wish? Will you commit to holding all meetings of your leaders and operators in public, with ample opportunity for members of the public to speak out?

Will you promise me that no matter what, you will never turn my child away from this school?

My suggestion to you? Find a place that will say yes to all of those, because without a foundation of stability, transparency, and commitment to your child, any other promises mean nothing. They are like getting a marriage proposal from a man who says, "I will be the greatest husband ever, but I do reserve the right to skip town any time that I feel like it." The charter school promise is not really a promise at all. If our pubic school promises seem smaller and less grand, it's because we know that whatever we promise, we'll have to stick around to deliver.

That would be my pitch. I know there are public schools that would have to step up their game to live up to that pitch, and they should start stepping today. I know that state and federal government have put obstacles in the way of living up to those promises, and that in some urban areas, much has been done to take the "public" out of public education. I know that the sales pitch would have to be tweaked by locality.

Most of all, I know that this sales pitch doesn't address the actual quality of education. But we have to start with the foundation, and the foundation (which we have previously taken for granted) is an institution dedicated to being a permanent provider, operated by and responsive to the community, and committed to meeting the needs of every student within its community. That foundation must be in place in order for a structure of quality education must be built.

Fixing Tenure

Conversations over the holiday break have reminded me that to the regular civilians, the removal of bad teachers remains a real policy issue. There is no way to argue against that as a policy issue-- "I didn't have a single bad teacher in all my years of school," said no person ever. Arguing against a system for removing incompetence from the classroom is like arguing against the heliocentric model of the solar system; it can be done, but you'll look like a dope.

But we aren't any closer to fixing whatever is supposedly wrong with tenure than we were a few years ago. Why not? Because there are certain obstacles to the brighter bad-teacher-firing future that some dream of.

Administration

In most districts there is a perfectly good mechanism in place to fire bad teachers. But to use it, administrators have to do work and fill out forms and, you know, just all this stuff. So if you're an administrator, it's much easier to shrug and say, "Boy, I wish I could do something about Mr. McSlugteach, but you know that tenure."

A natural reluctance is understandable. In many districts, the administrator who would do the firing would be the same one who did the hiring, and who wants to say, "Yeah, I totally failed in the Hiring Good People part of my job."

Yes, there are large urban districts where the firing process is a convoluted, expensive, time-wasting mess. But that process was negotiated at contract time; school leaders signed off on it. Could a better version be negotiated? I don't know, but I'll bet no teacher facing those kind of charges thinks, "Boy, I hope this process that's going to decide my career is going to be long and drawn out."

We know that administrators can move quickly when they want to. When a teacher has done something that smells like parent lawsuit material, many administrators have no trouble leaping right over that tenure obstacle.

All of which tells us that most administrators have the tools to get rid of incompetent teachers. They just lack either the knowledge or the will. So there's our first obstacle.

Metrics vs Quality

We don't have a valid, reliable tool for measuring teacher quality.

There can't be a serious grown-up left in this country who believes that VAM actually works, and that's all we've got. The Holy Grail of evaluation system is one that can't be tilted by a principal's personal judgment, except that would be a system where a good principal's good judgment would also be blocked, and that seems wrong, too. We need to allow local discretion except when we don't.

I have a whole system blocked out and I'm just waiting for a call to start my consulting career. The downside for national scalability fans is that my system would be customized to the local district, making it impossible to stack rank teachers across the country.

And even my system is challenged by the personal quality involved. I can have every graduate of my high school list their three best and worst teachers, and they can probably all do it-- but their lists won't match. Bad teaching is like pornography-- we know it when we see it. But we don't all see it the same way. Identifying how we know bad teaching is a huge challenge, as yet unsurmounted.

Metrics vs Time

But that hurdle is just about identifying who's doing a good or bad job right now. There's another question that also needs to be answered-- with support, will this teacher be better in the future?
Once we've spotted someone who's not doing well, can we make a projection about her prospects? I've known many teachers who started out kind of meh in the classroom, but got steadily better over the course of their careers (include me in that group). I've known several teachers who hit a bad patch in mid-career and slumped for a while before pulling things back together.

If I ask graduates from over two decades to list best and worst teachers, that will provide even more variety in the lists. So how do we decide whether someone is just done, or that some support and improvement will yield better results that trying to start from scratch with a new person.

Hiring replacements

Any system that facilitates removing bad teachers must also reckon with replacing them. In fact, if we were good at hiring in the first place, we'd have less need to fire.

For all the attention and money and lawyering thrown at tenure, precious little attention has been paid to where high-quality replacements are supposed to come from. Instead, we've got the feds preparing to "evaluate" ed programs with the same VAM that serious grown-ups know is not good for evaluating teachers.

But the lack of suitable replacements has to be part of the serious calculus of firing decisions. Beefing up the teacher pool must be part of the tenure discussion.

Holding onto quality

The constant gush, gush, gush of teachers abandoning the profession is also a factor. If I've just had two or three good teachers quit a department in the last year, I'm less inclined to fire the ones I have left (who at least already know the bell schedule and the detention procedures). There are many ways to address this, including many that don't cost all that much money. But if you are going to remove a feature of teaching that has always made it attractive-- job security-- you need to replace it with something.

This is why holding onto a few less-awesome teachers is better than firing some good ones-- you do not attract teachers by saying, "You might lose your job at any time for completely random reasons." If you can't hold onto your better people, your school will be a scene of constant churn and instability, which will go a long way toward turning your okay teachers into bad teachers.

The virtues of FILO

I know, I know. Just go to the comments and leave your story of some awesome young teacher who lost her job while some grizzled hag got to stay on. First In, Last Out may be much-hated, but it has the following virtues.

1)   It is completely predictable. You don't have to wonder whether or not your job is on the line. The school trades a handful of young staffers with job worries for the rest of the staff having job security.

2)   It's a ladder. As a nervous young staffer, you know that if things work out, you'll earn that job security soon enough.

3)   Youth. Young teachers at the beginning of their careers are best able to bounce back from losing a job. Being fired is least likely to be a career-ender for the newbs.

But in private industry--

Don't care. Schools are not combat troops, hospitals, or private corporations. I'll save the full argument for another day, but the short argument is this--

schools are not private industry, and there's no good reason to expect them to run like private industry.

Whose judgment

At the end of the day, any tenure and firing system is going to depend on somebody's judgment. When we use something like Danielson rubric or even a God-forsaken cup of VAM sauce, we are simply substituting the judgment of the person who created the system for the judgment of the people who actually work with the teacher.

True story. In a nearby district a few years ago, the teachers were called to a meeting, and as they entered the meeting, they pulled numbers out of a hat. Then as the meeting started they were told what the numbers meant-- certain numbers would have a job the next year, other numbers would not, and the last group were maybe's.

That's what an employment system that uses no personal judgment looks like, and it satisfies the needs of absolutely none of the stakeholders. What we need is a system that uses the best available judgment in the best possible way. But it will have to address all the issues above, or we're just back to numbers in a hat.

Testing: What Purposes?

As the Defenders of Big Standardized Tests have rushed to protect and preserve ~~this important revenue stream~~ this monster program, they have proposed a few gazillion reasons that testing must happen, that these big bubbly blunt force objects of education serve many important purposes.

The sheer volume of purported purposes makes it appear that BS Tests are almost magical. And yet, when we start working our way down the list and look at each purpose by itself...

Teacher Evaluation.

The notion that test results can be used to determine how much value a teacher added to an individual student (which is itself a creepy concept) has been debunked, disproven, and rejected by so many knowledgeable people it's hard to believe that anyone could still defend it. At this point, Arne Duncan would look wiser insisting that the earth is a giant flat disc on the back of a turtle. There's a whole argument to be had about what to do with teacher evaluations once we have them, but if we decide that we do want to evaluate teachers for whatever purpose, evaluations based on BS Tests do not even make the Top 100 list.

Inform Instruction: Micro Division

Can I use BS Tests to help me decide how to shape, direct and fine tune my classroom practices this year? Can I use the BS Tests results from the test given in March and sent back to us over the summer to better teach the students who won't be in my class by the time I can see their individual scores? Are you kidding me?

BS Tests are useless as methods of tuning and tweaking instruction of particular students in the same year. And we don't need a tool to do that any way because that's what teachers do every single day. I do dozens of micro-assessments on a daily basis, formal and informal, to determine just where my students stand on whatever I'm teaching. The notion that a BS Test can help with this is just bizarre.

Inform Instruction: Macro Division

Okay, so will year-to-year testing allow a school to say, "We need to tweak our program in this direction." The answer is yes, kind of. Many, many schools do this kind of study, and it boils down to coming together to say, "We've gotten as far as we can by actually teaching the subject matter. But test study shows that students are messing up this particular type of question, so we need to do more test prep--I mean, instructional focus, on answering these kinds of test questions."

But is giving every single student a BS Test every single year the best way to do this? Well, no. If we're just evaluating the program, a sampling would be sufficient. And as Catherine Gerwitz pointed out at EdWeek, this is one of many test functions that could already be handled by NAEP.

Measuring Quality for Accountability

It seems reasonable to ask the question, "How well are our schools doing, really?" It also seems reasonable to ask, "How good is my marriage, really?" or "How well do I kiss, really?" But if you imagine a standardized test is going to tell you, you're ready to buy swampland in Florida.

There are articles stretching back to before the days in which measuring quality didn't carry such political weight, and some of them provide highly technical answers. The less technical answer is to ask-- when people wonder about how good a school is, or ask about schools, or brag about schools, or complain about schools, how often is that directly related to BS Tests results. When someone says, "I want to send my kids to a great school," does that question have anything to do with how well their kid will be prepped to take a narrow bubble test?

BS Tests don't measure school quality.

Competition Among Schools

"If we don't give the BS Test," opine some advocates, "how will we be able to stack rank all the schools of this country." (I'm paraphrasing for them).

The most obvious question here is, why do we need to? What educational benefit do I get in my 11th grade English classroom out of know how my students compare to students in Iowa? In what parallel universe would we find me saying either, "Well, I wasn't actually going to try to teach you anything, but now that I see how well they're doing in Iowa, I'm going to actually try" or "Well, we were going to do some really cool stuff this week, but I don't want to get too far ahead of the Iowans."

But even if I were to accept the value of intra-school competition, why would I use this tool, and why would I use it every year for every student? Again, the NAEP is already a better tool. The current crop of BS Tests cover a narrow slice of what schools do. Using these to compare schools is like making every single musician in the orchestra audition by playing a selection on oboe.

The Achievement Gap

We used to talk about making the pig fatter by repeatedly measuring it. Now we have the argument that if we repeatedly weight two pigs, they will get closer to weighing the same.

The data are pretty clear-- in our more-than-a-decade of test-based accountability, the achievement gap has not closed. In fact, in some areas, it has gotten wider. It seems not-particularly-radical to point out that doubling down on what has not worked is unlikely to, well, work.

The "achievement gap" is, in fact, a standardized test score gap. Of all the gaps we can find related to social justice and equity in our nation-- the income gap, the mortality gap, the getting-sent-to-prison gap, the housing gap, the health care gap, the being-on-the-receiving-end-ofviolence gap-- of all these gaps, we really want to throw all our weight behind how well people score on the BS Tests?

Finding the Failures

Civil rights groups that back testing seem to feel that the BS Test and the reporting requirements of NCLB (regularly hailed as many people's favorite part of the law) made it impossible for schools and school districts to hide their failures. By dis-aggregating test results, we can quickly and easily see which schools are failing and address the issue. But what information have we really collected, and what are we actually doing about it?

We already know that the BS Tests correspond to family income. We haven't found out anything with BS Tests that we couldn't have predicted by looking at family income. And how have we responded? Certainly not by saying, "This school is woefully underfunded, lacking both the resources and the infrastructure to really educate these students." No, we can't do that. Instead we encourage students to show grit, or we offer us "failing" schools as turnaround/investment opportunities for privatizers. Remember-- you don't fix schools by throwing money at them. To fix schools, you have to throw money at charter operators.

Civil Rights

For me, this is the closest we come to a legit reason for BS Tests. Essentially, the civil rights argument is that test results provide a smoking gun that can be used to indict districts so steeped in racism that they routinely deny even the most rudimentary features of decent schooling.

But once again, it doesn't seem to work that way. First, we don't learn anything we didn't already know. Second, districts don't respond by trying to actually fix the problem, but simply by complying with whatever federal regulation demands, and that just turns into more investment opportunities. Name a school district that in the last decade of BS Testing has notably improved its service of minority and poor students because of test results. No, instead, we have districts where the influx of charter operations to fix "failing" schools has brought gentrification and renewed segregation.

BS Testing also replicates the worst side effect of snake oil cures-- it creates the illusion that you're actually working on the problem and keeps you from investing your resources in a search for real solutions.

Expectations

On the other hand, one of the dumbest supports of BS Testing is the idea, beloved by Arne Duncan, that expectations are the magical key to everything. Students with special needs don't perform well in school because nobody expects them to. So we must have BS Tests, and we must give them to everyone the same way. Also, in order to dominate the high jump in the next Olympics, schools will now require all students to clear a high jump bar set at 6' before they may eat lunch. That includes children who are wheelchair bound, because expectations.

Informing parents

Yes, somehow BS Test advocates imagine that parents have no idea how their children are doing in school unless they can see the results of a federally-mandated BS Test. The student's grades, the student's daily tests and quizzes and writing assignments and practice papers provide no information. Nor could a parent actually speak to a teacher face to face or through e-mail to ask about their child's progress.

Somehow BS Test advocates imagine a world where teachers are incompetent and parents are clueless. Even if that is true in one corner or another, how, exactly, would a BS Test score help? How would a terrible teacher or a dopey parent use that single set of scores to do...
anything? I can imagine there are places where parents want more transparency from their schools, but even so-- how do BS Tests, which measure so little and measure it so poorly, give them that?

Informing government

Without BS Testing, ask advocates, how will the federal government know how schools are doing? I have two questions in response.

1) What makes you think BS Tests will tell you that? Why not just the older, better NAEP test instead?

2) Why do the feds need to know?

Bottom Line

Many of the arguments for BS Testing depend on a non sequitor construction: "Nutrition is a problem in some countries, so I should buy a hat." Advocates start with a legitimate issue, like the problems of poverty in schools, and suggest BS Testing as a solution, even though it offers none.

In fact there's little that BS Tests can help with, because they are limited and poorly-made tools. "I need to nail this home together," say test advocates. "So hand me that banana." Tests simply can't deliver as advertised.

The arguments for testing are also backwards-manufactured. Instead of asking, "Of all the possible solutions in the world, how could we help a teacher steer instruction during the year," testing advocates start with the end ("We are going to give these tests") and then struggle to somehow connect those conclusions to the goal.

If you were going to address the problems of poverty and equity in this country, how would you do it? If you were going to figure out if someone was a good teacher or not, how could we tell that? How would you tell good schools from bad ones, and how would you fix the bad ones?

The first answer that pops into your mind for any of those questions is not, "Give a big computer-based bubble test on reading and math."

Nor can we say just give it a shot, because it might help and what does it really hurt? BS Tests come with tremendous costs, from the huge costs of the tests to the costs of the tech needed to administer them to the costs in a shorter school year and the human costs in stress and misery for the small humans forced to take these. And we have yet to see what the long-term costs are for raising a generation to think that a well-educated person is one who can do a good job of bubbling in answers on a BS Test.

The federal BS Test mandate needs to go away because the BS Testing does not deliver any of the outcomes that it promises and comes at too great costs.

The Biggest Failure: Defining Success

Time magazine ran an interview with Senator Lamar Alexander, discussing the future of testing and the ESEA. It concludes with this quote:

What I know is the biggest failure of No Child Left Behind is the idea that Washington should tell 100,000 public schools and their teachers whether they're succeeding, whether they're failing and what the consequences of that should be. That hasn't worked.

I think that's close, but perhaps not dead-on. Because implied by the idea of DC telling the public schools whether or not their succeeding is the idea of DC telling the schools what success really means.

No Child Left Behind didn't just legislate the idea that the feds would tell schools and teachers how well they were doing. It redefined what "success" means in education.

Defining success has always been one of the great challenges in education. Through the early part of my career (I graduated from college in 1979), there was a steady trend toward authentic assessment, because everything we knew and were learning about education said that an objective test was by far the worst way to decide how well a student was acquiring skills and knowledge.

If you are of a certain age, you recognize and tremble at these initials-- TSWBAT. For you youngsters, that's "The Student Will Be Able To," and it meant that your lesson plans would focus on what the student could actually do at the end of instruction. So if you were trying to teach a student the knowledge and skills necessary to analyze a full modern novel or write a complete analytical essay or assemble a carburetor or successfully bid out a hand of bridge, you weren't going to give some sort of bubble test. The student was going to demonstrate outcomes by doing the thing. That would be success.

The focus on outcomes was leading us to student portfolios. No longer would a test or two or ten define the student's achievements. Instead, a portfolio would be assembled showing progress, development, achievement, and success in a year's worth of projects, assignments, and accomplishments. That was going to be success.

And just as we were out in the trenches coming to grips with how exciting and terrifying it would be to come up with a portfolio system and they could be electronic portfolios, because with computer tech we could include videos and demonstrations and oh holy smokes on a shingle this would be completely individualized so that each student would graduate with twelve years' worth of broad, varied authentic achievements that would paint a completely personal picture of all the strengths and depths and awesomeness of that individual human being-- just as we were starting to get a grip on that, the feds stepped in, dragged the needle across the vinyl and said, "Nope-- we got your definition of success right here."

Success is a good score on a standardized test. And it looks exactly the same for every student.

And Race to the Top and RttT Lite (less filling, more waivery) doubled down on that by adding one-size-fits-all non-sequitorian justification. Success is a good score on a standardized test because success is a college education and a well-paying job.

Being an outstanding musician or welder? Not success. Being a middling student but a stand-up person who makes their community a better place? Not a success. Screwing up as a freshman and turning your life around to graduate after five years? Not a success.

Marching to the beat of a different drum? Hey, kid. Who said you could have a drum? Everybody in this band plays clarinet, and to be a success, you must take the standardized bubble test on clarineterry.

The most stunning obtusity, the most spectacular failure of NCLB/RTTT is the manner in which it has turned the goal and purpose of education into something small, cramped, meager and unvaried.

Success is a good score on a standardized test.

What a sad, tiny, uninspired definition of success. But NCLB introduced it and tied us all to it, like eagles chained to a stuffed turtle on the desk of the world's least ambitious accountant. The biggest failure of NCLB was to take the whole vast continent of possibilities, the promise and varied range of humanity that has always characterized this country-- to look at all that and say, "No, we're just going to say that success is a good score on a standardized test that only covers a couple of subjects, badly. And we'll demand that everyone achieve it at the same time in the same way. That's success."

That's the biggest failure of No Child Left Behind. If you see Senator Alexander, you can tell him I said so.

Sampling the PARCC

Today, I'm trying something new. I've gotten myself onto the PARCC sample item site and am going to look at the ELA sample items for high school. This set was updated in March of 2014, so, you know, it's entirely possible they are not fully representative, given that the folks at Pearson are reportedly working tirelessly to improve testing so that new generations of Even Very Betterer Tests can be released into the wild, like so many majestic lion-maned dolphins.

So I'm just going to live blog this in real-ish time, because we know that one important part of measuring reading skill is that it should not involve any time for reflection and thoughtful revisiting of the work being read. No, the Real Readers of this world are all Wham Bam Thank You Madam Librarian, so that's how we'll do this. There appear to be twenty-three sample items, and I have two hours to do this, so this could take a while. You've been warned.

PAGE ONE: DNA

Right off the bat I can see that taking the test on computer will be a massive pain in the ass. Do you remember frames, the website formatting that was universally loathed and rapidly abandoned? This reminds me of that. The reading selection is in its own little window and I have to scroll the reading within that window. The two questions run further down the page, so when I'm looking at the second question, the window with the selection in it is halfway off the screen, so to look back to the reading I have to scroll up in the main window and then scroll up and down in the selection window and then take a minute to punch myself in the brain in frustration.

The selection is about using DNA testing for crops, so fascinating stuff. Part A (what a normal person might call "question 1") asks us to select three out of seven terms used in the selection, picking those that "help clarify" the meaning of the term "DNA fingerprint," so here we are already ignoring the reader's role in reading. If I already understand the term, *none* of them help (what helped you learn how to write your name today?), and if I don't understand the term, apparently there is only one path to understanding. If I decide that I have to factor in the context in which the phrase is used, I'm back to scrolling in the little window and I rapidly want to punch the test designers in the face. I count at least four possible answers here, but only three are allowed. Three of them are the only answers to use "genetics" in the answer; I will answer this question based on guesswork and trying to second guess the writer.

Part B is a nonsense question, asking me to come up with an answer based on my first answer.

PAGE TWO: STILL FRICKIN' DNA

Still the same selection. Not getting any better at this scrolling-- whether my mouse roller scrolls the whole page or the selection window depends on where my cursor is sitting.

Part A is, well... hmm. If I asked you, "Explain how a bicycle is like a fish," I would expect an answer from you that mentioned both the bicycle and a fish. But PARCC asks how "solving crop crimes is like solving high-profile murder cases." But all four answers mention only the "crop crime" side of the comparison, and the selection itself says nothing about how high-profile murder cases are solved. So are students supposed to already know how high-profile murder cases are solved? Should they assume that things they've seen on CSI or Law and Order are accurate? To answer this we'll be reduced to figuring out which answer is an accurate summary of the crop crime techniques mentioned in the selection.

This is one of those types of questions that we have to test prep our students for-- how to "reduce" a seemingly complex question to the simpler question. This question pretends to be complex; it is actually asking, "Which one of these four items is actually mentioned in the selection?" It boils down to picky gotcha baloney-- one answer is going to be wrong because it says that crop detectives use computers "at crime scenes"

Part B. The old "which detail best supports" question. If you blew Part A, these answers will be bizarrely random.

PAGE THREE: DNA

Still on this same damn selection. I now hate crops and their DNA.

Part A wants to know what the word "search" means in the heading for the final graph. I believe it means that the article was poorly edited, but that selection is not available. The distractor in this set is absolutely true; it requires test-taking skills to eliminate it, not reading skills.
Part B "based on information from the text" is our cue (if we've been properly test prepped) to go look for the answer in the text, which would take a lot less time if not for this furshlugginer set up. The test writers have called for two correct answers, allowing them to pretend that a simple search-and-match question is actually complex.

PAGE FOUR: DNA GRAND FINALE, I HOPE

Ah, yes. A test question that assesses literally nothing useful whatsoever. At the top of the page is our selection in a full-screen width window instead of the narrow cramped one. At the bottom of the page is a list of statements, two of which are actual advantages of understanding crop DNA. Above them are click-and-drag details from the article. You are going to find the two advantages, then drag the supporting detail for each into the box next to it. Once you've done all this, you will have completed a task that does not mirror any real task done by real human beings anywhere in the world ever.

This is so stupid I am not even going to pretend to look for the "correct" answer. But I will remember this page clearly the next time somebody tries to unload the absolute baloney talking point that the PARCC does not require test prep. No students have ever seen questions like this unless a teacher showed them such a thing, and no teacher ever used such a thing in class unless she was trying to get her students ready for a cockamamie standardized test.

Oh, and when you drag the "answers," they often don't fit in the box and just spill past the edges, looking like you've made a mistake.

PAGE FIVE: FOR THE LOVE OF GOD, DNA

Here are the steps listed in the article. Drop and drag them into the same order as in the article. Again, the only thing that makes this remotely difficult is wrestling with the damn windows. This is a matching exercise, proving pretty much nothing.

PAGE SIX: APPARENTLY THIS IS A DNA TEST TEST

By now my lower-level students have stopped paying any attention to the selection and are just trying to get past it to whatever blessed page of the test will show them something else.

Part A asks us to figure out which question is answered by the selection. This is one of the better questions I've seen so far. Part B asks which quote "best" supports the answer for A. I hate these "best" questions, because they reinforce the notion that there is only one immutable approach for any given piece of text. It's the very Colemanian idea that every text represents only a single destination and there is only one road by which to get there. That's simply wrong, and reinforcing it through testing is also wrong. Not only wrong, but a cramped, tiny, sad version of the richness of human understanding and experience.

PAGE SEVEN: SOMETHING NEW

Here comes the literature. First we get 110 lines of Ovid re: Daedelus and Icarus (in a little scrolling window). Part A asks which one of four readings is the correct one for lines 9 and 10 (because reading, interpreting and experiencing the richness of literature is all about selecting the one correct reading). None of the answers are great, particularly if you look at the lines in context, but only one really makes sense. But then Part B asks which other lines support your Part A answer and the answer here is "None of them," though there is one answer for B that would support one of the wrong answers for A, so now I'm wondering if the writers and I are on a different page here.

PAGE EIGHT: STILL OVID

Two more questions focusing on a particular quote, asking for an interpretation and a quote to back it up. You know, when I say it like that, it seems like a perfectly legitimate reading assessment. But when you turn that assessment task into a multiple choice question, you break the whole business. "Find a nice person, get married and settle down," seems like decent-ish life advice, but if you turn it into "Select one of these four people, get married in one of these four ceremonies, and buy one of these four houses" suddenly it's something else.

And we haven't twisted this reading task for the benefit of anybody except the people who sell, administer, score and play with data from these tests.

PAGE NINE: OVID

The test is still telling me that I'm going to read two selections but only showing me one. If I were not already fully prepped for this type of test and test question, I might wonder if something were wrong with my screen. So, more test prep required.

Part A asks what certain lines "most" suggest about Daedelus, as if that is an absolute objective thing. Then you get to choose what exact quotes (two, because that makes it more complex) back you up. This is not constructing and interpretation of a piece of literature. Every one of these questions makes me angrier as a teacher of literature and reading.

PAGE TEN: ON TO SEXTON

Here's our second poem-- "To a Friend Whose Work Has Come To Triumph." The two questions are completely bogus-- Sexton has chosen the word "tunneling" which is a great choice in both its complexity and duality of meaning, a great image for the moment she's describing. But of course in test land the word choice only "reveals" one thing, and only one other piece of the poem keys that single meaning. I would call this poetry being explained by a mechanic, but that's disrespectful to mechanics.

PAGE ELEVEN: MORE BUTCHERY

Determine the central idea of Sexton's poem, as well as specific details that develop the idea over the course of the poem. From the list of Possible Central Ideas, drag the best Central Idea into the Central Idea box.

Good God! This at least avoids making explicit what is implied here-- "Determine the central idea, then look for it on our list. If it's not there, you're wrong." Three of the four choices are okay-ish, two are arguable, and none would impress me if they came in as part of a student paper.

I'm also supposed to drag-and-drop three quotes that help develop the One Right Idea. So, more test prep required.

PAGE TWELVE: CONTRAST

Now my text window has tabs to toggle back and forth between the two works. I'm supposed to come up with a "key" difference between the two works (from their list of four, of course) and two quotes to back up my answer. Your answer will depend on what you think "key" means to the test writers. Hope your teacher did good test prep with you.

PAGE THIRTEEN: ESSAY TIME

In this tiny text box that will let you view about six lines of your essay at a time, write an essay "that provides and analysis of how Sexton transforms Daedelus and Icarus." Use evidence from both texts. No kidding-- this text box is tiny. And no, you can't cut and paste quotes directly from the texts.

But the big question here-- who is going to assess this, and on what basis? Somehow I don't think it's going to be a big room full of people who know both their mythology and their Sexton.

PAGE FOURTEEN: ABIGAIL ADAMS

So now we're on to biography. It's a selection from the National Women's History Museum, so you know it is going to be a vibrant and exciting text. I suppose it could be worse--we could be reading from an encyclopedia.

The questions want to know what "advocate for women" means, and to pick an example of Adams being an advocate. In other words, the kinds of questions that my students would immediately id as questions that don't require them to actually read the selection.

PAGE FIFTEEN: ADAMS

This page wants to know which question goes unanswered by the selection, and then for Part B asks to select a statement that is true about the biography but which supports the answer for A. Not hopelessly twisty.

PAGE SIXTEEN: MORE BIO

Connect the two central ideas of this selection. So, figure out what the writers believe are the two main ideas, and then try figure out what they think the writers see as a connection. Like most of these questions, these will be handled backwards. I'm not going to do a close reading of the selection-- I'm going to close read the questions and answers and then use the selection just as a set of clues about which answer to pick. And this is how answering multiple choice questions about a short selection is a task not much like authentic reading or pretty much any other task in the world.

PAGE SEVENTEEN: ABIGAIL LETTER

Now we're going to read the Adams family mail. This is one of her letters agitating for the rights of women; our questions will focus on her use of "tyrant" based entirely on the text itself, because no conversation between Abigail and John Adams mentioning tyranny in 1776 could possibly be informed by any historical or personal context.

PAGE EIGHTEEN: STILL VIOLATING FOUNDING FATHER & MOTHER PRIVACY

Same letter. Now I'm supposed to decide what the second graph most contributes to the text as a whole. Maybe I'm just a Below basic kind of guy, but I am pretty sure that the correct answer is not among the four choices. That just makes it harder to decide which other two paragraphs expand on the idea of graph #2.

PAGE NINETEEN: BOSTON

Now we'll decide what her main point about Boston is in the letter. This is a pretty straightforward and literal reading for details kind of question. Maybe the PARCC folks are trying to boost some morale on the home stretch here.

Oh hell. I have a message telling me I have less than five minutes left.

PAGE TWENTY: JOHN'S TURN

Now we have to pick the paraphrase of a quote from Adams that the test writers think is the berries. Another set of questions that do not require me to actually read the selection, so thank goodness for small favors.

PAGE TWENTY-ONE: MORE JOHN

Again, interpretation and support. Because making sense out of colonial letter-writing English is just like current reading. I mean, we've tested me on a boring general science piece, classical poetry, modern poetry, and a pair of colonial letters. Does it seem like that sampling should tell us everything there is to know about the full width and breadth of student reading ability?

PAGE TWENTY-TWO: BOTH LETTERS

Again, in one page, we have two sets of scrollers, tabs for toggling between works, and drag and drop boxes for the answers. Does it really not occur to these people that there are students in this country who rarely-if-ever lay hands on a computer?

This is a multitask page. We're asking for a claim made by the writer and a detail to back up that claim, but we're doing both letters on the same page and we're selecting ideas and support only from the options provided by the test. This is not complex. It does not involve any special Depth of Knowledge. It's just a confusing mess.

PAGE TWENTY-THREE: FINAL ESSAY

Contrast the Adams' views of freedom and independence. Support your response with details from the three sources (yes, we've got three tabs now). Write it in this tiny text box.

Do you suppose that somebody's previous knowledge of John and Abigail and the American Revolution might be part of what we're inadvertently testing here? Do you suppose that the readers who grade these essays will themselves be history scholars and writing instructors? What, if anything, will this essay tell us about the student's reading skills?

DONE

Man. I have put this off for a long time because I knew it would give me a rage headache, and I was not wrong. How anybody can claim that the results from a test like this would give us a clear, nuanced picture of student reading skills is beyond my comprehension. Unnecessarily complicated, heavily favoring students who have prior background knowledge, and absolutely demanding that test prep be done with students, this is everything one could want in an inauthentic assessment that provides those of us in the classroom with little or no actual useful data about our students.

If this test came as part of a packaged bunch of materials for my classroom, it would go in the Big Circular File of publishers materials that I never, ever use because they are crap. What a bunch of junk. If you have stuck it out with me here, God bless you. I don't recommend that you give yourself the full PARCC sample treatment, but I heartily recommend it to every person who declares that these are wonderful tests that will help revolutionize education. Good luck to them as well.

Reformster Fallacious Argument Made Simple

It is one of the great fallacies you will frequently encounter in the work of education reform.

I most recently encountered a very striking version of it in a new position-paper-advocacy-research-report-white-paper-thingy from FEE, the reformster group previously working for Jeb Bush and handed over (at least until Bush finishes trying to be President) to Condoleezza Rice.

The report wants to make the case for charters and choice in education, and it starts by arguing that soon there will be way too few employed people paying for way too many children and retired geezers, therefore, school choice. The "report" runs to almost 100 pages, and ninety-some of those are devoted to mapping out the severe scrariosity of the upcoming crisis. The part that explains how school choice would fix this-- that gets a couple of pages. At its most critical juncture, the argument depends on one previously debunked study.

This is a relatively common fallacious argument structure, but if you are going to spend time in the education debates, it's useful to know it when you see it. The basic outline of the argument looks like this:

1) SOMETHING AWFUL IS GOING TO HAPPEN OH MY GOOD LORD IN HEAVEN LOOOK I EVEN HAVE CHARTS AND GRAPHS AND IT IS SOOOOOOOOO TERRIBLE THAT IT WILL MAKE AWFUL THINGS HAPPEN, REALLY TERRIBLE AWFUL THINGS LET ME TELL YOU JUST HOW AWFUL OH GOD HEAVENS WE MUST ALL BEWARE--- BEEE WAAAARREEEEEEE!!!!!!!!!

2) therefore for some reason

3) You must let me do X to save us!

The trick here is to load up #1 with facts and figures and details and specifics. Make it as facty and credible as you possibly can (even if you need to gin up some fake facts to do it).

#3 is where you load in your PR for whatever initiative you're pushing.

And #2 you just try to skate past as quickly as possible, because #2 is the part that most needs support and proof and fact-like content, but #2 is also the place where you probably don't have any.

In a normal, non-baloney argument, #2 is the strongest point, because the rational, supportable connection between the problem and the solution is what matters most. But if you are selling baloney, that connection is precisely what you don't have. So instead of actual substance in #2, you just do your best to drive up the urgency in #1.

For example:

1) The volcano is gigantic and scary and when lava comes pouring out of it WE ARE ALL GOING TO DIE HOT FLAMING DEATHS AND SUFFOCATE IN ASH AND IT WILL BE TERRIBLE

2) Therefore, for some reason

3) We should sacrifice some virgins

Or:

1) We are falling behind other countries and if we don't get caught back up we will be BEHIND ESTONIA!! ESTONIA!!!! GOOD GOD, WE MUST NOT FALL BEHIND THESE OTHER NATIONS ON THE TOTALLY MADE-UP INTERNATIONAL AWESOMENESS INDEX

2) Therefore, for some reason

3) We should adopt Common Core

You can manufacture the #1 crisis if necessary. But this can be even more effective if you use an actual real problem for #1:

1) Poor and minority children in this country keep getting the short end of the stick educationally, with fewer resources and less opportunity to break out of the cycle of poverty. This is a crappy way for our fellow Americans to have to live, and certainly leaving no pathway out of poverty is a violation of the American dream

2) Therefore, for some reason

3) We should make sure they all have to take a Big Standardized Test every year.

You just have to convey a sense of urgency about #1 and never ever let the conversation drift to #2. If people start trying to ask exactly how #3 actually helps with #1, you just rhetorical question them into silence.

Treat questioning #2 as if it's the same as questioning #1.Can't for the life of you see how the #1 of poverty and under-resourced schools is solved by more charter schools that drain resources from public education and only agree to teach the handful of students that they accept, while remaining unaccountable to anyone? Condoleezza Rice says you're a racist.

But it's #2 where the most important questions lie. Even if I accept that US schools are in some sort of crisis (which I don't, but if), exactly how would Common Core fix that? I do believe that we have a real problem with poverty in this country, but how, exactly, will giving poor kids standardized tests help with that?

If you have a gut feeling that a great deal of the reformster just doesn't make sense, #2 is where the problem mostly lies. Most reformster arguments involve using a loud #1 and a slick #3 to cover up a nonexistent #2.

1) Some students score low on Big Standardized Tests-- They GET LOW SCORES! LOW SCORES THAT ARE A BAAAAAAD THING! True, they're a bad thing because we've set up a system of artificial imposed punishments for low scores but hey, still-- LOOOOWWWW SCOOORESSSSSS!!!!!

2) Therefore, for some reason

3) There should be no tenure for teachers

There's no connection at all. We could just as easily say

3) Taxpayers should buy charter operators a pony

3) The National Guard should shoot a badger

3) We should sacrifice a virgin

But of course badgers and ponies and virgins aren't nearly as profitable as charters and tests. That, and I think some folks really believe that #2 is there when it just isn't. Either way, it's important to know what the real connection is before you start sacrificing virgins.

Students As Vending Machines

One of the most pernicious yet subtle side effects of test-driven accountability is that it flips the mission of a school on its head.

The proper view of a school is that it exists to serve the students, to help them become the people they can best be, to become better wiser citizens and members of the community. A school's mission is to help with that process.

But under a regime of high stakes testing, that mission is thrown out. The school's mission is to Get Good Numbers out of the students. The institution is no longer there to meet the needs of the students-- the students are there to meet the needs of the institution. The students are there to produce the numbers that the school needs to produce.

Proponents of test-driven accountability will say that there's no problem. The drive to get good test scores out of students will motivate schools to meet the student's needs. This kind of reasoning would also suggest that there's no difference between a person who is your friend because he likes you and a person who is your friend because he wants to get money from you. If you cannot tell the difference between those two relationships, I would rather not be your friend.

In the upside-down world of high stakes testing, schools only need to care about student needs that might affect test scores. They need only give the students what will get the school what it wants-- a good score on a bad test of a narrow sliver of skills.

In the world of test-driven accountability, students are simply vending machines. Put in the correct change. Kick and shake the machine a little if the candy won't fall all the way to the bottom.

If you haven't witnessed this, it's hard to imagine how pervasive the effect can become. Let's assign students to teachers based not on who would be a good fit, but who might get the best scores out of the kid. Let's structure the day, the curriculum, the organization of grades within the district strictly on what will generate the best numbers.

What the students want or need from us doesn't matter. What matters is what we want from them-- good numbers. They are no longer customers or clients; they are employees. Meeting their needs is no longer our goal; their needs are now an obstacle in the path of our goal, which is to get good numbers.

There's no question that not all schools have always embodied my high ideals for schools. But there's no question that test-driven accountability moves us further from that ideal, not closer.

Doublespeak Studies: "Student Achievement"

If you frame the argument, you win the argument before it even starts. And the best way to frame the argument is to choose the language that will be used to argue.

That's why, for instance, there's so much wrestling over whether to talk about "pro-choice" or "pro-life"-- because each term tilts the playing field.

Reformsters have framed the argument with precisely this technique, and nowhere have they been as successful as with the term "student achievement." It's a great re-construction, like renaming lifeobliterating nuclear weapons as peacekeeper missiles, or remarketing GI Joe's not as dolls for boys, but as action figures.

The essence of doublespeak is to use a word that has two meanings-- one is the meaning that I actually have in mind when I use the term, and the other meaning is the one the audience will supply based on their own assumptions (which are based on what the word ordinarily means). So I tell my prom date we're taking a "limo" because to most people, "limo" means big elegant fancy car; but I actually mean a hotelowned van. I use the language to conjure up a happy picture in your head, rather than confront you with smelly reality.

If you asked any 100 random people to explain what they thought student achievement meant, you would likely get a rich and varied set of answers. Student achievement sounds like it covers the full range of accomplishments, talents, skills and knowledge that we would find within a student body. It might echo the way in which I sometimes describe classes of students as a Legion of Super-Heroes (my personal preference over the Avengers or Justice League)-- a group of accomplished individuals, each with a different but exciting super power. Student achievement sounds great. It sounds like lots of young folks Getting Things Done and Fulfilling Their Promise.

But of course that's not what student achievement means at all.

"Student achievement" means "student test scores."

That's all. That's it. But reformsters have been excrutiatingly effective in getting people to think we're talking about actual student achievement while we're only talking about student test scores.

A google of "student achievement" returns 37,700,000 results. They are not encouraging.

Lots of folks want to talk about the student achievement gap. This always means the student test score gap.

When Arne Duncan tells audiences that the nation must "focus on improving teacher quality and support in order to boost student achievement," he means "to boost student test scores."

When a study last year asserted that teacher strikes hurt student achievement, fully reading the study shows that they mean the strike hurt student test scores (they didn't prove it, but they meant it).

Whenever a study talks about whether or not TFA boosts student achievement, the study is inevitably talking about whether or not TFA boost student test scores.

Whenever there's an attempt to connect teacher tenure to effects on student achievement, we turn out to actually be talking about correlations between tenure and student test scores.

In short, it has become commonplace to say "student achievement" when we really, honestly mean "student test scores." It serves reformsters well, because few people are really all that concerned about student standardized tests scores. "Chris seemed happy and thriving at school, and was coming home excited about new learning every day. Chris was just blossoming and becoming a great little person. But Chris kept got a low standardized test score last year, so we had no choice but to look for another school," said no parent ever. Ever!

As advocates for public education, here's one of the things we need to keep doing. When reformsters start saying student achievement, we need to speak up and ask, "So are you really just talking about student test scores?" Over and over.

By allowing them to say "achievement" when they mean "test scores" we are allowing them to skip over the entire discussion of whether or not the Big Standardized Test measures anything worth measuring. We allow them to skip over the discussion of whether the BS Test can be a useful proxy for anything (spoiler alert: it can't).

One of the ways to control a conversation is not to say what you mean, but to say something else so that your audience will hear something else, something different from what you are really saying. Let's stop saying "student achievement" when we're really talking about "student test scores."

The Trouble with Belief

Belief is a big part of the reformster narrative put forth by the administration and its various proxies. The problem with low-achieving minority students and students with special needs, goes the narrative, is that both individual teachers and the institution of school itself do not believe that these students can learn or grow or achieve, and therefor they are denied a full-on education.

At the heart of this narrative is something that is absolutely, undeniably true-- so undeniably true that I don't know a single competent teacher who denies it.

To teach students, you must believe that they can learn. The degree to which you believe in their power and potential has a huge effect on what those students will actually achieve.

I think we would be hard-pressed to find anybody who disagrees with that. But once we get past that point, we start to encounter a great deal of argument and disagreement.

Some of the disagreement is manufactured, the result of a new attempt to use belief to bolster the stance of reformsters, particularly those in the charter camp. The stance goes something like this: "This charter school has achieved great and wonderful success. If you question our statements about that success, it can only be because you don't believe that our students could possibly be that successful." This is another variation on the Condoleezza Rice "charter opponents are racists" argument; it's not about establishing a dialogue, but about shutting people up.

In fact, we know the secrets of charter success, and one of them is the exact opposite of believing all students can learn. That story goes something like this: in every low-achieving under-served school you will find a mix of students who could really achieve and students who are part of the problem, so we should use charters to rescue the students who can actually accomplish something.

Where charters succeed (or do at least as well as their public counterparts) it is because they believe only in certain students who meet certain qualifications and behave in certain ways and produce certain results. There are very few charters out there using a sales pitch of, "We believe that all students can succeed and we will accept any and all students and keep them till the bitter end, no matter what, because we will find a way to help them succeed."

Most charters are an expression of the same old belief system that has always marred the face of US public education-- there are some students who we believe in and some we don't. Charters just have the opportunity to gather only the students they believe in. That does not necessarily make charters evil or venal or dastardly, but it does mean that they have nothing to teach public schools, which must take all comers all year, about success and believing in students.

So when I say I'm not impressed by your story of charter success, I'm not saying that I don't believe that your students couldn't succeed or even didn't succeed. I am saying that 1) I have no reason to believe they wouldn't have been just as successful in a public school and 2) that there's very little that you've done in your charter school that is any help to me in a public school, where I will take any student at any time. And if I seem angry, I'm angry on behalf of all the other students that you abandoned in public schools where they must now make do with fewer resources because money and resources were stripped for the select few chosen for charterdom.

Belief is also a problem when it's used as an excuse to ignore the nuts and bolts of education. When belief becomes the linchpin of an argument that says, "You don't need money or a roof that doesn't leak or current textbooks for every single student or enrichment programs or a functional gym or the best administrators we have in the system or the best resources that money can buy-- you just need teachers who believe in those kids."

Do students in poor, minority schools deserve and need teachers who believe in them, in their promise, in their ability, in their potential? Absolutely. Is that the only thing they need? Absolutely not. Find me a rich white school in the 'burbs where the parents say, "Yeah, let's not spend any money on resources or upkeep for the school. Our kids have teachers who believe in them, so they don't need to have anything else at all."
For politicians and policymakers to say, "Yes, we believe in these young people, and that's why we're not going to fully fund their school," is a shameless crock. I'm in Pennsylvania, where the state government leads the nation in making school districts depend on local taxpayers for the bulk of school funding. This has had the predictable effect of making schools in poor areas poor. Belief is important and fundamental and essential, but the students of our poor districts also need resources, tools, a means of attracting and retaining top teaching talent. If politicians want to show how much they believe in the potential of young people, they need to put their money where their mouths are.

Belief is essential. Faith is great. But faith without works is a hollow, empty exercise.

That's because belief has limits. There's a point at which believing in a student goes past the point of being supportive and turns into being abusive. Good teachers try to find that balance every day. If I don't ask enough of a student, I have failed that student. But if I demand more than the student can give, I have also failed that student. There are hundreds of reasons not to believe in students, and they are all wrong and inexcusable. But it is also inexcusable to expect students to leap great barriers without help, support or guidance, just because we expect them to. Believing in the student means the whole student, including her challenges. We cannot overcome what we refuse to acknowledge, but we also can't overcome what we see as insurmountable. This is a hugely difficult balance, and it's here, more than anywhere else in the ongoing debate, we seem to find people refusing to acknowledge the difficulty and importance of this balance. Not all SPED students are placed because of institutional bias and lies, and not all of them are placed because they should be.

This, I think, is one of the reasons that we need more teachers who are rooted in the community where they teach. To actually teach a student, it's not just enough to believe in that student's ability and potential-- you have to be able to understand their world, their life, their background, their culture well enough to see past all of that to where their potential lies and what odds and ends it's hiding behind. This is why the theory of "Let's just move the effective teachers around" strikes me as a waste. I'm pretty effective where I am, but where I am is where I grew up-- I know the territory, I know the background, I know the culture. Transplant me to inner-city Philly, and I would be far less effective. I wouldn't believe in the students any less, but my ignorance of the neighborhood, the families, the culture would all be real deficiencies in me as a teacher and would stand in the way of my ability find connections between student potential and the world they want to enter. I would do my damnedest to learn what I needed to learn, to listen and watch and try to understand and overcome my ignorance, but I doubt that I could ever raise my game to the level of a teacher who has lived there for decades

There are other challenges with belief in the modern reformster era. We need, for instance, measures of student achievement broad enough to encompass all the many ways in which students can achieve. Saying "student achievement" when we mean "student scores on a narrow standardized math and reading test" is disingenuous, and grossly unfair to the students whose awesomeness lies in places other than standardized test taking.

And yes, teachers get testy and defensive when they are confronted with what amounts to the accusation, "Your students failed because you didn't believe in them," as if there isn't any other possible explanation. Blaming the player (We lost the game because you didn't want it enough) is sometimes the truth, but sometimes it's the first and last resort of the bad coach.

And the area where we will probably never find large-scale consensus is in the question of how student potential is affected by student circumstances. Do the most challenging circumstances actually change a child's potential, or do they just lock that potential away behind harder-to-breach barriers? How do we navigate the area between what the child can achieve and what the child will achieve?

I do agree with the core assertion-- teachers must believe that all students can achieve. It is hugely hard to do for every single student, but it's necessary. I know teachers who fail at it occasionally and teachers whose daily failure to believe in their students is the surest sign that they should get out of the teaching biz. But using "belief" as a rhetorical bludgeon or an excuse to sit on your hands does not help us move education forward.

Why Critical Thinking Won't Be on the Test

Critical thinking is one of the Great White Whales of education. Every new education reform promises to foster it, and every new generation of Big Standardized Tests promises to measure it.

Everybody working in education has some idea of what it is, and yet it can be hard to put into a few words. There are entire websites devoted to it, and organizations and foundations dedicated to it. Here, for example, at the website of the Foundation for Critical Thinking, is a definition of critical thinking from the 1987 National Council for Excellence in Critical Thinking that goes on for five paragraphs. One of the shortest definitions I can pull out of their site is this one:

The intellectually disciplined process of actively and skillfully conceptualizing, applying, analyzing, synthesizing, and/or evaluating information gathered from, or generated by, observation, experience, reflection, reasoning, or communication, as a guide to belief and action.

Bottom line-- critical thinking is complicated.

So can we believe test manufacturers when they say that their test measures critical thinking skills? Can a series of questions that can be delivered and scored on a national scale be designed that would actually measure the critical thinking skills of the test takers?

I think the obstacles to creating such a standardized test are huge. Here are the hurdles that test manufacturers would have to leap.

Critical thinking takes time.

Certainly there are people who can make rapid leaps to a conclusion, who can see patterns and structure of ideas quickly and clearly (though we could argue that's more intuitive thinking than critical thinking, but then, intuition might just be critical thinking that runs below the level of clear consciousness, so, again, complicated). But mostly the kind of analyses and evaluation that we associate with critical thinking takes time.

There's a reason that English teachers rarely give the assignment, "The instant you finish reading the last page of the assigned novel, immediately start writing the assigned paper and complete it within a half hour." Critical thinking is most often applied to complex constructions, and for most people it takes a while to examine, reflect, re-examine and pull apart the pieces of the matter.

If you are asking a question that must be answered right now, this second, you are at the very best asking a question that measures how quickly the student can critically think-- but you're probably not measuring critical thinking at all.

Critical thinking takes place in a personal context.

We do not do our critical thinking in a vacuum. We are all standing in a particular spot in space and time, and that vantage point gives us a particular perspective. What we bring to the problem in terms of prior understanding, background, and our own mental constructs, profoundly influences how we critically think about any problem.

We tend to make sense out of unfamiliar things by looking for familiar structures and patterns within them, and so our thinking is influenced by what we already know. I've been an amateur musician my whole life, so I can readily spot structures and patterns that mimic the sorts of things I know form the world of music. However, I am to athletics what Justin Bieber is to quantum physics, and my mental default is not to look at things in athletic terms. Think about your favorite teachers and explainers-- they are people who took something you couldn't understand and put it in terms you could understand. They connected what you didn't know to what you did know.

None of this is a revolutionary new insight, but we have to remember that it means every individual human beings brings a different set of tools to each critical thinking problem. That means it is impossible to design a critical thinking question that is a level playing field for all test takers. Impossible.

Critical thinking is social.

How many big critical thinking problems of the world were solved single-handedly by a single, isolated human being?

Our sciences have a finely-tuned carefully-structured method for both carrying on and acknowledging dialogue with the critical thinkers of the past. If a scientist popped up claiming to have written a groundbreaking paper for which he needed no citations nor footnotes because he had done it all himself, he would be lucky to be taken seriously for five minutes. The Einsteins of history worked in constant dialogue with other scientists; quantum theories were hammered out in part by dialogue by a disbelieving Einstein ("God does not play dice") and the wave of scientists building on the implications of his work.

On the less grand scale, we find our own students who want to talk about the test, want to compare answers, want to (and sometimes love to) argue about the finer points of every thinking assignment.

Look at our own field. We've all been working on a big final test question-- "What is the best way to take American education forward?"- and almost everyone on every side of the question is involved in a huge sprawling debate that sees most of us pushing forward by trying to articulate our own perspective and thoughts while in dialogue with hundreds of other thinkers in varying degrees of agreement and disagreement. One of the reasons I trust and believe David Coleman far less than other reformsters is that he almost never acknowledges the value of any other thinker in his development of Common Core. To watch Coleman talk, you would think he developed the entire thing single-handedly in his own head. That is not the mark of a serious person.

Do people occasionally single-handedly solve critical thinking problems on their own, in isolation, like a keep-your-eyes-on-your-own-paper test? It's certainly not unheard of-- but it's not the norm. If your goal is to make the student answer the question in an isolation chamber, you are not testing critical thinking.

Critical thinking is divergent.

Let's go back to that critical thinking problem about how to best move forward with public education. You may have noticed that people have arrived a wide variety of conclusions about what the answer might be. There are two possible explanations for the wide variety of answers.

The first explanation is the childish one, and folks from both sides indulge in it-- people who have reached a conclusion other than mine are some combination of stupid, uninformed, and evil.

The more likely explanation is that, given a wide variety of different perspectives, different histories, and different values, intelligent people will use critical thinking skills and arrive at different conclusions.

Critical thinking is NOT starting with the conclusion that you want to reach and then constructing a bridge of arguments specifically designed to get you there, and yet this is perilously close to the kind of thinking a standardized test requires.

But here's a good rule of thumb for anyone trying to test critical thinking skills-- if you are designing your assessment and thinking, "Okay, any student who is really using critical thinking skills must come up with answer B," you are not testing critical thinking skills. No-- I take that back. Oddly enough this is a sort of critical thinking question, but the actual question is, "Given what you know about the people giving you the test and the clues they have left for you, what answer do you think the testmakers want you to select?" But that is probably not the question that you thought you were asking. As soon as you ask a question with one right answer (even if the one right answer is to select both correct answers), you are not testing critical thinking.

Critical thinking must be assessed by critical thinking.

How do you assess the answer to your critical thinking question? Again, I direct you to the education debates, where we "grade" each others' work all the time, checking and analyzing, probing for logical fallacies, mis-presentation of data, mis-reading of other peoples' writing, honesty of logic, etc etc etc.

To assess how well someone has answered a critical thinking question, you need to be knowledgeable about the answerer, the subject matter, and whatever background knowledge they have brought to the table (if I answer a question using a music analogy and you know nothing about music, will you know if my analogy holds up). On top of all that, you need some critical thinking skills of your own. And that means all of the issues listed above come back into play.

What are the odds that you can get all that in a cadre of minimumwage test-scorers who can wade through a nation's worth of tests quickly, efficiently, and accurately?

Can it be done?

When I look at all those hurdles and try to imagine a nationally scaled test that gets deals with all of them, I'm stumped. Heck, it's a challenge to come up with good measure for my own classroom, and that's because critical thinking is more of a tool than an end in itself. Testing for critical thinking skills is kind of like testing for hammering skills-- it can be done, but it will be an artificial situation and not as compelling and useful and telling as having the student actually build something.

So I try to come up with assessments that require critical thinking as a tool for completion of the assignment. Then I try to come up with the time to grade them. Could I come up with something for the entire nation? Practically speaking, no. Even if I get past the first few hurdles, when I reach the point that I need a couple million teachers to score it, I'm stumped. Plus, standardized test fans are not going to like the lack of standardization in my test.

No, I think that standardized testing and critical thinking are permanently at odds and we'd be further ahead trying to develop a test to compare the flammability of the water from different rivers.

Critical thinking is not on the BS Tests. It will not be on the new generations of the BS Tests. It will never be on the BS Tests. Test manufacturers should stop promising what they cannot hope to deliver.

Embrace the Core

You know, perhaps we're looking at this the wrong way. Perhaps we are missing a golden opportunity.

After all-- at this point, very few people know what the hell the Common Core Standards actually are. We've learned that the vast majority of Common Core textbook materials are actually not aligned at all. We know that the Common Core tests are a random crapshoot. We know that what Common Core looks like tends to depend on who's interpreting it for your district.

If the Common Core Standards were supposed to create a common, shared framework that would put students and teachers across this country on the same educational page, then they have failed spectacularly and completely.

Pushers of professional development use the CCSS brand to push their favorite ideas. Teacher-advocates describe their programs, based on nothing more than their own best teacher judgment, and give all the credit to the Core. Opponents of the Core blame it for every dumb homework paper ever created, whether that assignment has anything to do with the Core or not.

Those last groups are the ones we can learn from, really.

It's so simple, I can't believe I didn't see it sooner.

Do whatever the hell you want, and blame it on the Core.

Teaching students to research material before reading it? I'll call that core-aligned. Forbidding students to research material before reading it? Also core-aligned. Want to do writing-based assessments? Why, that's totally core. Drilling reading assignments with bubble question quiz at the end? Also complete core. I have a great new idea for a program that integrates research, literature and video presentations. Pitch it as aligned to the core.

My home ec students have to read recipes, so I'm a core teacher. I'm a band director? Create a new tweak to the program-- web-based video pre-reviews of works as concert advertisement. Declare it aligned to the Core. Increase in the budget? I need it for Core-related stuff. Teaching students to make a souffle? It's a Common Core souffle.

Teacher core advocates and publishing companies have shown us the way-- there is literally nothing that can't be claimed as a Core-aligned program. Slap "common core" on anything-- there is nobody who can tell you you aren't allowed.

I'm going to have an extra order of fries-- for the Common Core. I am going to get the red Porsche instead of the mini-van because I need it for the Common Core. I did not have sex with that woman-- we were just aligning some Common Core. Please put more frosting on my cupcakes-- it's required by the Core. If anyone tries to question you, just exclaim, "Critical thinking! Alignment! Why are you against higher standards?"

If you happen to be deep in red state Common Core hating territory, just flip the script. Anything you dislike can be blamed on Common Core.

I'm not going to teach Herman Melville because he's part of the Common Core. Don't order that cheap recycled papers-- it's part of the Common Core. Don't you dare put any of that low-fat dressing on my salad-- that's just another way to promote Common Core. I had to punch that guy; he looked like he was going to talk to my kids about Common Core. If anybody questions you on this, just holler, "Communism! Indoctrination! Why do you hate freedom!"

The Common Core, primarily through the efforts of its alleged friends, has been reduced to a meaningless ball of mush. In hindsight, this seems like a completely predictable result-- there is no hard underlying structure of solid sound education ideas based on research and professional experience. Just blobs of personal preferences slapped together by educational amateurs. There is no solid framework, no sturdy skeleton to stay standing when bits and pieces are chipped away. When you dig into CCSS, there's no there there. And so under stress, exploitation, and just being passed along like a nonsense message in a game of telephone, the Core is being reduced to its most basic parts-- nothing at all.

We can take advantage of that by raising the CCSS flag over any and all territory we want to explore (or want to forbid). We were worried that CCSS would be a concrete straightjacket, but as its allies have tweaked and twisted and slanted and squeezed until it's a soggy mess of nothing, a document written on unobtainium with a unicorn horn dipped in invisible ink. And then, with rare exceptions, they've run off so that they don't have to defend the weak sauce they've left behind.

Now, there's no question that on the state and local level, we still have officials doing their best to slavishly enforce their version of the core-- but the vast majority of them aren't enforcing the standards as actually written, either. Andrew Cuomo would be the same size tyrant whether CCSS existed or not. If your district is in the steely grip of Test Prep Mania, the core really doesn't have anything to do with your problems-- the Core can go away, but until the Big Standardized Test goes away, your troubles will remain.

So do whatever you like and use the Common Core as your excuse. Slap the Core justification on every single thing you do in the classroom-- all the cool kids are doing it. Not only will it give you ammunition to defend your teaching choices, but you will help hasten the ongoing disintegration of the standards into a mushy, meaningless, irrelevant mess. The Common Core Standards are over and done. If we do embrace it, perhaps we can embrace it extra hard and help finish it off. I would say to stick a fork in them, but you'll probably need a spoon, and it will be much more fun to use a blender.

Voucher Party

One of the foundational assertions of the charter movement is that public school tax dollars, once collected, should be attached to the child, maybe in a backpack, or perhaps surgically. "This public money... belongs to the student, not the failing school" wrote a commenter on one of my HuffPost pieces today. And I've heard variations on that over and over from charter advocates.

The money belongs to the student.

I've resisted this notion for a long time. The money, I liked to say, belongs to the taxpayers, who have used it to create a school system that serves the entire community by filling that community with welleducated adults who make better employees, customers, voters, neighbors, parents, and citizens. But hey-- maybe I've been wrong. Maybe that money, once collected really does belong to the student. In which case, let's really do this.

Let's let the student spend his voucher money (and let's stop pussyfooting around this-- when we talk about the money following the students, we're talking about vouchers) on the education of his dreams.

Does she want to go to the shiny new charter school? Let her go (as long as they'll take her, of course). But why stop there? Travel has long been considered a broadening experience-- what if she wants to take the voucher and spend it on a world cruise? Why not? It's her money. Perhaps she wants to become a champion basketball player-- would her time not be well spent hiring a coach and shooting hoops all day? Maybe she would like to develop her skills playing PS4 games, pursuant to a career in video-game tournaments. That's educational. In fact, as I recall the misspent youth of many of my cohort, I seem to recall that many found smoking weed and contemplating the universe to be highly educational. I bet a voucher would buy a lot of weed.

What's that, charter advocate? Do I hear you saying that's an unfair comparison, that obviously a high quality charter school is way different from smoking a lot of weed. I agree, but that's beside the point.

The money belongs to the student.

You didn't say that the money was the student's to be used on educational experiences that met with the approval of some overseeing government body. You didn't say that the money was the student's on the condition that the student got somebody's permission to use it first.

You didn't say that we'd need to put strings on how the money is spent because students and their parents might not always make responsible choices.

You said the money belongs to the student.

Heck, let's really go all in. Why use the odd fiction of a voucher at all-- let's just collect taxes and cut every single student an annual check for $10,000 (or whatever the going rate is in your neighborhood). Let's just hand them the money that we're asserting belongs to them, and let them spend it as they wish. Maybe they'd like a nice couch, or a new iPad, or a sweet skateboard, or a giant voucher party, or food and clothing for themselves and their family.

Unless of course you'd like to suggest that the taxpayers who handed over that money and the community that collected it have an interest in making sure that it's spent well and responsibly in a way that serves the community's greater good. In which case we can go back to discussing how those needs of the stakeholders--ALL the stakeholders-- are best served by an all-inclusive community-based taxpayercontrolled educational system, and stop saying silly things like, "The money belongs to the student."

The Rewards of Teaching

Many reformsters have built their confused, misguided and just plain bad ideas on one very big misconception, a gap in their belief system that informs a hundred other flawed ideas.

Many reformsters do not believe that teaching is intrinsically rewarding.

This has always been there in the worst denigrations of teacher-haters. Teachers are just in it for the paycheck, for the summer vacation, for the cushy ease of the job. You can only believe this if you also believe that there is nothing rewarding about the job itself, if there is nothing to enjoy about working with students and helping them grow and understand and become more fully themselves, more fully human.

It's also there in so-called teacher supporters. We need raise pay. We need to offer financial incentives, merit pay, just higher pay levels across the board. Those are all lovely things, but don't think those have to be there because there's no other reason we'd be in the classroom.

Even Teach for America, a group that more than any other has mastered the rhetoric of teacher idealism about changing the world and touching children-- TFA may laud teaching in its ad copy, but their actions belie their pretty words. "Come be a teacher. Touch the future. Change a life. But for God's sake get the hell out of there and on to a real job." It's nice to touch lives for a year or two, but that couldn't possibly sustain you for an entire career.

Virtually every reformy program now comes with one form of incentivization or another, seemingly borrowed from the world of business cogs, grey flannel suits passing through a series of offices chasing ever-increasing stacks of cash.

If we want teachers to follow one program or another, we must incentivize it with money. Why else would teachers teach?

Mind you, I don't want to roll back to the more traditional argument for keeping teachers poor-- "If you were really doing it for the kids and the good warm feeling you get, then we shouldn't need to pay you more than minimum wage."

But the constant waving about of money is a sign that many reformsters have a fundamental misunderstanding of the work and the people who do it.

For example, lots of reformsters like the idea of setting up a system, because the way you get people to do work is you line them up in various coggy functions, allowing them to work their way up to higher levels of cogsmanship, which they'll do because each cog level offers new incentives (with lots of structure and direction). This is what you do with work that has no intrinsic motivation. Incentives, because why else would people pursue doing it right, and structure, because we don't believe that there's any natural feedback that tells the cog whether it's doing well or not.

This is dumb. It's like assuming that kissing does not have any natural feedback loop, so we need a system to let people know if they're kissing correctly or not. That same thinking says that a teacher can't tell whether a class is going well or poorly because there's no intrinsically rewarding feedback loop. This is a fundamental misunderstanding of how a classroom works.

For another example, we return frequently to the problem of getting super-duper teachers to go work in America's most hard-to-staff schools, and we always return with a discussion of how we could create some financial incentives for teachers to go work there. But teachers do not go to work at Shiny New High School because the pay is great (often the cost of living in SNHS's neighborhood eats up the higher pay). Teachers go to work at SNHS because it's a great place to work.

I could try to lay out all the specifics of what makes a school or district a great place to work, but I think I can simplify it--

A great school to work in is one where there are the fewest possible obstacles between the teachers and the intrinsic rewards of teaching. And the intrinsic rewards of teaching are, most simply stated, using your skills, knowledge, judgment and efforts to help your students learn and grow, and getting to see the real life results of that growth.

The more obstacles stand between a teacher and the use of those personal skills, knowledge, judgment and effort, the less rewarding it is to work there.

So a plan like, say, "We'll give you a scripted program, and you are never to use your own judgment. We have no interest in what skills and knowledge you bring to the table as an individual-- just do as your told when you're told. But we'll give you a few thousand more dollars to do it"-- well, that's not a plan. And while you may find takers for it, they are not the teachers that you want.

Likewise a plan like, "Yes, take all your passion and care and dedication into that classroom, but we're not going to give you any tools such a books or paper, and we won't give you any support to help maintain discipline, and we'll never fix that broken window. but we will give you some extra pay"-- also not a plan.

Yes, teachers need money (we have families and we like to eat food and wear clothes), but if you don't understand that there is something exciting and joyful and rewarding for us in the work we do, you will never come up with a plan or program or system that motivates us. In fact, if you don't get that we're still in the classroom because we're already motivated, then you don't understand the work situation well enough to have a positive effect on it.

Teaching is intrinsically rewarding. You know when things are going well, and it feels good. You know when things are going poorly, and that feels lousy. You also know when people are trying to help you become your best teachery self so that you can have more good days, great moments. And you know when people are not trying to help, but are just trying to take away all the tools that allow you to create the good days.

Charter Laboratory Is Failing

President Obama has called charter schools "incubators of innovation" and "laboratories of innovation," and he has done so for several years, despite the fact that, so far, the laboratories have yielded nothing.

One of the standard justifications for the modern charter movement is that these laboratories of innovation will develop new techniques and programs that will then be transported out to public schools. Each charter school will be Patient Zero in a spreading viral infection of educational excellence.

Yet, after years-- no viral infection. No bouncing baby miracle cure from the incubator. The laboratory has shown us nothing.

Here's my challenge for charter fans-- name one educational technique, one pedagogical breakthrough, that started at a charter school and has since spread throughout the country to all sorts of public schools.

After all these years of getting everything they wanted, modern charter schools have nothing to teach the public schools of the US.

The widely-lauded Success Academy model of New York is based on the emotional brutalization of children and tunnel-vision focus on The Test. This is justified by an ugly lie-- that if poor kids can get the same kind of test scores as rich kids, the doors will open to the same kind of success.

Put all that together with a mission to weed out those students who just can't cut it the SA way, and you have a model that cannot, and should not, be exported to public schools. Success Academy demonstrates that charters don't necessarily need to cream for the best and the brightest, but just for the students who can withstand their particular narrow techniques.

But then, most modern charters are fundamentally incompatible with the core mission of public schools, which is to teach every single child. Examination of charters show over and over and over again that they have developed techniques which work-- as long as they get to choose which students to apply them to. New Jersey has been rather fully examined in this light, and the lesson of New Jersey charters is clear-- if you get to pick and choose the students you teach, you can get better results.

This is the equivalent of a laboratory that announces, "We can show you a drug that produces fabulous hair growth, as long as you don't make us demonstrate it on any bald guys."

Modern charters have tried to shift the conversation, to back away from the "laboratory" narrative. Nowadays, they just like to talk about how they have been successful. These "successes" are frequently debatable and often minute, but they all lack one key ingredient for legitimate laboratory work-- replication by independent researchers.

Replication is the backbone of science. Legit scientists do not declare, "This machine will show you the power of cold fusion, but only when I'm in the room with it." The proof is in replicating results by other researchers whose fame and income does not depend on making sure the cold fusion reactor succeeds.

If your charter has really discovered the Secret of Success, here's what comes next. You hand over your policies and procedures manual, your teaching materials, your super-duper training techniques to some public school to use with their already-there student body. If they get the excellent results, results that exceed the kind of results they've been getting previously, results measured by their own measures of success, then you may be on to something.

But if you only ever get results in your own lab with your own researchers working on your own selected subjects measured with your own instruments, you have nothing to teach the rest of us.

Andy Smarick recently charted up some charter results, looking at how they relate to CREDO and NACSA ratings. He did not make any wild or crazy claims for what he found, but he did note and chart correlations. The more CREDO likes a city (it offers more opportunities for chartering), the higher its charter testing results. The more NACSA thinks charters are regulated in a city, the lower the testing results. There are many possible explanations, but here are two that occur to me: the more charters you let open, the more they can set the rules and collect the students that they want, and the more that regulations force charters to play by the same rules as public schools, the more their results look just like public school results.

Maybe, as Mike Petrilli suggested, it's time to stop talking about charters as laboratories and stop pretending that they're discovering anything other than "If you get to pick which students you're going to teach, you can get stuff done" (which as discoveries go is on the order of discovering that water is wet). There may well be an argument to make about charters as a means of providing special salvation for one or two special starfish. But if that's the argument we're going to have, let's just drop the whole pretense that charters are discovering anything new or creating new educational methods that will benefit all schools, and start talking about the real issue-- the establishment of a two-tier schools system to separate the worthy from the rabble.

College Ready, My Butt

There are some parts of the ed reform debates that have repeated so many times, we almost forget that they don't actually make sense.

For instance, the beloved mantra "college and career ready."

What the heck does that even mean?

David Conley, Ph.D, of the Education Policy Improvement Center, has presented on this many times-- and he offers this definition:

The level of preparation a student needs in order to enroll and succeed-- without remediation-- in a credit-bearing course at a postsecondary institution that offers a baccalaureate degree or transfer to a baccalaureate program, or in a high-quality certificate program that enables students to enter a career pathway with potential future advancement.

In case you're wondering, he goes on to define "succeed" as basically "pass the course well enough to continue to the next course or complete the program." So, the Peter Principle is not invoked, I guess.

Note that the "career" portion of readiness doesn't include anything that you can do with a high school diploma. He has also disqualified any job that doesn't allow for future advancement, which is unfortunate since that rules out teaching as an actual career. Go figure.

But even as a measure of college readiness, this is an unhelpful mess. "Enroll and succeed in a credit-bearing course." Any course? As long as I can pass any one entry level course, I'm college ready? If I'm ready to take a music theory course, am I college-ready? And if so, why isn't any instrument in place to mark me college ready? And if not, then why not? Because it would seem that a student is only college ready if she scores well on a math and ELA test, but lots of people go on to college for other things. Is a brilliant young musician or scientist or historian or welder who can't pass a Big Standardized Math test not ready for college, even if they won't take a single math class once they get there?

And really-- which college? Because I'm pretty sure that college ready for the University of Southern North Dakota at Hoople looks a great deal different from college ready for Harvard. For that matter, I'm pretty sure that college ready for Harvard looks a lot different from college ready for the Tulsa Welding School.

The whole complex of questions is further confused by frequent conflation of "college ready," "on grade level," and "scoring proficient." These three ideas are often discussed as if they are interchangeable, but they are not.

We're also ignoring all the non-academic issues. Every year, students slink home from college carrying failing grades that are not the result of any academic, intellectual, or skill issues, but instead resulting from a failure to master their own Hey I'm At College independence. There is no standardized test for self-discipline and responsibility.

We especially have no clue what college readiness looks like on the elementary level. You can see where we're headed-- we'll find a correlation between third grade reading scores and college success, but we'll call it causation rather than look for the common cause of both (spoiler alert: it's wealth).

We'll continue to pretend that out of the hundreds of factors that prepare a student for college, the only one that counts is the test score. There are a hundred things to check before you go skydiving, but the reformster way is to say, "Well, you've got a handle thing to pull and shoes on your feet, so everything's great" without ever checking to see if there's even a parachute on your back before they shove you out of the plane.

In fact, we have no clear, complete, scientifically supported picture of what a college ready student looks like, nor any proven way to measure the complex of qualities (that we still can't name and quantify). Standardized test scores are not a proxy, not even a bad one. "Sorry, honey. I couldn't find any ingredients to make you a birthday cake, so I pan fried some pillow stuffing in some engine oil, instead."

Colleges, who have more incentive than anyone to figure out the magic secret of what college ready looks like, still have only moderate success. After all-- all those not-ready students who supposedly need super-remediation?-- the college accepted those students in the first place! Every student who flunks out is a student that the college accepted in the first place! How can that be? Don't we know exactly how to tell that a student is ready for college??

The answer, of course, is no, no, we don't. So instead we demand that teachers coach students to run faster, even though we can't find the track and aren't sure exactly where the finish line is. But run faster anyway. And we'll check how well your shoes are tied regularly, because that's how we'll know whether you're on track to win or not.

Yes, at the root of Common Core and all this other reforminess is a quality we can't identify and don't know how to measure. Is it any wonder that the mansion built on this foundation of dust bunnies and dreams is not safe to live in.

Who Has Been Saved?

Who has been saved?

We have had this regimen of testing, this revenue-generating stream of dis-aggregated data collection for over a decade. For over ten years we have been collecting test scores so that, having measured, we can then fix. So again I ask.

Who has been saved?

Where is the urban school system where the state has said, "Damn-- this school is in trouble. Get some resources and help and support in there stat. Divert tax dollars and raise more. Hire the best educational experts to help." And then, having sent the educational marines, the state could then watch their efforts pay off and declare, "Thank God for the test results. We have saved this school system."

Where is that school? Who has been saved?

Now, we've identified plenty of "failing systems." But from New Orleans to Newark, from Detroit to Little Rock to Holyoke, the response has not been to help the school or community. The response has been to cancel democracy, shut down the duly-elected school board, and effectively silence the parents, students and taxpayers of the community. Then, once governance of the school system has been stripped from the community and handed over to other interests, the schools have not been repaired, but replaced. Charter operators have been handed the keys to the candy store and allowed to reap profits while "rescuing" some small percentage of the students while leaving the rest to stew in public schools that now have-- well, not MORE resources than before their problems were "discovered," but LESS.

The community members are disenfranchised. The public schools are stripped of resources, not assisted. And some students (only those found worthy) are allowed to "escape" to charters that may not be in their community, may not be doing anything different than the public school except carefully skimming students, may be rolling back the clock on segregation, may not even be getting results any better than the public school.

Who has been saved? What has been fixed?

Test supporters run the litany of problems in failing schools. Low graduation rates. Achievement (aka test score) gaps. Low-income students with low college completion rates. These are just a few of the absolutely true, absolutely critical issues that we need to be addressing. Nobody explains how taking a standardized test will help.

Here's a suggestion. Speak honestly.

If your argument for the tests is, "We need to find and label the schools that must be closed. We must find the communities that are not fit to have a voice in their own governance so that we can take democracy away from them because their test scores suck and that is why they can't have nice things--" Even if what you should really be saying is, "Look, we're not going to try to save all the kids; some just aren't worth it. We'll save a select few and dump the rest like ballast on an overburdened balloon--" If that's the true purpose of the Big Standardized Test, then just say so. Let's have an honest conversation about that. Let's talk about what the BS Test can actually tell us. Let's talk about what the "data" from the test can tell us, and what we can do about it.

Because this story about how the tests are like a big diagnostic medical test and the doctors are just waiting to whisk the worst patients to an operating room where they will receive the best care that modern science and top dollar can buy-- well, that story is getting old. We have been doing this for over a decade, and we keep watching patients get whisked away to that magical operating room, and yet not one of them has emerged alive and healthy. Most have not emerged at all. And in the meantime, more patients keep showing up, suffering from diseases spawned by inequity and injustice.

Maybe test results could be used to fix education. I tend to doubt it, but let's say it's possible. That's not how the data has been used for the past decade-plus.

If you are going to insist on this story of how we need the data in order to save students or schools or communities, then, please, answer just one question.

Who has been saved?

The Narrow Path

Yesterday was grad project day at my school. On this in-service day every year our seniors come in to present for evaluation their senior projects. It is, for many of us on staff, one of the best days of the year.

Pennsylvania installed a graduation project requirement years ago, leaving every school free to decide what their local version would be. Some required every student to write a paper (and the English department to grade all of them-- thanks a lot), some required a service project, and some incorporated the project into classwork students were already taking.

We took a different approach, allowing students to select from five different types of projects-- everything from a career research project to service project to building a cabinet to performing an original work. The project is student chosen, and as you might imagine, some students choose more wisely than others. But as I tell them at their project kick-off meeting, if the project is a waste of their time, they have nobody to blame but themselves. This is one time that a major element of their school career is based on what they value, not on what the school values.

Do some students half-ass it, or create some desultory bland project? Sure. But we also see so many awesome things on this day. Numerous beautiful pieces of cabinetry. An album of photographs. the models our students with hair and make-up by the photographer. A home-built logsplitter. A delicious meal. A refurbished game room for children staying at a battered women's shelter. A student weeping as she tells the story of going to Puerto Rico to meet her extended family. A student explaining the training he goes through to be a volunteer fireman, and what he thinks about going into a burning building to rescue a person.

Every grad project day reminds me that our students are so much more than the handful of classes that we teach, and that when they are allowed to display their competencies on their own terms (and those competencies fall outside "sit in desk for forty-five minute increments all day"), the vast majority of them turn out to be pretty great people. They are passionate about stuff-- it's just not all stuff that has a direct and clear connection to classroom and School Stuff.

We complain that the Big Standardized Tests measure just a small sliver of what we do in schools, and we are right to do so. In fact, the meagerness of BS Tests is doubly inadequate, because these students live lives so much bigger than the small sliver of existence that we deal with in school.

We are also right to complain about the narrowing of school under the reformster regime, reducing education to a narrow path for narrow purposes. That has happened, and it's not a good thing-- not for students, schools, or the nation.

But let's be honest. Public education in this country has always flirted with the narrow path, the idea that what we could fit within our school walls was a complete and sufficient view of life and the world and what it means to be fully human in that world. The architects of Common Core and NCLB did not try to take education in a completely new direction; we've been dallying at the trailhead of the narrow path for-- well, forever.

What we see on grad project day is that there are so many and varied versions of success, and that, in many cases, we would never have seen them in our classrooms. Grad project day always prompts me to reflect, to remind myself that part of my obligation as a teacher is to make sure that the path through my classroom is as broad as I can make it, to make sure that I have left as much space as I can for the full range of who my students are and who they aspire to be. There is so much to see and do, and the view from the narrow path is so limited and restrictive.

The Two Critical Testing Questions

The full range of debate about the Big Standardized Tests really comes down to answering two critical questions about the testing.

1. Does the test collect good data?

The whole justification for the BS Tests is that they will collect all sorts of rich and useful data about students, schools, and educational programs.

I have been amazed at the widespread, childlike, bland faith that many people have in anything called a "standardized test." If it's a "standardized test," then surely it must measure real stuff with accuracy, reliability and validity. Sure, the reasoning goes, they wouldn't be putting the test out there if it weren't really measuring stuff.

But to date, no evidence has appeared that the BS Tests are reliable, valid, or actually measuring anything that they claim to measure. The test contents are locked under a Giant Cone of Secrecy, as if the test is some sort of educational vampire that will evaporate if sunlight hits it. Nor have the data collected by the BS Test been clearly linked to anything useful. "Well, since she got a great score on the PARCC, we can be assured that she will be a happy, productive, and rich member of society," said nobody, ever.

Nor is the data rich with any level of data at all. Instead, we get reports that are the equivalent of saying the student was either "Pathetic," "Sad," "Okee dokee-ish," and "Mighty Swell."

Do the BS Tests measure anything other than the students' ability to take the BS Tests? Do the test results actually mean anything? If the test fans can't answer those questions, we're wasting everyone's time.

2. What action is taken with the data?

The tests are supposed to provide data on which to act. Does that-- can that-- happen?

On the classroom level, no. Data is too meager, non-transparent, and just plain late to do anybody any good. "Well, last year you score Okeedokee-ish because you missed some questions that I'm not allowed to see, so I've customized an educational program to address what I imagine your problem areas used to be," is not a useful thing to say to a student.

But what about identifying schools that need help? Is the data used to help those schools? Not unless by "help" you mean "close" or "take over" or "strip of resources so students can go to a charter instead." Our current system does not identify schools for help; it identifies schools for punishment.

Of course, it's hard to come up with a good action plan based on bad data, which is why we need answers to Question #1 before we can do anything with Question #2.

We can't fix what we don't measure.

Well, maybe, but it doesn't matter because right now our process is as follows:

1) Hey, your bicycle looks like it's not working right.

2) I've measured the lead content of the paint on the bicycle by squeezing the bouncy part of the seat. Your bike is definitely defective.

3) I have thrown your bicycle in the dumpster.

We aren't measuring anything, and we aren't fixing anything. Outside

Whose Voice Is Heard?

The "ed reform" crowd has been working hard at dressing its corporate wolves up in the clothing of civil rights sheep. Charter schools, high stakes testing, and the destruction of teacher job protections have all been billed as some version of the New Civil Rights battle.

This is a wise and powerful PR shift for the reformsters. Unlike the skyis-falling crises of other reformy sales pitches ("OMGZ! Our failing schools will soon make the USA economically subservient to Estonia!!"), civil rights issue are real. The problems of systemic racism and social injustice are real. The needs of poor and minority students and their communities-- those issues are real.

But as post-Katrina New Orleans has thoroughly demonstrated, you can use a real problem to promote a fake solution.

So how do we sort the policies and proposals, the reformsters and the shysters. How do we know if people work as true reformers and not, as Jitu Brown put it in Chicago at 2015's NPE convention, simply colonizers. The key question is simple: whose voice is being heard?

I don't mean whose voice is used to provide cover and camouflage. I don't mean the pretend plaintiffs for groups like Students Matter or the Partnership for Educational Justice; I mean the voices who are truly speaking, who are making the decisions, whose concerns are guiding the ship and calling the shots.

We can see the same old pattern playing out again and again. In Arkansas, Little Rock has become one more school system stripped of a democratically-elected school board by the state. In Massachusetts, the state ignored the voices of citizens in order to strip democracy from the Holyoke school system. I could get into the details, but at this point we have seen this story over and over and over again, from New Jersey to Chicago. In city after city, "reformers" have arrived to "help" by silencing the voice of democracy and community.

We use the Big Standardized Test to "prove" that a school system is "failing." Here are all the things we don't do next.

We do not offer this failure as proof that the state has failed to properly support and supply the school. We do not release additional funds and resources from the state to the local district so that duly elected school board members and local community members can best decide how to use the new support.

We do not bring together a group of stakeholders to ask them what they need to turn their school around.

We do not launch a drive to make sure that local stakeholders have the tools necessary to steer their schools to the solutions the community desires.

We do not hear politicians or policymakers or reformy astroturf groups say things like "We have no way of knowing what solutions are needed here, and we look to the community to take the lead and set priorities" or "It's most important that we develop a strategy that honors the democratic process and involves community members" or even "We want to be very careful to share resources with the community without trying to sell them something. These are human beings, families, and children-- not potential market fodder."

Instead, people from outside the community bring in other people from outside the community, and the voices inside the community are dismissed, ignored, silenced. Occasionally local folks are allowed to speak-- as long as they're the Right Kind of People and they stay on message.

"We are here to get you your civil rights, but you're going to have to shut up and do as we say." There is no context in which that is not some kind of absurdist baloney, and yet that is repeatedly the message of reformy "civil rights" activists. "The tests are a civil rights issue. The charters are a civil rights issue. We are here to help, but to get our help, you will have to stay silent, because we know better than you. We ARE better than you."

Any real reform will involve the vigorous pursuit of democratic processes and the active involvement of local voices. Any real reform will be driven by decisions made by the people there in the community. Any real reform will be focused on engaging, involving, and amplifying the members of the community-- not finding ways to commandeer or cancel elected school boards and other home-grown local leaders.

Giving people permission to speak is not an act of reform; recognizing their right to speak is. Treating them as honored guests is not an act of reform; recognizing that you are a guest in their home is. Here's a hint- if the students of your community have to stage a sit-in to get a meeting with you, you are not a reformer.

"Shut up while I fix this for you. I will tell you what you need," is not the motto of the civil rights activist. It's the language of the colonizer, and it has no place in true education reform.

Welcome Aboard Big Test Airlines

This week is Big Standardized Test week in Pennsylvania high schools. I have the great good fortune to be a proctor, which means of course that I earned my Super-Secret High Security Test Guardian Certificate. And that means I can't tell you anything about the test itself.

Technically speaking, I'm not even supposed to look at it, though the state seems to recognize that my proctoring duties would be more challenging were I blindfolded. But I am not supposed to retain, remember, in part or in whole, any test items-- not even the general idea of a test item. You might think that the results of unseen test questions to inform instruction might be challenging or impossible or just plain stupid, but that is why you are sitting there reading some silly teacher blog and not making either policy decisions in a capitol or big piles of money in a test manufacturing company.

Yes, we now live in a world where I may well be risking legal penalties for saying that the test includes old-fashioned vocab questions where the student must match a semi-unfamiliar word with its synonym among four other semi-unfamiliar odds. Or that there are interpretation questions with at least three equally correct answers, only one of which will be accepted by the state.

By saying that, I may have said too much. I'm certain that if I tell you more, I have to kill both you and myself.

But I can, as near as I can tell, talk about giving instructions.

BS Test instructions are a unique piece of tone-setting, the classroom equivalent of pre-flight safety instructions on any airline that is not Southwest. These instructions accomplish many goals, none of which are desirable in a classroom.

Right off the bat, the scripting sets a tone. The usual tone (or should I say mood?) of a classroom recognizes that we are all human beings, and that I am an adult human being here to help you manage our next challenge. But the script establishes that I am not here to help you-- in fact, I am not even supposed to interact with you in the same manner as we would any other place in the universe.

Immediately, we are both stripped of agency. You are not to do the simplest action-- not even turn a page-- until I read the instructions to do so. And because I must announce even my simplest action ("I will now pass out pieces of scratch paper"), it is clear I have no agency, either. We are both just subject to a Greater Power-- the Power of the Test.

We then move into a ridiculous dance. I say turn to page two and read the paragraph (the one threatening you with vague, ominous punishment if you dare to violate test security), and you of course do not. Certainly not the fourth time you've been told to read it in two days. Again, we are establishing a tone, delivering a message.

In six modules of testing, you will be told to sign a Code of Test Taker Ethics Pledge (don't cheat or violate security) three times. You will be told to read the section about test security six times. Test security gets a paragraph, all on its own page. Encouragement ("do your best") gets eighteen words over six modules. How many times will we tell you something encouraging, affirming, reminding you of your value as a student and a human being. None times. The allocation of space in the script makes it clear what is most important here, and it's not the students.

I will read the directions out loud as you read them silently just about as much as air travelers read the card in the seat-back pocket. I will ask you repeatedly if you have any questions, but of course by the time we get to those, it's clear that none of us is supposed to say or do anything that's not in the script.

I am supposed to tell you one bald-faced lie-- when looking at the scoring guides, the script makes reference to "professional scorers." That is a lie. There are no such people.

Sometimes I will use vocal inflection or facial expression to indicate that I am, in fact, a live human being and not a Borg-trained flight attendant. I don't know if that makes things better or worse-- is it sadder just to see the bars of a cage, or to see the face of the person shut in behind them?

It is hard to imagine an atmosphere more artificial and offputting. I imagine that for the youngest students it is the saddest, most alienating experience they have ever had. For some very young students I'll bet it is the first time in their lives they've found themselves in a difficult place with no friendly face to be found. When I was little I had nightmares about being lost in a store, unable to find my parents and surrounding by cold, distant strangers. If I were that young today, would I have nightmares about BS Tests instead?

It is all just one more reason that I doubt the validity of the test. Is this really the situation under which we think students will demonstrate their very best? Did test manufacturers stop just short of saying, "What if we left a Slim Whitman album playing full blast the whole time, and every fifteen minutes the proctor had to punch each kid in the face?"

I am not saying that the poor, fragile children need to be coddled through every test. But if I were setting out to discover exactly what my students knew and could do, this is not the first, or even the one thousandth, way I would think of going about it. The direction script is just one more indicator that there are many priorities in play here, and finding out what our students really know is far from the top of the list.

Two Turnaround Questions

From Pennsylvania to Arizona, reformsters are hitting the streets (well, the legislatures) to push the value of turning schools around. More specifically, they're pushing for a New Orleans style handover of schools to charter operators. The seeds of slow-motion disaster (financial starvation and bogus failure rates for bogus standardized tests) are finally yielding fruit that is ready to harvest.

Hear the touching chorus. "Give us your tired, your poor, your huddled low-scoring students yearning to hand their funding to charter operators who may let them breathe free, but that's the last free thing anybody is going to get because we have some Return On Investment numbers to make this quarter." Or something like that. One can hardly expect hedge funders to be great poets, too.

There is one strategic problem with selling the idea of turning failing schools around-- pretty much nobody has ever actually done it. Charteristas have had a decade or so to show off how they can transform failing schools into gardens of glorious success, and so far the best they can come up with is a two-step process:

1) Make sure you get all the loser students out of your building. 2) Write really well-spun press releases and get news outlets to run the uncritically.

I have a standing offer for anyone who can tell me about a single technique, program or approach developed in charter schools that has gone on to be widely successful in public schools. The "successful" charter model is generally the same-- do pretty much what the public schools do, but do it with a different (better) group of students.

So when a turnaround expert turns up in your neighborhood and starts asking for control of public schools, here are the two questions to ask:

1)   What specific successful techniques and programs do you propose to use in turning around the school?

2)   Is there any reason those techniques could not be used in the current public school?

Without clear, compelling, and evidence-supported answers to those questions, there is simply no reason to close a public school just to open a money-making (and that includes money-making "non-profits") charter operation.

It is the great charter secret-- charter operators don't know a damn thing that public schools don't know. They have had years to try every trick that they thought would transform schools into factories of excellence; of all these tricks, only careful management of which students are in the building has been consistently successful. I believe there are some charter successes out there, and I believe there could be more-- but not on a large scale. The most successful charter ideas would be location specific, and not scaleable. But that's not what charteristas are selling. What they are selling is snake oil and smoke, and they need to be called on it repeatedly.

The Ballast

I worry about the ballast.

Charter fans brag about their successes. They tell the starfish story. They will occasionally own that their successes are, in fact, about selecting out the strivers, the winners, the students who are, in fact, their own children and allowing them to rise. And it is no small thing that many students have had an opportunity to rise in a charter setting.

But I worry about the ballast.

How do these lucky few rise? The charter doesn't have better teachers. In many cases the charter doesn't have a single pedagogical technique or instructional program that is a bit different from its public school counterparts. What it has is a concentration of students who are supported, committed, and capable.

Those students are able to rise because the school, like the pilot of a hot air balloon, has shed the ballast, the extra weight that is holding them down. It's left behind, abandoned. There's no plan to go back for it, rescue it somehow. Just cut it loose. Let it go. Out of sight, out of mind. We dump those students in a public school, but we take the supplies, the resources, the money, and send it on with the students we've decided are Worth Saving.

This may be why the charter model so often involves starting over in another school-- because the alternative would be to stay in the same school and tell Those Students, the ones without motivation or support or unhindered learning tools, to get out. As those students were sent away so that strivers could succeed, it would just be too obvious that we are achieving success for some students by discarding others.

The ballast model is an echo of a common attitude about poverty. If you are poor, it's because you chose badly, because you didn't try hard enough, because you don't have grit, because you lack character, because you deserve to be poor. Insert story here of some person who was born poor and use grit and determination and hard work to become successful, thereby proving that anyone who is still poor has nobody to blame but himself. Just repeat that narrative, but instead of saying "if you are poor" say "if you are a poor student."

This is a societal model based on discarding people. This is a school model based on discarding students.

Because after all, if a student is failing, that is because the student is faulty, or possibly the teacher. Even learning disabilities, we've been told, have no effect on the student's achievement if the teacher's expectations are high and the student has grit.

So I guess that makes it okay to discard the ballast, the extra weight that is holding the Better People back.

I repeat-- it is no small thing that some students are carried aloft, lifted high among the clouds in that basket of high achievement.

But I keep thinking of the ballast. Somebody cuts a rope, and the heavy bag goes rocketing downward, plummeting to earth and disappear in a cloud of impact far below. Except they aren't just bags of dirt. They are human beings.

That's the charter model. Cut loose all the dead weight, all the students who aren't good enough, who cost too much time and trouble and money to lift up. This is one more reason that public school folks remain unimpressed by charter "success"-- we always knew that cutting loose the ballast would help everyone else, but our mandate is to lift everyone, not just the chosen few.

Maybe cutting loose the ballast is necessary. Maybe we've decided that's how school should work now. But we should at least be honest and have that discussion, not just cut the ballast loose while nobody is paying attention and then declare, "Well, look, we're headed up now. It's like magic!" If we're going to abandon ten students in order to rescue one, we need to talk about whether or not we're okay with that. We might even have conversation about getting a bigger balloon, one with enough lift to carry everyone and not just the chosen few.

I am glad that a few more students are being lifted up, and that is no small thing. But still, I worry about the ballast.

Proficient?

"Proficient" is having a moment right now, so perhaps this is an opportune moment to stop and reflect, to sit and think about how the term, like "all natural" and "college and career ready," doesn't actually mean a thing.

Okay, that's not entirely true. "Proficient" does have one very specific meaning-- "having scored above an arbitrarily set cut score on a Big Standardized Test." But like "student achievement" (which actually means "test scores"), it has been carefully chosen because it suggests so much more than it actually means. Like much of education reform rhetoric, it is that smouldering hottie that gives you a look across the room that promises all sort of soft, sweaty delights but who never delivers so much as a friendly peck on the cheek.

What could it even mean to call someone a proficient reader? Does it mean she can finish an entire novel? Does she have to understand it? Does she have to finish it in less than a month? A week? A year? Can it be any novel? Does it have to be a modern one, or can it be a classic? If I can get through *The Adventures of Huckleberry Finn* but not *Moby Dick,* am I still a proficient reader? If I read Huck Finn, but I just think it's a boy's adventure novel, and I proficient, or do I have to grasp the levels of satire to be proficient? Must I also be able to see symbolism tied to the search for identity in order to be proficient? What about poetry? Does someone have to be able to read poetry to be proficient? Any poetry? From any period? Is a proficient reader moved by what she reads, or does reading proficiency have to do only with the mechanics and thinky parts? And should proficient reader be able to read and follow instructions, say, for assembling a new media center? Would a proficient reader be able to follow the instructions even if the writer of the instructions was not a proficient English language writer? Can a proficient reader deal with any non-fiction reading? How about, say, Julian Jaynes *Origin of Consciousness in the Breakdown of the Bicameral Mind?* Can a proficient reader read a whole Glenn Beck book and spot which parts are crap? Because that was some pretty heavy stuff! How about legal documents? Does a proficient reader read legal documents well enough to understand them sort of, or completely, or well enough to mount a capable counter-argument to the legal document? Would I count as proficient if I only ever read chunks of reading that were all 1000 words or less (like, say, blog posts), or does proficiency mean dealing with longer, more involved stuff? If college readiness is part of proficiency, does that mean a proficient reader is ready to do the assigned reading for a class on Italian Literature at Harvard or a class on Engineering at MIT or How To Talk Good at West Bogswallup Junior College? Will a proficient reader get A's? C's? And speaking of levels of ability, would a proficient reader read all of a Dan Brown or Stephanie Myers novel and know that it was terribly written? Would a proficient reader have made it all the way through this unnecessarily lengthy paragraph, or would a proficient reader have figured out that I was using bulk to make a rhetorical point and just skipped to the end?

Or does "proficient" just mean "able to manage the dribs and drabs of reading-related tasks that we can easily work into a standardized test"?

Because not only do we have to pretend that we actually know what "proficient" means, but we after we have drawn our lines around all of the complicated questions above, we have to go on to claim that we can glean a clear and accurate picture of that constellation of complex skills with one standardized test. In Pennsylvania, we are going to assess your proficiency with fifty-four questions, half of which are just plain old multiple choice bubble questions.

So the next time you read a piece like this thinky tank piece or this piece of ridiculous editorializing, keep in mind that all these people waxing philosophic about "proficient" might just as well be discussing the hair care preferences of yetis.

Standards: Agreements and Assurances

When we talk about standards, we are really talking about two different things-- and only one of them is real.

Agreements

For a while it was in vogue to compare educational standards to manufacturing standards like the standards for electrical outlets.

Those sorts of standards represent an agreement-- the interested parties come to an understanding that in order to play together successfully, we will all agree to play by the same rules. These agreements do not always come easily-- while the AC power that flows into all our homes may now seem like a no-brainer, it is, in fact, the victor of the War of Currents, a battle over whether US homes would be powered by AC or DC power. Think also VHS vs. Betamax, HD vs. Bluray, and Microsoft vs. Apple operating systems. Think about how many various charger cords you have for electronic devices; standards don't always get worked out.

When they do get worked out, it's a matter of folks saying, "Let's make it easier to play together by all driving on the right side of the road" or "Let's make it easier to make money by all using the same currency" or "Let's keep refusing to use the metric system."

Some times the terms of agreement can be dictated by power players. If I control the game, then you must agree to my rules if you want to play. "We control access to the North American continent, so if you want a piece of the action, you must build your railroad cars to our agreed-upon gauge." Microsoft and Apple have not set universal standards, but they dominate the market so effectively that they can dictate the terms of agreement for anyone who wished to play in their sandbox.

Folks who want to set the terms of agreement have two basic avenues open to them-- seduction or force. Seduction has been the preferred method in game platform wars-- "Buy our console and you will get to play the awesome new game Robotic Beavers Disembowel Ninja Cowboys" on the front end and "Create a game for our platform and you'll make a gazzillion dollars" on the back end.

Seduction works best with quality (Betamax) or opportunity to profit (VHS), but when you don't have either going for you (asbestos removal), you need brute force. That would be the part where John D. Rockefeller bludgeons the rest of the oil industry into economic submission, or the part where Wall

Street makes sure that the standards for ethical and responsible behavior set by the feds do not actually forbid unethical and irresponsible behavior.

The architects of the Common Core Standards used seduction successfully with industry insiders ("Pearson, this is going to make you so rich") and tried hard to wrap their product in Robes of Excellence (Thanks, Fordham), but ultimately they had not fully reckoned with the millions and millions of end-users of their product who were unwilling to enter a standards agreement either way. That led to the use of brute force (Race to the Top, waivers, and the installation of Coreenforcing goons in state capitals). But sensing that was a long bridge to cross, the CCSS-pushing forces also tried to portray the Core as the other type of standard.

Assurances

People love standards because every standard is a promise-- Do X and you will be sure to get Y.

Do this and you will be sure to get rich. Do this and you will be sure to get a spouse. Do this and you will be sure to get great children. Do this and you will be sure to go to heaven.

There are folks out there making small mountains of money writing books that make these claims. People want to know what rules to follow to get the outcomes they want from life. The marketing genius of the Core (and all its attached education programs) is to say to parents and legislators, "If your kids do this, they are sure to go to college and get a good job."

Standards as assurances appeal to the human desire to Know What To Do. They promise a clear future, with clear choices leading to the desired outcome. And they are completely imaginary. All standards of this sort are completely imaginary. Nobody can tell you exactly what you have to do to become successful or have a happy spouse or rear perfect children. At best, people can tell what has often worked for many people of a certain type under certain conditions at some times in the past. But none of that guarantees that any person who follows those standardized steps will be certain to arrive at the same destination. Insisting that life be whittled down to just the narrow path described by such standards does guarantee that you will miss a great deal of what could have been good and rich and rewarding in your life. You will be the person throwing away diamonds because your rulebook told you to look only for gold.

Promising that following these standards will make every child college and career ready is codswallup. It's baloney. We don't even know what "college and career ready" actually means, and we certainly don't know a set of steps to follow that will bring every student to that place. Collapsing education (and life) down to a single narrow path is for cowards and fools. It's trading the richness of life for the empty promise of a guaranteed future, a promise on which no standard can deliver.

The First Hurdle

Watching a roomful of students slog through Pennsylvania's algebraflavored Big Standardized Test today, I'm reminded of one of the many flawed assumptions of test promoters.

Before you can compile the test answers, before you can crunch the numbers and sift the data and build your house of test-driven cards-- before you can do all that, you have a first hurdle to fling yourself over.

The students taking the test have to care.

Of all the bizarre, imaginary scenarios that test-promoters believe, this is perhaps the most reality impaired: a room full of sixteen year olds coming to school and thinking, "Boy, I cannot wait to do my very best on these. I can think of nothing more important to me right now than making sure that the state and federal government have accurate data about the kind of job my school is doing."

All discussions of test-generated data start with the assumption that the students were really trying, that they really wanted to do the very best that they could. I do not know where that assumption comes from. I can't help noticing that while many reformsters are parents, very few are parents of teenagers.

People often act as if teenagers are mysterious, otherworldly creatures. I've spent my entire life around teens, and I can tell you the secret to understanding them-- they are human beings. That's it. Teens are essentially rough cut version of their adult selves with some impulse control and long-term vision issues. But they're just people.

So imagine the following scenario. At work, you are periodically required to complete a series of tasks. These tasks are not really related to your usual job, and what connection they do have is only to a very small sliver of your total job. Performing these tasks does not help you do your job better, nor does it help your supervisor lead you. The tasks themselves are long and boring and require your actual work to come to a halt for days at a time. There's no benefit at all to doing really well; you just need to do well enough so that you can be done and get back to your regular work.

I would present you with a clearer analogy, but there really isn't anything like BS Testing in the adult world. Maybe when you have to go on line and watch one of those workplace slide shows and take an idiot quiz at the end (True or False: Stealing equipment from the office is okay.)

In that situation, do you imagine that you are trying your hardest, doing your best, or caring at all?

Test promoters have spent so much time pushing PR about the high noble valuable purposes of the BS Test that they've convinced themselves that students believe it, too. They do not.

In fact, getting older students to take any test seriously has always been one of the challenges of school (for the littler ones, who would eat fried weasel brains just to make the beloved Miss Othmar happy, motivation is less of a challenge). The entire institution is organized to coerce students into telling us what we want to know. You can't "pass" this course unless you try on this test. You can't "pass" this grade until you "pass" the course. This is why that smart-ass smart kid drives some of her teachers into a rage-- they all know she's not trying at all, but they don't have enough leverage to get her to really care about doing her best.

A small sub-industry of BS Testing has sprung up. Pep rallies. Bribes. Threats. Up the road, an administrator hauled all of students into an auditorium just to berate them for their lackluster test efforts. Occasionally, there's success-- the SAT and ACT command fear and attention because students are convinced that Big Things are riding on the test results. This is why BS Tests are destined to be high stakes-- because it's the only way we can think of to make students at least pretend to care.

And if the students don't care, the data aren't there.

Behind the test results are not students intent on showing The State what they know, but students with a hundred other thoughts in their mind, and not one of them was "Boy, this is really important." The BS Tests offer nothing relevant or beneficial to students, and our older students are perfectly capable of seeing that. The flop-sweaty pep rallies and super-secret swears of silence just underline that the whole exercise is a waste of their time, and guess what-- teenagers don't react any better to having their time wasted than anyone else.

You can say that it's my job to fix that, my job to convince them that the BS Test is Valuable and Important and they should totally care, that because I have the classroom relationship with them, I have the juice to make it happen. But the very first step in that relationship with my students came last fall on Day One, when I promised them several things including 1) I would never willingly waste their time and 2) I would never lie to them.

So here we sit, stuck at the first hurdle, a room full of teens calculating just how much effort and care they can afford to throw at what appears to be a pointless waste of their time. I wish very testtouting reformster who ever tried to sell the data as being True and Real and Valuable had to sit here with me and actually watch these students take the test. Better yet, I wish those reformsters had to apologize to my students for wasting their time.

Betterocracy

This thread runs through many reformster ideas and many of my responses to them. I just wanted to gather thoughts about betterocracy in one place.

Many reformsters have one fundamental point in common-- they don't really believe in democracy. They believe in betterocracy.

Betterocracy rests on one simple fundamental belief-- some people really are better than others. It's not necessarily the possession of a particular quality, though Betters are usually smarter, wiser, and possessed of superior character. It's that Betters are made of the right stuff. They come from good stock. They are just better than others.

This is not a new thing. Back in the earlier days of romance and story, we find tales of princes who were reduced to tatters and penury, but whose Inner Quality always shone through, and they always rose to their proper princely place. Our Puritan forefathers believed that God had chosen certain people, and you would be able to spot the Chosen because God would reward them for being Better. Horatio Alger made a career out of penning stories of young men possessed of fine character and plucky grit, whose innate superiority eventually lifted them to the level of society to which they truly belonged.

Some folks interpret the idea of American Democracy to be, "All humans are equal."

But other folks believe that promise is, "Any human can become a Better."

We have always had signifiers of Betterness. In the bad old days, those signs that you might be a better include traits such as Being White or Having a Penis. More progressive bettercrats have come to understand that such signifiers are unreliable, but when they talk about opening the tent to folks of all race, gender and religion, it's not that they believe that all Black Muslim women are equal to white Christian guys. They just mean they are open to the possibility that a Black Muslim woman could turn out to be a Better, too. In fact, many bettercrats are delighted to find non-white, non-wealthy, or non-men who are Betters because it proves we really do live in an enlightened and liberal age. But they still don't believe in democracy, and they still believe that some people are better than others.

Non-believers in betterocracy often imagine that Betters are simply greedhounds in pursuit of stuff and money and power and prestige just to have those things. I don't believe that's true. Bettercrats like those things because they are signfiers of Quality. They are proof that the Betters really are Better. The money, the prestige, the stuff-- why would they have all of that unless they were Better? The right schools, the right clubs, the right houses in the right neighborhoods-- these are all proof that they really are Better.

Bettercrats can actually be dismissive of the stuff. After all, they have the stuff because they deserve it, and so if fate somehow burned down the house and rabble took the money, the Betters would still get it back. They deserve it, and as long as the universe is functioning properly, the Betters will not be denied their due. Failure is a temporary glitch and only happens on a real or permanent scale to Lessers.

Betters can come in all political stripes, defined mostly by disagreements about what the signifiers of Betterness actually are. Conservative vs. liberal bettercrats mostly argue whether anyone who's not white and penis-deprived can be a Better (mostly no), and how to treat the Lessers.

Because a bettercratic country has to be organized in strata. We must sort and stack, because Betters and Lessers should be subject to different regulations, different laws, different punishments, and, of course, different educational systems.

Betters can be allowed to roam free, and while they may need to get an occasional course-correction or wake-up call, we know they're The Right Kind of People. Lessers, however, have all sorts of Naughty Tendencies and we must do what we can to hold their Lesser natures in check. So a Better who is, say, busted for drugs, shouldn't have to suffer the rest of his life for a youthful indiscretion, but a Lesser who is busted needs to be taught a lesson without mercy. Betters should be cut some slack, but if you give a Lesser an inch, he'll take a mile.

Betters occasionally need a hand or some help, and that's only right. Betters owe it to other Betters to lend a hand, and of course Betters deserve every bit of help they get. But Lessers are always looking for a handout, and to give them help is just to encourage their dependent, lazy, lesser nature. Betters who have had a hard moment or two need understanding and support, but Lessers should be allowed No Excuses.

Bettercrats are in a tizzy these days because we have a problem as a country-- too many portions of the government have been taken over by Lessers, who in turn are pandering to large groups of Special Interest Lessers. This is Very Bad, because unchecked, Lessers will do Terrible, Bad Things. In fact, they might demand money and power and other trappings of success to which they are not entitled (though Better's will use the word "entitled" to mean "thinking they deserve things that they do not deserve"). They don't seem to understand that the fact they need help proves that they don't deserve help.

Bettercrats expect Lessers to know their place. After all, they wouldn't be poor and powerless if that wasn't what they deserved. After all, the nicer word for betterocracy is "meritocracy," the system in which people get what they deserve-- and not everybody deserves the best. If they deserved it, they would have it. Trying to give it to them is just violating the natural order.

So we need different education systems-- one to prepare Betters for lives of well-deserved privilege, money and power, and another to prepare Lessers for their proper role in society. Better schools are for providing opportunities and enrichment for America's future leaders. Lesser schools are for training America's future employees. In addition, in the dreams of liberal-minded bettercrats, the system should also provide a means of discovering and rescuing Betters who are, by some accident of birth and zip code, trapped amongst the Lessers. This rescue mission makes bettercrats feel more progressive. But, again-- progressive bettercrats do not believe that all humans are created equal; they believe that individuals from almost any background could turn out to be Betters (but only if rescued from the influence of Lessers).

And if the two-tier system is set up and managed in such a way that it reverse the regrettable trend of giving Lessers too much control, too much power, too much say-- well, that's a bonus.

Bettercrats know that not everybody should have a say. Betters should be in charge. Lessers should not. Letting just anybody have a vote, even if he's a Lesser, leads to bad, messy, stupid decisions. Better to sweep away voting rights (from electing Presidents to choosing school boards) in predominantly Lesser communities. Dump the school board, and install leadership by a Better. Do not engage or discuss with the members of the community; if they deserved to have money, power,or a say, they would already have it.

Bettercrats sometimes succumb to anger-- why don't these Lessers see that their schools suck, their children are ignorant, their neighborhoods are holes, and that their communities are awash in unworthy Lessers. Some of them don't even have the decency to feel bad about it. Man, if we could just get some solid proof that their world sucks and rub their faces in it until they finally hollered uncle and begged for their Betters to come straighten everything out for them. But some of them just keep acting like they deserve to have a voice, like they have a right to love their lives and their families and their communities.

The bottom line is that bettercrats believe that democracy is, really, a bad idea. Some people just don't deserve to have a say. Some people just don't deserve to be in charge of anything. Some people just aren't important. Some people just don't matter. Some people just can't have nice things. Bettercrats may, out of generosity and a general sense of noblesse oblige, give Lessers the nice things that they don't deserve, but those will be nice things that the Betters have selected, and Lessers can have the nice things under terms dictated by the Betters. Why shouldn't Betters have an outsized disproportionate influence on government? The fact that they have the money and power to wield influence is proof that they are right to do so.

None of this is democracy, not even a watered-down republic-styled democracy. Bettercrats mostly would not recognize democracy (they most commonly call it "socialism").

And that's why we've got the refomster programs that we have. Our Betters are trying to give the Lessers the system they deserve while rescuing Betters who have been trapped by zip codes in dens of Lesser iniquity. Our Betters are creating a system that disenfranchises Lessers (who, after all, do not deserve to be enfranchised in the first place because if they deserved to have power, they would have it). Our Betters are trying to create a system that further reinforces their own power and control, because they deserve to have them. Our Betters are even trying to get Lessers to understand that they are, in fact, Lessers.

The genius of America is that of a country that makes room for all voices and treats them all as equals, tied together and forced to create systems that accommodate all our citizens. It envisions a level playing field in which all voices and ideas can compete in the grand marketplace of thought. We have never fully lived up to that genius, but Betters do not even recognize it as genius to begin with. Right now their lack of vision is bad for education, but in the long run, it's bad for the entire country.

Stop "Defending" Music

Today I ran across one more xeroxed handout touting the test-taking benefits of music education, defending music as a great tool for raising test scores and making students smarter. It was just one more example among many of the "keep music because it helps with other things" pieces out there.

I really wish people would stop "defending" music education like this.

I get that music programs are under intense pressure, that all across America they are sitting hunched over with one nervous eye on a hooded figure stalking the halls with a big budgetary ax. Music programs are watching administrators race by, frantically chasing test scores and ignoring music in schools. So it may seem like a natural step to go running after the testing crowd hollering, "Hey, I can help with that, too."

Don't. Just don't.

First of all, it's a tactical error. If your state gets swept up in the winds of test dumpage and suddenly tests are not driving your school, what will you say to the ax guy (because, tests or not, the ax guy is not going away any time soon)? If your big selling point for your program has been that it's actually test prep with a horn, you've made yourself dependent on the future of testing. That's a bad horse on which to bet the farm.

Second, it's just sad. And it's extra sad to hear it come from music teachers. Just as sad as if I started telling everyone that reading Shakespeare is a great idea only because it helps with math class.

There are so many reasons for music education. Soooooooo many. And "it helps with testing" or "makes you do better in other classes" belong near the bottom of that list. Here are just a few items that should be further up the list.

Music is universal. It's a gabillion dollar industry, and it is omnipresent. How many hours in a row do you ever go without listening to music? Everywhere you go, everything you watch-- music. Always music. We are surrounded in it, bathe in it, soak in it. Why would we not want to know more about something constantly present in our lives? Would you want to live in a world without music? Then why would you want to have a school without music?

Listening to music is profoundly human. It lets us touch and understand some of our most complicated feelings. It helps us know who we are, what we want, how to be ourselves in the world. And because we live in an age of vast musical riches from both past and present, we all have access to exactly the music that suits our personality and mood. Music makes the fingers we can use to reach into our own hearts.

Making music is even more so. With all that music can do just for us as listeners, why would we not want to unlock the secrets of expressing ourselves through it? We human beings are driven to make music as surely as we are driven to speak, to touch, to come closer to other humans. Why would we not want to give students the chance to learn how to express themselves in this manner?

Music is freakin' magical. In forty-some years I have never gotten over it-- you take some seemingly random marks on a page, you blow air through a carefully constructed tube, and what comes out the other side is a sound that can convey things that words cannot. And you just blow air through a tube. Or pull on a string. Or whack something. And while we can do a million random things with a million random objects, somehow, when we just blow some air through a tube, we create sounds that can move other human beings, can reach right into our brains and our hearts. That is freakin' magical.

Music connects us to other humans in amazing ways. I have played in concert bands, a couple of jazz bands, and pit orchestras; I have directed church choirs and community musical theater. It is both indescribable and enormously compelling to see the many ways in which humans making music come together and connect to each other. I imagine the experience of playing team sports is something similar. You are part of something-- something bigger than yourself and more than the sum of the parts. I can't think of any other school subject that so completely fosters cooperation, collaboration, and connection between students. Students learn to help and mentor each other, support each other, lift each other up, and come together into something glorious and way, way cool.

In music, everyone's a winner. In sports, when two teams try their hardest and give everything they've got, there's just one winner. When a group of bands or choirs give their all, everybody wins. Regrettably, the growth of musical "competitions" has led to many programs that have forgotten this-- but music is the opposite of a zero-sum game. The better some folks do, the better everybody does. In music, you can pursue excellence and awesomeness without having to worry that you might get beat or defeated or humiliated. Everybody can be awesome.

Music programs give back to communities forever. See that big list of community music groups I've worked with? I am not in a large community, but all those groups exist, and they can all exist because every single person in them came through a school music program. Your community band, your church choir, your local theater-- all those groups that enrich the cultural life of your community are the result of school music programs.

Music programs can be a huge source of pride for school and community. Just like a football team, a band or choir can draw a crowd of fans who take great pride in the traditions and accomplishments of the groups. And if you're not getting your program out in front of the public to help build that following and support, you're messing up.

My high school band director is a hell of a guy, and he absolutely altered the trajectory of my life. When people talk about him, they often talk about all the music teachers and professional musicians that came out of his program, but I think his greatest success was all the students like me who went on to do something else, but whose lives have always been enriched by music.

Music is awesome. It's human. It's universal. It's big business precisely because it is something that everybody wants.

Music does not need to make excuses for itself, as if it had no intrinsic worth. It does not have to dress itself up in test-taking robes or mathematical masks. It has deep, powerful human value, and all of us who love it should be saying so, over and over and over again.

Do not defend a music program because it's good for other things. That's like defending kissing because it gives you stronger lip muscles for eating soup neatly. Defend it because music is awesome in ways that no other field is awesome. Defend it because it is music, and that's all the reason it needs. As Emerson wrote, "Beauty is its own excuse for being." A school without music is less whole, less human, less valuable, less complete. Stand up for music as itself, and stop making excuses.

Showing Up

Teaching is a relationship, and the first rule of relationships is that you have to show up.

Take it from a previously-divorced guy. You cannot maintain a relationship through proxies, in absentia, on autopilot, or by wearing a big, thick mask. You have to be present. You have to be honest. You have to show up.

Many teacher-reforming ideas trip over this simple truth.

Attempts to "teacher-proof" classrooms by using carefully constructed lessons and word-for-word scripting are attempts to make showing up irrelevant. Whoever shows up in the classroom, the reasoning goes, the lesson will go on exactly the same. But teacher-proofing a classroom is like husband-proofing a marriage, trying to come up with some set of rules so that it won't matter who shows up to fill the husband role, the marriage will work just fine. That's crazy talk. If the teacher doesn't really show up as a living, breathing human being, students cannot be engaged.

Likewise, I doubt the usefulness of computer-based learning. Certainly for limited amounts of drill or simple instruction, a computer screen works as well as a book. But if there is no context of a relationship to go with it, nothing happens. I can imagine a day when something might-- after all, readers enter relationships with the works that they read. But that's because the authors enter their own works as living human voices. The default in computerland is still to create an inhuman, person-free voice, and when it comes to relationship, that will always make a better barrier than a door.

I don't mean to suggest that we show up in the classroom like a raw exposed nerve or searching to have our own needs met. It is still a teacher's role to be a responsible, professional adult.

But we have to be honest. We have to be available. We have to be present. We cannot be effective with messages such as "I would be honest with you, but we have to move on with this lesson plan" or "I'm not going to be open to what you have to say because it's not on my script."

Showing up, really listening, really looking, speaking honestly-- these are all the most fundamental way we show that we care. To follow the script or the mandated pacing plan is to send the message, intentional or not, that we don't really care about our students or what is going on in our classroom.

This is the scary challenge that some teacher wanna-be's can't bring themselves to face. I remember still the moment during student teaching when I realized that I could not just keep the important parts of myself locked safely away from the classroom, only to be used when I was out of school. Not if I ever wanted to be any good. I would have to listen-- not just pretend to listen or try to construct some proper but artificial response. This is one of the reasons that we can all use the down time of summer-- it is hard to be in a classroom when you aren't sure how to be in the world.

One of the fatal flaws of almost every teacher reform program is an soul-strangling inauthenticity, a desire to have the teacher perform certain tasks almost by remote control, without actually showing up in the classroom.

But by showing up, by being our actual selves (still, mind you, grown up professionals), and by being present with our students, we actually model for them a whole approach to life. And we model courage. Because hiding behind a mask sends a message of, "Don't go out there-- it's not safe," but walking out into the world, head up, eyes wide, tells them that the world (even this little classroom corner of it) is a place where they can thrive and grow and more fully be themselves. The most fundamental thing we all teach is how to be more fully human in the world, and to do that we must be present, in a relationship with the world and the people in it.

We must show up.

Made in the USA
Columbia, SC
29 December 2017